China's Belt and Road Initiative
and
RMB Internationalization

Series on China's Belt and Road Initiative

Print ISSN: 2591-7730
Online ISSN: 2591-7749

Series Editors: ZHENG Yongnian *(National University of Singapore, Singapore)*
Kerry BROWN *(King's College London, UK)*
WANG Yiwei *(Renmin University of China, China)*
LIU Weidong *(Chinese Academy of Sciences, China)*

This book series showcases the most up-to-date and significant research on China's Belt and Road Initiative (BRI) by leading scholars from inside and outside China. It presents a panoramic view on the BRI, from the perspectives of China's domestic policy, China's foreign investment, international relations, cultural cooperation and historical inheritance. As the first English book series on the BRI, this series offers a valuable English-language resource for researchers, policymakers, professionals and students to better understand the challenges and opportunities brought by the BRI.

Published:

For the complete list of volumes in this series, please visit
www.worldscientific.com/series/scbri

Series on China's Belt and Road Initiative – Vol. 9

China's Belt and Road Initiative and RMB Internationalization

MENG Gang

China Development Bank, China

W✺ World Scientific

NEW JERSEY · LONDON · SINGAPORE · BEIJING · SHANGHAI · HONG KONG · TAIPEI · CHENNAI · TOKYO

Published by

World Scientific Publishing Co. Pte. Ltd.
5 Toh Tuck Link, Singapore 596224
USA office: 27 Warren Street, Suite 401-402, Hackensack, NJ 07601
UK office: 57 Shelton Street, Covent Garden, London WC2H 9HE

British Library Cataloguing-in-Publication Data
A catalogue record for this book is available from the British Library.

Series on China's Belt and Road Initiative — Vol. 9
CHINA'S BELT AND ROAD INITIATIVE AND RMB INTERNATIONALIZATION

Copyright © 2020 by World Scientific Publishing Co. Pte. Ltd.

ISBN 978-981-3278-89-9

For any available supplementary material, please visit
https://www.worldscientific.com/worldscibooks/10.1142/11230#t=suppl

Desk Editor: Tan Boon Hui

Typeset by Stallion Press
Email: enquiries@stallionpress.com

Author's Disclaimer

This book is based on personal, independent and academic research. All views, analyses and opinions expressed in this book belong solely to the author and do not represent the stands of the institutions that the author is currently working for or had worked for in the past.

About the Author

Meng Gang, China Development Bank, Doctor of Law, Post-Doctoral in Practical Economics; Senior Economist and Special Research Fellow of Peking University and Zhejiang University, China.

About the Editor

Wu Zheneng, Visiting Scholar of Harvard University (2015–2016); Senior Economist and Special Research Fellow of Nankai University China; Director of Beijing Representative Office, Singapore Temasek International Pte. Ltd; formerly worked for the China-Africa Development Fund.

Foreword

The Historical Opportunity of Belt and Road Initiative and RMB Internationalization

Chinese economy has long been deeply incorporated into globalization. On one hand, the overflow impact and systematic risks of external macro-policies in an open-world pattern might be passed on to the country. Many factors, including domestic currency policies, exchange policies and cross-border capital flow are becoming increasingly complex. On the other hand, China is steadily pushing forward RMB internationalization to meet the market requirements emerging due to global cooperation, based on the Belt and Road Initiative (BRI). The authors of this book once worked in global development-oriented financial cooperation in many developed and developing countries, and this book mainly studies RMB internationalization pushed forward by the BRI. This book not only reflects the thoughts of overseas front-line financial workers, but also constitutes the academic results achieved by a financial theory researcher after thoughtful considerations.

Currently, the Chinese economy has stepped into the "new normal" phase. As proposed in the 19th National Congress, our country should focus on the construction of the Belt and Road Initiative, and by doing so, it will open up a new pattern, create new relationships with foreign countries and build a world in which countries are closely united. Along with the dynamic shift of our country's comparative advantages, companies are stepping out of the border in a faster pace. As a result, higher requirements are imposed on the depth and width of the financial support system. To steadily push forward RMB internationalization, we need to facilitate the marketization reform of RMB exchange formation mechanism, take advantage of the opportunity of RMB's inclusion into the special drawing rights basket, and strengthen RMB's position as a reserve currency. Meanwhile, we should increase the free usability of RMB, adjust the macro-policies based on our position as a reserve currency issuer, and achieve more effective macro-control. We need a financial system that is healthier and more stable, and more advanced, reliable financial infrastructure to boost the world's confidence in RMB.

China is a large developing country on the rise. In the perspective of currency development, the internationalization of RMB is a general trend and a historical choice. As an important measure of China to fully open up and unite with foreign countries, the BRI intends to effectively connect relevant countries in different aspects, such as policies, roads, trade, capital and popular support. Financial cooperation based on domestic currency is an important aspect of BRI in its construction, and an important means to meet the financial needs. Financing in the BRI project is obviously helpful for China in adopting more active policies in capital account convertibility and RMB internationalization; and therefore, accelerates the process of RMB internationalization.

The 19th National Congress of the Communist Party of China was successfully held in Beijing, on October 18–24, 2017. The meeting's resolution on the revised Constitution of the Communist Party of China explicitly requested to incorporate the BRI into the Constitution. The Constitution sets the basic law and the representation of the common will of the entire Party. It can be seen that China is strongly determined, and with solid confidence, to construct the BRI, push forward global cooperation based on the BRI, open up fully, build new international relationships, and create a world community. Human history has shown us that the internationalization of a currency indicates the political and economic positions of the corresponding country's sovereign credit in the world. RMB internationalization has made substantial progress since China issued the Management Methods for Trials of Settling Cross-Border Trade Accounts in RMB in 2009. On October 1, 2016, RMB was formally included in the special drawing rights basket of International Monetary Fund. The BRI incorporated into the Party's *Constitution* in the new age will bring about new historical opportunities for RMB internationalization.

The BRI is a road of globalization which will facilitate the formation of the RMB currency area. However, incidents of "de-globalization" has been taking place now and then in recent years. Major countries have quit the *Paris Agreement*, and trade protectionism is rising. According to history, "de-globalization" is always against the trend of the times and often produces new leading forces, pushing forward globalization. The BRI advocated by President Xi is the embodiment of the peaceful development concept of joint business, joint construction and sharing, and will push forward globalization on a higher level and set up a new growth point of the world economy. China is the largest trading nation and the second largest economy in the world and pushing forward RMB internationalization during construction of the BRI is fair for both China and the world. According to the optimal currency area theory, several conditions are required to form an optimal currency area across multiple countries. These conditions include the flow of production factors, economic openness, integration of financial market, diversification of products, complementation of trade structures, policy coordination and more. As China build infrastructure connection with relevant countries, deepen investment and trade cooperation, and enhance policy coordination capabilities, the coordinated advancement of BRI construction and RMB internationalization will bring about more positive effects.

The BRI is a road of cooperation which advances hand-in-hand with RMB internationalization. BRI covers Asia, Africa and Europe, a population of over 4.4 billion, accounting for 63% of world population. The economic aggregate of the covered area accounts for 30% of the world number, and 65 relevant countries have different resource advantages, strong economic complementation capacity and huge potential for cooperation. Major aspects of BRI construction, such as financing, facility connection, trade connection, policy communication, and popular connection advance hand-in-hand with RMB globalization. Financing can help enlarge the scale of bilateral domestic currency swap of relevant countries, strengthen RMB's payment and settlement functions, and push forward the construction of a global currency stability system and credit system. Facility connection requires a large amount of credit funds, and helps boost RMB demands and fills the financing gaps of major projects. Trade connection helps different countries discuss more convenient ways to conduct trade and investment, eliminate trade and investment barriers and improve the circulation speed and quality of regional economy. Policy communication helps China cooperate with relevant countries in development strategies and plans, strengthen cooperation in traditional fields, open up new fields of cooperation and build a regional integrated economy. Popular connection allows ordinary people to understand that RMB's internationalization could expand capital channels, reduce financial costs, avoid exchange risks and bring about tangible benefits for companies and the people.

The BRI is the road of benefit for all and a major driving force of RMB internationalization. BRI construction requires a large amount of capital. According to estimates of Development Research Center of the State Council, infrastructure investment of BRI in the next five years will require 10.6 trillion USD. BRI requires long-term stable investment, which helps RMB output under capital account and back-flow through cross-border trade under current account. RMB internationalization starts from trade settlement, but it can be predicted that investments will be an important driving force in the future. Meanwhile, many countries along the BRI route lack sufficient financial services. Financing is a problem for their micro, small and medium enterprises, and the cost of capital is generally high. For example, the loan interest rate of Egypt has reached 10–20%. Due to lack of funds, micro, small and mediumcompanies have difficulties in "self-advancement", and are unable to produce competitive products. Such a vicious cycle of industrial structure has a negative huge impact on the development of real economy of the relevant countries. Our country has become one of the largest capital export countries and strengthening financing connection with countries along the BRI route is beneficial for all. Pushing forward RMB internationalization while controlling risks helps our country conduct win-win economic diplomacy, encourages Chinese companies to "step out of the border" and facilitates capacity cooperation between China and foreign countries.

The BRI is "a road of greenness" and an important means to achieve global acceptance of RMB internationalization. The green development concept of BRI is widely supported by governments, corporations and the public, and serves the common interests of relevant countries. By developing green finance during BRI construction, our country could add green properties to traditional cross-border financial products, and boost requirements for green financial products valuated and settled in RMB. As a result, more choices could be offered for RMB to "step out" through green finance. Green credit is the precondition for financial institutions following the "equator principles" to support major projects, and an important means for RMB internationalization to be widely accepted by financial institutions of many countries. It could lead the development of global finances. Green bonds have a large market at present. The green bonds issued by China are already playing a significant role in the world, and the green bonds valuated in RMB will have a large space of development and strongly push forward RMB internationalization in future. Global carbon market is becoming increasingly active, and China's carbon market will become the largest spot carbon market in the world. Along with deepened cooperation in global carbon emission trade, our country could strive to develop carbon financial market and increase RMB's weighting in carbon financial trade. Green finance will certainly provide more financial tools to facilitate RMB internationalization during construction of the BRI.

The BRI is a road of financial innovation and a strategic opportunity to overcome weaknesses in RMB internationalization. The Belt and Road Summit for International Cooperation and the National Conference on Financial Work in 2017 have emphasized financial innovation in BRI construction. I worked in development-oriented financial field in multiple countries along the BRI route and learned that financial cooperation based on BRI has the prominent problem of "too much and too few". Firstly, many major projects are supported by traditional credits, but few breakthroughs are made in top-level design of international credit standards. Secondly, many participants are Chinese financial institutions, but the financial institutions of countries along the BRI route and international financial institutions are not involved sufficiently. Setting up overseas branches is a time-consuming task, and the Chinese financial institutions have difficulties integrating into the local society. The problem of financing cannot be solved from the root. Thirdly, cross-border investment and financing are still heavily dependent on USD, and there are few RMB financial products. Finance is a nation's core competitive force, and our country needs to strengthen top-level design in financial innovation, lead the formulation of global credit policies such as green finance, establish mechanisms of financial cooperation between China and foreign countries, and encourage creations of financial products valuated in RMB, in order to push forward RMB internationalization during the BRI construction.

In the future, RMB internationalization should be pushed forward by taking advantage of the historical opportunities of BRI construction. Firstly, advancements should be made in a steady fashion under the condition of healthy development of the domestic economy. We should achieve tangible results in supply-side structural reform, and our overseas investment should not lead to domestic industry hollowing. Secondly, the principle of currency policy independence should be followed. The managed floating exchange rate system should always be adopted to ensure the relative stability of

RMB value, and we should steadily push forward the opening-up of managed capital accounts. Thirdly, we should strive to develop an RMB-centered regional currency cooperation system in which the central banks of relevant countries are extensively involved. The countries along the BRI route will be directed to set up an RMB payment system and enlarge the scale of currency swap to facilitate investment, financing and trade cooperation. Fourthly, by taking advantage of RMB special loans and funds for BRI and directing social capital to major projects, we should solve the financing gaps and foreign exchange risks in the beginning of major project constructions. Fifthly, our country should vigorously push forward RMB valuation and settlement for bulk commodities such as petroleum in relevant countries, in order to gradually popularize RMB in international trade and achieve RMB internationalization. Sixthly, diversified offshore centers for RMB should be established in countries along the BRI route. Financial innovations should be accelerated in cross-border RMB businesses such as international settlements, foreign exchange trade, bond issue, international clearing and international credit, in order to set up a multi-level development model of multiple driving factors such as trade, investment valuation and financial product innovation. Lastly, by strengthening financial innovation, learning from global experiences, gradually following the equator principles, developing green finance, setting up enlending platforms and promoting inclusive finance, our country could share our concept of green and all-inclusive development with foreign countries and facilitate RMB internationalization with their participation.

MENG Gang
July 2018

Contents

Introduction

1.1 The Basic Meaning of RMB Internationalization

1.1.1 *The Concept of RMB Internationalization*

According to Meng Gang's research (2017), RMB internationalization refers to the process of achieving overseas circulation of RMB and the wide use of RMB as a valuation, settlement, investment and reserve currency in the world. A currency's internationalization is a process of gradual development of the currency's function and follows a basic pattern: domestic currency settlement in cross-border trade and investment (cross-border valuation and settlement) → overseas holding and trade in domestic currency (cross-border currency investment) → overseas holders participating in the financial market of domestic currency (deepened opening-up of capital account of the currency) → overseas holding and reserving of domestic currency asset (internationalization of the currency's reserve function). According to Cheng Siwei's research (2014), a currency's internationalization means the sovereign currency of a nation could be circulated and used normally in the world. An internationalized currency is not only a vehicle currency commonly used in the world, but is also provided with a lot of new functions, which mainly include value reserve, transaction medium and unit of account. Five objectives should be reached in RMB internationalization: (1) RMB can be freely exchanged into foreign currencies in China and overseas; (2) RMB can be used as a unit of valuation in international investment and trade; (3) RMB can be used as the payment currency in international investment and trade settlement; (4) RMB can serve as the investment and financing currency in international finance; (5) RMB can serve as a reserve currency.

1.1.2 *Historical Development of RMB Internationalization*

In 2003 and 2004, our country provided clearing arrangements for individual RMB businesses in Hong Kong and Macao in succession. In 2009, our country issued the Management Methods for Trials of Settling Cross-Border Trade Accounts in RMB, and gradually removed limitations of using RMB in cross-border trade. In 2011, the Management Methods for Trials of RMB Settlement in Overseas Direct Investment and the Management Methods for RMB Settlement in Direct Investment of Foreign Businesses were issued. Domestic organizations were allowed to conduct direct overseas investments, and foreign investors were allowed to conduct direct investments in China, both in RMB. Since then, cross-border usage of RMB has been developing rapidly, and major breakthroughs has been made in cross-border trades and investments, foreign exchange transactions, international payments and international bonds.

1.1.3 *Current Situation of RMB Internationalization*

Currently, the degree of RMB internationalization still falls behind our position as the second in economic aggregate and the first in total volume of trade in the world. According to statistics of Society for Worldwide Interbank Financial Telecommunications (SWIFT), RMB has been the second in trade financing currency, the fifth in payment currency and the sixth in foreign exchange transaction currency by December 2014, and the USD, EUR, JPY and GBP are still the currencies with the highest degree of internationalization. In November 2015, the International Monetary Fund (IMF) declared to include RMB in the special drawing rights (SDR) basket, and the declaration has taken effect since October 1, 2016. RMB is the fifth currency included into SDR currency basket, with a weightage of 10.92%, ranked the third, higher than JPY and GBP. The weightage of USD, EUR, JPY and GBP were 41.73%, 30.93%, 8.33% and 8.09%, respectively. The inclusion signifies that the international community highly recognizes China market's economy reformations and RMB internationalization. It helps strengthen RMB's credibility and global influence and indicates that RMB may surpass other currencies in its internationalization.

As far as trade settlement is concerned, the total import and export value of our country reached 24.33 trillion yuan in 2016, in which 4.12 trillion yuan was settled in RMB, accounting for a proportion of 16.93%, and the proportion of RMB settlement in global trade was even lower, at 2.17%. Meanwhile, the USA's cross-border trade in goods was mostly settled in USD, and USD settlement in global trade accounted for 42.09%. As far as official reserve is concerned, RMB had a share of 1.07% in global official foreign exchange reserve by December 2016, and USD had a share of up to 63.96%. As far as valuation and investment are concerned, international bonds and bills valuated in RMB had a balance equivalent to 98 billion USD, accounting for 0.48% of the world; while international bonds and bills valuated in USD accounted for 43.73% of the world balance. Obviously, RMB internationalization still has a long way to go.

1.1.4 *Difficulties in RMB Internationalization*

Although RMB internationalization has a huge potential, some difficulties are gradually rising to the surface. Firstly, breakthrough points can hardly be found in developing RMB's function as an international currency. Leading currencies such as USD and EUR have strong inertia in international investment and trade, financial transactions and foreign exchange reserves. After achieving a certain market scale, RMB's substitution effect will decrease. Secondly, the global value chain works in favor of western developed countries. Chinese corporations are mostly in the downstream of the global value chain and are similar to Japanese companies in the old days, which had to use USD and EUR due to competition. Thirdly, the China-centered global investment and trade cooperation is insufficient. Overseas investment and trades require China to optimize structure, expand fields, identify new growth points and enlarge RMB's "friend circle". Fourthly, our financial institutions lack sufficient capacity to provide services for Chinese corporations. Chinese banks should cooperate to provide convenience for Chinese companies and facilitate RMB internationalization. Lastly, RMB's offshore financial market is still under-developed. Since overseas RMB financial products lack sufficient innovation, and overseas RMB assets lack sufficient liquidity, it is hard to attract the interest of overseas investors in RMB asset investment.

1.2 The Significance of RMB Internationalization

1.2.1 *RMB Internationalization Reflects China's Political and Economic Positions in the World*

In essence, RMB internationalization reflects the political and economic positions of China's sovereign credit in the world. According to history, a regime's founding, prosperity, weakening and downfall has always been accompanied by the circulation, strengthening, weakening, abolition and disappearance of its legal currency. In the perspective of political economy, currency serves the corresponding regime and is restricted by power. A high degree of RMB internationalization could enhance our competitive strength in the international financial market and help us maintain a leading position in economic globalization. RMB internationalization was proposed during a period of slow growth of international economy and China's "new normal" phase. It is an economic strategy of China and reflects China's mission and power as a large country. By analyzing the international currency system during this period of time, we can find ever-prominent conflicts in leading currencies, such as insufficient supply or demand and unbalanced development, which had serious impacts on the global economy. As a leading country among emerging economies, China is obliged to play a leading role in this respect.

1.2.2 *RMB Internationalization can Facilitate Domestic Economic Transition*

RMB internationalization is favorable for China, undoubtedly. China is a large country of trade, with high dependency on resources. If RMB could be used in international trade settlement, it will help Chinese trading companies to increase their competitive force and reduce the influence of bulk commodity price fluctuations on our country. With a complete transaction function in the global market, RMB will allow our country to issue bonds with lower interest rates and reduce the cost of financing. RMB has been formally included into the SDR basket and has become the reserve currency of multiple countries. As a result, the value of RMB will become more stable, and China's global influence will increase. China is the largest developing country and the country with the most foreign exchange reserves, but it is on a disadvantageous position due to the low degree of RMB internationalization. Accelerating RMB internationalization will significantly increase our country's comprehensive national strength, while maintaining a steady political climate, a medium-high speed of economic development, a balanced import and export in foreign trade, a basically stable RMB currency and a sufficient and balanced foreign exchange reserve. And if RMB is widely accepted by all countries as a reserve currency, China will also benefit from the seigniorage bonus.

1.2.3 *RMB Internationalization can Help Enhance China's Competitive Force on the Global Stage*

Capacity and trade cooperations in BRI require a large amount of capital. According to history, America vigorously promoted the use of US dollars in its "Marshall Plan". As a result, the import of goods and services of western European countries increased, and the US dollar became the major settlement currency of western European countries in their trade with the USA. A new world system and order which facilitate economic integration of the USA and Western Europe was established. Since China is a major economy with GDP and trade volume ranking among the tops in the world, a high degree of RMB internationalization should be a fair choice. For countries receiving capital, RMB internationalization can help them save exchange cost, reduce exchange rate risks and attract more international capitals. Additionally, financial cooperation with our domestic currency in a global credit currency system can help maintain stability of the financial system along the BRI route, and even the entire world, and promote globalization, convenience and security of trade and investment.

1.2.4 *RMB Internationalization can Facilitate Domestic Financial Reforms*

RMB internationalization can effectively accelerate reforms of our financial market and facilitate steady growth of the market economy. It is favorable for the sustainable development of the domestic financial market. Currently, China's financial system has several problems, such as low degree of openness, low efficiency and weak competitive force, and RMB internationalization could help deepen China's financial system reforms. Based on the real cases from the BRI construction, we would encourage Chinese financial institutions to set up overseas branches and create green and inclusive financial products valuated in RMB. In this way, we can provide policy support for RMB to "step out" in the investment and financing field and meet the huge capital requirement of BRI construction.

1.2.5 *RMB Internationalization Serves the Common Interest of the International Community*

It has been common knowledge of the international community that if the international financial market is monopolized by a currency, the global economy will be deeply affected by the issuing country of the currency. In the 1970s, after undergoing two US dollar crises, America declared to abandon the "Bretton Woods System" which had been in force for 30 years. Since then, US dollar has been unhooked from gold, and the new age of credit currency system has arrived. America was no longer limited in dollar issuance. When the Federal Reserve raises the interest rate, dollar rises and global economy sags; when the Federal Reserve reduces the interest rate, dollar weakens and global economy booms. To some extent, US dollar has become a "rogue currency". Through quantitative easing and tightening, US dollar had robbed developing countries and emerging economies over and over again, and countries along BRI had suffered the most. Countries urgently need diversified foreign exchange reserves to protect themselves from financial risks, and RMB stood out as the fifth currency formally included into SDR basket and a high-quality choice for countries along the BRI route.

1.3 Research Summary

BRI and RMB internationalization are two important strategies of our country to establish a new pattern of full openness and facilitate economic growth. They are internally connected with each other and have huge potentials for co-development. According to Zhou Xiaochuan (2017), there is a great deal of experience to learn from working on domestic currency, with regard to pushing forward BRI construction. China could explore with relevant countries on how to increase usage of the domestic currency in investments and financing, while pushing forward RMB internationalization. Hu Huaibang (2015) pointed out that RMB internationalization will facilitate trade and investment of countries along the BRI route, help China and countries along the BRI route in effectively avoiding exchange losses, strengthen the countries' capabilities in withstanding financial risks, reduce capital and transaction costs, increase international competitive strength of local economy, financial institutions and corporations, and provide a strong driving force for BRI construction. Chen Yulu (2015) pointed out that China should push forward RMB internationalization and create a coordinated development model of international economy and finance through BRI construction. Meng Gang (2017) conducted a systematic research on pushing forward RMB internationalization through BRI construction based on the internationalization experiences of major currencies, and pointed out that China should carry through in supply-side structural reform, conduct top-level design for RMB internationalization, cooperate with relevant countries in economy and finance, optimize the investment and trade environment, and strengthen RMB's functions in valuation, settlement, investment and reserves.

Our country's capital account opening is progressing smoothly on the whole. It is a gradual process, and the corresponding academic research is conducted carefully to the depth. According to Zhou Xiaochuan's research (2012), our country should push forward RMB's capital account convertibility with plans and procedures. We could formulate objectives in multiple dimensions, and moreover, push forward this process with far sight, and strive to create more advantages than disadvantages. According to Cheng Siwei's research (2014), foreign exchange management of our country is in transition from "loose in and strict out" to "two-way balanced management". Administrative control is gradually being reduced, and differential treatments between domestic and foreign companies, state-owned and private companies, and organizations and individuals is also gradually removed. According to Cao Yuanzheng's research (2016), the major objective of RMB capital account's opening is to develop an in-depth financial market with liquidity which can provide secure, stable products, and realization of the objective determines how far RMB internationalization can go. According to Yu Yongding's research (2016), fragility still exists in our capital market and even the entire financial system, therefore the government can decisively adjust the process of capital account convertibility based on actual needs. According to Han Long's research (2016), RMB internationalization mainly faces three obstacles — capital account control, exchange rate regime and financial market system. Legal problems are the risks accompanying RMB internationalization from the beginning till the end and should be prevented through the innovation of macro-prudential regulation system and the temporary re-bound mechanism of capital account control. According to Ye Zhendong's research (2016), a new round of capital account opening should be conducted, RMB back-flow channels should be expanded, and RMB security market construction should be pushed forward in order to activate two-way direct investment.

As pointed out by Wen Xueguo (2016), the Shanghai-centered urban agglomeration at Yangtze River Delta is an important platform for our country to take part in global competitions, and an important intersection of the BRI and Yangtze River Economic Belt. Therefore, the urban agglomeration should be comprehensively opened up to serve as an international financial center, and investment and trade systems fitting common international rules should be established. From the perspective of political economy, Huang Xiaoyong (2017) analyzed the market force and political logic of the formation of natural gas RMB, the feasibility of natural gas RMB strategy, potential measures to push forward its development, and the challenges and opportunities in the process. He also explored effective means to push forward the implementation of natural gas RMB. According to Shen Jianya's research (2013), the essence of currency internationalization is currency substitution. It means foreign currencies have replaced the domestic currency in its function. In other words, when citizens of a country have lost confidence in the domestic currency, or the domestic currency's return on assets has fallen significantly, the citizens will start holding more foreign currencies and gradually reduce holding of the domestic currency. As a result, foreign currencies will replace the domestic currency in many aspects. The scholar, Cohen (1971), pointed out that the substitution of a foreign currency for domestic currency is called currency substitution; but in international trade, substitution of the domestic currency for a foreign currency is called currency internationalization. Chen Miaoxin (2002) analyzed the optimal currency area theory and proposed the concept of substitutability competition and increasing a currency's competitive force through cooperation. He mentioned that different countries could form a currency union and adopt single currency in a specific area; or allow free exchange of their respective currencies in order to stabilize domestic price of commodities, reduce unemployment rate and maintain balance of payment in the international market. According to Jiang Boke (2005), the academic circle has reached a consensus on the criteria of whether a currency can be deemed as an international currency, i.e. the currency is widely used in international trade settlement, various financial derivatives associated with the currency are widely traded in the foreign exchange market, and assets valued in the currency are included as foreign exchange reserves of multiple countries.

According to Ma Jun (2015), along with the rapid rise of China's overseas investments, the overseas investment organizations are facing more and more environmental and social risks. Our country should push forward green investments in BRI construction to fulfill our promise of green actions and maintain our image as a responsible great nation. According to Li Mei and Ding Hui (2016), we should persist in green and ecological development during BRI construction, set up a green financial system, adhere to the principle of sustainable development, push forward greenization reforms of financial institutions and strengthen top-level designing, especially in mechanism and platform construction. Zhou Yueqiu (2017) researched the relationship between green finance and RMB internationalization and indicated that both should be pushed forward in a coordinated fashion. Mai Junhong *et al.* (2015) conducted research on the influence factors of green finance of our country and indicated that the government should formulate appropriate policies to direct and encourage financial institutions to implement green finance. According to Yu Qi's research (2016), the BRI has produced lots of opportunities of industrial and capacity cooperation as well as investment and financing, therefore the traditional green finance should be combined with BRI construction to set up a green financial system on levels of strategic plans and system construction. Li Guohua (2017) analyzed the unique advantages of Postal Savings Bank and indicated that financial institutions should fulfill the social responsibility of "benefiting all people in cities and villages" during the BRI construction. According to Zhang Guangyuan and Liu Xiangbo's research (2017), inclusive finance is urgently needed in the BRI construction, which accomplishes economic integration, co-development and sharing of successful results. Guo Tianyong and Ding Xiao (2015) conducted an international comparison of inclusive finance from the perspective of banking services and indicated that factors influencing the development of inclusive finance in different countries mainly include economic strength, level of financial development, and credit price. Li Junfeng *et al.* (2017) conducted research on the core principles of inclusive finance development. He indicated that our country should not only incorporate inclusive finance into the framework of tolerance, development and financial stability, but also direct inclusive finance suppliers to strengthen self-governance, and fulfill social responsibilities on the basis of commercial sustainability. Li Jianjun *et al.* (2015) compared the small and micro financing of internet loan platforms and commercial banks and pointed out that internet financing and mobile payment industries are important suppliers of inclusive financial services.

1.4 Research Framework

By considering the theories and practice of pushing forward RMB internationalization through BRI construction, this book attempts to establish a three-dimensional framework of thought and research in four aspects: (1) Emphasizing fundamental theory research; (2) Thinking on policy and strategic levels; (3) Using historical and current situation analysis as the support; (4) Putting forward pragmatic advice on the operational level. This book has 15 chapters excluding the foreword and epilogue. The foreword summarized the coordinated relationship between BRI and RMB internationalization. Chapter 1 is an overview and introduction of the basic meaning and significance of RMB internationalization and provides a literature summary and research framework. Chapter 2 is the theoretical foundation of RMB internationalization. It introduces the currency substitution theory, optimal currency area theory, impossible trinity, Gresham's Law and currency grades. Chapter 3 explains the coordinated relationship between BRI and RMB internationalization and analyzes on how to push forward RMB internationalization on levels including financing, facility connection, trade connection, policy communication, and popular connection. According to the chapter, cooperation in trade, investment and finance should be strengthened. Chapter 4 introduces the internationalization experiences of several major currencies, including GBP, USD, JPY and EUR, and the foundations of cooperation in trade, investment, finance, and government. It also summarizes on the referential value of those experiences for RMB internationalization. Chapter 5 introduces financial innovations of BRI led by green finance, inclusive of finance and domestic currency finance. It emphasizes that our country's green and inclusive development concept and practice should be shared with relevant countries; indicates that construction fund deficiency and foreign exchange risks should be solved; and that the support of governments, corporations and the public of relevant countries should be gained. Chapter 6 provides path choices of capital account opening during the comprehensive opening of our country. It analyzes the scope, current situation and path choices of capital account opening based on new orientations put forth in the Party's 19th National Congress, and also provides policy suggestions. Chapter 7 provides strategic considerations on developing RMB offshore financial market during BRI construction. It explains the meaning of offshore financial market and the significance of developing RMB offshore financial market. Multi-level development is proposed in the chapter from the angles of geographical quartering, core objectives and determining factors. Major challenges are analyzed and policy suggestions are put forward. In Chapter 8, the development of petroleum RMB during BRI construction is introduced. The chapter studies the formation and disadvantages of petrodollar system, and analyzes the urgency, key nations and current obstacles of creating the petroleum RMB system. Meanwhile, policy suggestions are also provided. Chapter 9 introduces RMB internationalization pushed forward by green finance. It mentions that countries along BRI are facing severe challenges of sustainable development and introduces the origin and theoretical foundation of green finance as well as definitions and policies of green finance in China and foreign countries. The tools of green finance in RMB internationalization are also introduced, which includes green credit, green bonds and carbon finance. Meanwhile, existing obstacles are analyzed and solutions are offered. Chapter 10 provides an overseas case study — setting up overseas RMB funds in France. It introduces the current situation of RMB internationalization in the European Union, especially France, analyzes the major problems, advantages and disadvantages of setting up RMB overseas fund in France, and provides relevant suggestions. Chapter 11 provides case study on a region — the Arab League countries. It introduces the current situation of RMB internationalization in Arab League countries, studies the cooperation basis and major problems of pushing forward RMB internationalization in Arab League countries, and provides relevant suggestions. Chapter 12 provides case study on a nation — Russia. It introduces the current situation of RMB internationalization in Russia, studies Russia's political and economic situation, analyzes the feasibility of pushing forward RMB internationalization in Russia, and provides relevant suggestions. Chapter 13 provides case study on institutions — especially the advantages of and suggestions for China Development Bank to push forward RMB internationalization. It introduces the institutional orientation and mission of China Development Bank, analyzes the advantages of the Bank in pushing forward RMB internationalization, and puts forward relevant strategies. Chapter 14 provides the case study of a project — SAI-Bank project, which was the first breakthrough of RMB internationalization in Egypt. The chapter studies the nation, project, and background of borrowers in RMB internationalization in Egypt, and analyzes the process and significance of pushing forward RMB internationalization. Chapter 15 is a conclusive chapter. It provides policy suggestions on pushing forward RMB internationalization through BRI. According to the chapter, domestic economic foundation should be strengthened to push forward RMB internationalization steadily; economic and financial cooperation should be strengthened on the principle of "discussion, co-development and sharing"; investment and trade cooperation environment of BRI should be optimized; and lastly, RMB's function of valuation and settlement in international trade, and its functions of financial transaction and reserves should be strengthened, in order to improve the quality of financial services. The epilogue provides the authors' thoughts in writing this book.

Theoretical Foundation of RMB Internationalization

According to history, international currencies compete with each other in the following pathway: They break through the limitations of metal currency and gradually develop into credit currencies. Various competition relationships emerge in the long development process, and the competition model is transformed from substitution to cooperation, from diversification to simplification, and at last, to diversification, again. Various currency theories have also been put forward in this historical process.

2.1 Currency Substitution Theory

In March 1969, American economist V.K. Chetty published an article on American Economic Review, and it was the first mention of currency substitution. According to currency substitution theory, major factors influencing RMB internationalization include macro-economy, scale and systems. The macro-economy factor refers to currency substitution caused by variation of cost-benefit of holding a foreign currency, caused by the macro-environment, such as difference of true yields of the domestic and foreign currencies, foreign exchange factors, inflation rate and political and economic risks. The scale factor refers to the situation where the foreign currency amount of the trading party would increase with the value of international trade under the driving force of trade and prevention motives, such as the level of national income, level of wealth and scale of international trade. The system factor refers to the transaction cost differences due to different economic and exchange systems of various countries, such as convertibility of a currency, transaction cost of the foreign exchange market and the market factors.

2.2 Optimal Currency Area Theory

In 1961, the American economist Robert A. Mundell put forward the concept of optimal currency area, and the contemporary American economist Ronald I. Mckinnon also provided an in-depth explanation of the theory. According to the optimal currency area theory, several conditions are required to create an optimal currency area across multiple countries: (1) liquidity of production factors; (2) economic openness; (3) financial market integration; (4) product diversification; (5) synchronism of economic cycles; (6) similarities in inflation rate; (7) flexibility in salaries and prices; (8) similarities in trade structure; (9) policy integration. Currently, RMB has become the "hard currency" in neighboring countries, and is playing a significant role in border trade. As China has deepened investment and trade in countries along the BRI route, set up infrastructure connections, and strengthened coordination with the countries, creating an optimal currency area along the BRI route should be an objective of RMB internationalization.

2.3 The Impossible Trinity

In 1998, the American economist Krugman first put forward the "impossible trinity" principle after the Asian financial crisis. He indicated it is impossible for a country to realize the three policy objectives of currency policy independence, exchange rate stability and free flow of capital all at the same time, and only two of them can be selected. According to the "impossible trinity" principle, a country's foreign exchange reserve is always insufficient, compared with the large amount of international hot money. Once the international hot money is expected to have a huge impact on the country's currency, the country will be unable to maintain exchange rate stability even if it uses up all of its foreign exchange reserve. With RMB internationalization and the impact of overseas hot money, it will be difficult to maintain exchange rate stability of RMB and currency policy independence. While pushing forward RMB internationalization, our country should adhere to currency policy independence. As to free flow of capital and exchange rate stability, we need to choose the key item and make transitions. In other words, we need to realize managed flow of capital and a basically stable exchange rate with flexibility.

2.4 Gresham's Law

The Gresham's Law reflects the phenomenon of "bad money drives out good money" under the precious metal currency system. The law was explained by the world-renowned scholar Thomas Gresham in the 16th century. According to Gresham's Law, when two currencies are in circulation at the same time, even if they have the same nominal value, their real values will be different. And the currency with the higher real value will be collected or flow into other countries. On the contrary, the currency with lower real value will be used by the public and be widely circulated. Along with the circulation of credit currencies, the Gresham's Law is reversed, and the phenomenon of "good money drives out bad money" occurs in currency competition. For example, due to the collapse of the Soviet Union and the devaluation of rouble, the trading parties selected more RMB in their transaction and did not accept rouble in border trade between Russia and China.

2.5 Currency Grade Theory

Cohen (1998) divided currencies into 7 grades from the angle of currency geography based on different competitive advantages. The

7 grades include: top currencies, which are widely used in the world, such as USD; noble currencies, which are widely used in a specific region, but are not playing a leading role in international market, such as EUR; outstanding currencies, which are widely recognized but only have a small global influence, such as GBP and JPY; ordinary currencies, which are widely used in its corresponding countries, but are seldom used globally, such as South Korean Won; infiltrated currencies, which are influenced by foreign currencies and are gradually replaced, such as Latin American currencies; quasi-currencies, which are facing serious threats in their applications, such as the currencies of weak economies, for example, Cambodia; and pseudo-currencies, which exist in name only, such as Panama currency.

3

Coordination between Belt and Road Initiative and RMB Internationalization

Belt and Road Initiative (BRI) construction is the key to opening the international market and an accelerator of RMB internationalization. As BRI construction is gradually pushed forward and more Chinese companies step out of the border, more investment and trading activities will be settled in RMB. Meanwhile, countries along BRI will have larger and larger demand for RMB, the first of which is the liquidity demand. For example, People's Bank of China has signed currency swap agreements of more than 3 trillion yuan with other countries. Secondly, there are trading and reserve demands. The central banks of various countries are motivated to invest in bonds and security assets valuated in RMB and increase liquidity of RMB assets to share risks of their reserve assets.

The BRI, put forth by Chinese government in accordance with the times, signifies that the developing countries, which center on emerging great powers, have become new engines of global economy and important entities of global governance. The situation has brought about historical strategic opportunities for RMB internationalization. The countries along BRI have different resource endowments, complement each other in economy and have huge potentials for cooperation. Therefore, policy communication, facility connection, trade connection, financing, and popular connection could be pushed forward in coordination with RMB internationalization.

3.1 Belt and Road Initiative is a Strategic Historical Opportunity for RMB Internationalization

The "connections and communications" in BRI construction has provided a strategic historical opportunity for RMB internationalization. China is one of the fastest growing economies in the world. According to economic development rules, if a country's industry has reached a certain scale and is globalized, the country's currency internationalization will progress as a consequence.

The Belt and Road Summit for International Cooperation 2017 was successfully held, and 270 results under 76 items have been achieved in policy communication, facility connection, trade connection, financing and popular connection. President Xi especially announced multiple major moves with expected significance in pushing forward RMB internationalization. For example, 100 billion yuan's capital will be added to the Silk Road Fund, financial institutions will be encouraged to conduct overseas fund businesses with a scale of about 300 billion yuan, the China Development Bank and Exim Bank of China will provide special loans of 250 billion yuan and 130 billion yuan for BRI construction, respectively. The horns of pushing forward RMB internationalization in BRI construction have sounded, and front-line financial workers are already on the way.

To push forward RMB internationalization in BRI construction, we need to conduct top-level designs, construct an economic cooperation framework for relevant countries, and set up a central bank cooperation organization. Meanwhile, we should enhance flexibility of RMB exchange rate, push forward managed capital account convertibility, accelerate overall arrangement of financial institutions, implement RMB valuation and settlement for bulk commodities and cross-border e-commerce, and strengthen RMB's transaction and reserve functions with currency exchanges. Additionally, we should also improve RMB's financial infrastructure, push forward construction of RMB offshore centers, and create diversified financial products.

3.2 The "Connections and Communications" of Belt and Road Initiative Helps Push Forward RMB Internationalization

3.2.1 *Financing Helps Increase the Degree of RMB Internationalization*

Financing is an important support of the BRI's construction. It deepens financial cooperation of relevant countries in trade and investment, strengthens RMB's payment and settlement functions, enlarges the scopes and scales of bilateral exchanges and settlements with domestic currencies of relevant countries, pushes forward the opening and development of the Asian bond market, widens RMB's investment and reserve functions, and establishes a channel for two-way benign circulation of RMB. Moreover, financing could accelerate reforms of the domestic financial system, push forward construction of the stability system and credit system of Asian currencies, increase RMB's use in surrounding countries and specific regions, and finally, generate a resultant force to push forward RMB internationalization.

3.2.2 *Facility Connection Helps Boost Demands for RMB Internationalization*

The key point of facility connection is to strengthen our country's infrastructure connections with countries along the BRI route. Roads, railways, port logistics and communication pipelines are typical public projects with a long construction duration, and their economic benefit cannot be realized in a short term. Therefore, they require large amount of credit capital. Since China has a rich supply of high-quality resources, such as building materials, accelerating RMB internationalization could solve financing gaps in infrastructure projects, and help achieve the grand objective of connecting countries along "Belt and Road". Therefore, BRI construction can activate the huge demand for RMB internationalization.

3.2.3 *Trade Connection Helps Strengthen the Foundation of RMB Internationalization*

China is discussing with countries along the BRI route, on trade and investment convenience, and trying to remove barriers in investment and trade to improve the cycling speed and quality of regional economy. As to selection of valuation and settlement currency in international trade, the most influential factor is the currency's cost of use. Therefore, trade connection and RMB internationalization will facilitate each other. There is a huge potential for trade cooperation between China and countries along the BRI route. Trade connection not only facilitates the economic development of relevant countries and recovery of global economy, but also opens up a large space of cooperation for RMB internationalization.

3.2.4 *Policy Communication Provides an Assurance for RMB Internationalization*

Policy communication enables China to formulate development strategies, discuss cooperation plans, create regional economy integration, and lay a solid foundation for RMB internationalization with countries along the BRI route. By conducting high-level reciprocal visits and following the principle of "discussion, co-development and sharing", we have built political trust with countries along the BRI route, achieved a win-win situation, strengthened traditional fields of cooperation, opened up new cooperative space, and deepened multi-lateral and bi-lateral cooperation in finance and currencies. As a result, we have provided a great historical opportunity for pushing forward RMB internationalization and created necessary policy conditions.

3.2.5 *Popular Connection Helps Create a Suitable Atmosphere for RMB Internationalization*

The relationship between two countries depend on intimacy of their people. The progress of RMB internationalization during BRI construction requires "solid popularity" and social support. RMB internationalization could enhance capital-use efficiency, reduce financial cost, prevent exchange rate risks, and is immensely beneficial for companies and individuals from countries along the BRI route. According to history, a currency's internationalization is also a process of the corresponding country's civilization being recognized around the world. Popular connection is highly valued during the BRI construction, and it reflects our country's strategic and global far-sightedness. It is a wise decision, beneficial in the long run and has created a benign atmosphere for RMB internationalization.

3.3 Trade, Investment and Financial Cooperation Should be Emphasized in RMB Internationalization During the Belt and Road Initiative Construction

3.3.1 *Trade Cooperation*

(1) *Restricting Factors of RMB Internationalization in the Trading Field*

Compared with our country's position as a global trading power, RMB settlement and valuation in cross-border trade is still in its starting phase, and significantly less than the use of domestic currency of America, Germany, Great Britain, Japan and Australia in their own cross-border trade. In the cross-border trading field, RMB valuation and settlement are mainly restricted by the following factors: Firstly, Chinese companies mainly conduct low-end manufacturing in their starting phase of international trade. They are mostly dependent on foreign trade partners, therefore they are at the downstream of global value chain system and only had a weak pricing power. It takes some effort to accumulate the power to push forward RMB valuation and settlement in trade. Secondly, currency inertia exists in international trade. Trade partners do not choose a substitute currency immediately. Thirdly, the RMB exchange market and financial derivatives are not complete, and are unable to meet the needs of companies to finance and prevent exchange risks. Fourthly, it is not convenient enough for companies to use RMB.

(2) *Trade Cooperation on BRI will Effectively Push Forward RMB Valuation and Settlement*

By strengthening trade contacts and capital flow with countries along "Belt and Road", and reducing tariff and non-tariff barriers, China and countries along BRI are deepening their economic mutual dependence and creating a huge demand for RMB valuation and settlement in the trading field. The use of RMB will expand from surrounding countries to specific regions and then the entire world, and an "RMB investment and trade circle" with RMB as the major currency in circulation will be created. For example, RMB valuation and settlement for bulk commodities might achieve a major breakthrough in the trading field of the BRI. And in cross-border e-commerce, currency substitution effect could be produced by adopting dual-valuation mechanism of RMB and the domestic currency of another country. In this way, we can lay a solid foundation for RMB valuation and settlement in the trading field. Additionally, RMB financial market and financial products can follow up and even make innovations to meet the huge demand for RMB internationalization in the trading field.

3.3.2 *Investment Cooperation*

(1) *Restricting Factors of RMB Internationalization in the Investment Field*

Since our country's launch of the RMB settlement trials for overseas direct investment in 2011, RMB internationalization has been advancing in a fast pace. However, the use of RMB in cross-border investment is still restricted by several factors: Firstly, complete capital account convertibility for RMB is still unpractical. Overly fast opening of the capital account will produce negative results. Supervision of overseas investment must be strengthened to regulate the industry. In recent years, there have been some unregulated conducts in overseas investments of Chinese companies, which has had an impact on our USD exchange reserve. Secondly, convenience is still a problem factor for Chinese and foreign companies, in using RMB in trades. Two-way flow of RMB is still not smooth. Thirdly, RMB has two markets — the domestic and overseas, therefore, effective supervision is required to prevent excessive interest arbitrage and currency arbitrage. Fourthly, the destination countries of investment have different and diversified political and economic situations, and therefore, it is difficult to conduct cross-border capital flow monitoring and risk management.

(2) *Investments and Cooperation on Belt and Road Initiative will Produce a Huge Demand for RMB Capital*

In BRI construction, the development strategies of China and relevant countries will be connected, therefore the countries will have a huge demand for capital, capacity and technology in aspects of infrastructure and energy development. Implementation of those projects requires long-term and stable capital input, therefore it could facilitate RMB output under capital account, and back-flow under current account through cross-border trade. RMB internationalization starts from trade settlement, but it can be predicted that capital account opening will become the major driving force of RMB internationalization in future. Complete opening of capital account does not mean that all 11 sub-accounts must be convertible. Capital flow of countries along BRI route should be protected from extra-territorial interferences and hot money speculations. Capital account opening of our country must be steadily pushed forward under careful supervision, and the managed convertibility principle should always be followed, in order to coordinate currency policies and exchange policies in a reasonable scope.

3.3.3 *Financial Cooperation*

(1) *Restricting Factors of RMB Internationalization in the Financial Field*

Finance should always serve real economy. Deepening of trade and investment cooperation between China and countries along BRI route is certainly accompanied by the deepening of financial cooperation. RMB internationalization is mainly restricted by the following factors in the field of financial cooperation: Firstly, the service scope of Chinese financial institutions does not meet the needs of companies in "stepping out of the country", and there is insufficient convenience in RMB investment and trade. Secondly, currency swap innovation should still be strengthened, and foreign exchange reserve cooperation should be vigorously pushed forward. Thirdly, there are still disputes on flexibility of RMB exchange rate and the extent of capital account convertibility. Fourthly, the RMB clearing and settlement system is not complete, and our financial infrastructure is still weak. Fifthly, RMB is still not a leading currency in the international financial market. RMB offshore financial market construction still has a long way to go, and channels of RMB to flow in and out are still not smooth.

(2) *BRI Financial Cooperation Should have a Clear Direction*

Financial cooperation reduces companies' cost of currency use, facilitates investment and trade cooperation, and provides maximum benefits for countries along the BRI route. In terms of financing, Asian Infrastructure Investment Bank, China Development Bank and Exim Bank of China are quickly setting up bank-government-corporation platforms in countries along the BRI route and have supported lots of important cooperation projects. In terms of RMB clearing, China has set up RMB clearing banks in more than 20 countries and districts, among which, 7 are in countries along the BRI route. In terms of currency exchange, China has signed bilateral domestic currency swap agreements, with a scale exceeding 3.3 trillion yuan, with 33 countries and districts. In terms of foreign exchange transaction, RMB can be traded directly with more than 20 currencies. And in terms of reserve currency, IMF has listed RMB holdings for the first time. The listing will greatly facilitate various countries' acceptance of RMB in their foreign exchange reserve configuration.

4

Internationalization Experience of Several Major Currencies

GBP, USD, JPY and EUR are major international currencies. Studies of internationalization experience of the above currencies in trade, investment, finance and government will provide enlightening significance for RMB internationalization pushed forward by the Belt and Road Initiative (BRI). To push forward RMB internationalization in BRI construction, China needs to strengthen domestic economic foundation and move forward steadily, discuss, co-develop and share economic results with countries along the BRI route, strengthen economic and financial cooperation, optimize investment and trade environment, and strengthen RMB's valuation, settlement, trade and reserve functions.

4.1 Great Britain Pound

4.1.1 *Overview of GBP Internationalization*

(1) *The Solid Foundation of "The Empire on which The Sun Never Sets"*

GBP is the first international currency in modern sense, and its dominance in the world was basically from 1816 when England first implemented the gold standard system to 1945 when the Bretton Woods System was formally established. Internationalization of GBP basically put an end to the loose condition of independent working of different currencies and signified the initial establishment of the international currency system. From the 1760s to the 1840s, the first industrial revolution took place, and the production force of England made a huge advancement. In the middle of the 19th century, England became the largest industrialized country and suzerain in the world, with colonies distributed in Europe, America, Oceania, Asia and Africa, and was called "the empire on which the sun never sets". Internationalization of GBP is attributed to the first industrial revolution, which replaced handwork with machine production and laid a solid political and economic foundation for England, and the foreign trade, investment and financial cooperation conducted through colonial expansion.

(2) *The Decline of the Comprehensive National Strength of England and the Position of GBP*

After World War I, British economy started declining, and with America's rise, GBP and USD were leading the global currency system together for some time. In 1945, the Bretton Woods System was formally established, and the USD became the only leading international currency in the world. In September 1949, GBP devalued 30.5% at once, and the exchange rate of GBP/USD fell from the fixed rate of 1:4.03 in 1940 to 1:2.8. However, GBP has not since quit the world currency system, but stood on a subordinate position based on regionalization. England's economic aggregate was surpassed by former

West Germany in 1961, by France in 1964 and by Japan in 1967. And finally, the international currency position of GBP fell behind those countries. According to statistics of IMF, GBP/USD exchange rate was about 1:1.23 by the end of December 2016. In the international currency system, GBP was ranked after USD, EUR and JPY, and took up a percentage of 2.1–4.9% in international reserve currencies.

4.1.2 *Foreign Trade Basis of GBP Internationalization*

(1) *The First Position in International Trade*

In 1860, England's total industrial output value accounted for nearly 50% of the world. In 1870, England's economic aggregate reached up to 9.1% of the world economic aggregate. Overseas colonies provided large amount of raw materials and a trading market for England, and surplus product could be sold overseas in cross-border trades. After acquiring abundant financial resources and advanced technology, England conducted large-scale investment in relevant countries, and further strengthened its position as a large trading country. In 1850–1880, the value of export commodities of England increased fourfold. In 1880, England's international trade volume accounted for 40% of the world. GBP was widely used with a strong overseas influence, and its value preservation capacity and transaction capacity were recognized by all countries.

(2) *GBP had a Prominent Function of Valuation and Settlement in Trade*

In the 1750s, England accomplished a transition from mercantilism to free trade. England's international free trade policy directly pushed forward GBP internationalization. In 1860, England and France signed the trade agreement *Cobden-Chevalier Treaty*, which signified the beginning of England's overseas free trade. In the subsequent years, England and other countries in Europe entered into similar trade agreements and created a comprehensive regional trade network centering on England. In the 1870s, England's total trade volume accounted for over 40% of the export volume of major developed countries. On the ground of trade convenience, England required most trade partner countries to valuate and settle in GBP. The rapid development of England's foreign trade greatly strengthened GBP's international currency functions of payment and circulation.

4.1.3 *Overseas Investment Basis of GBP Internationalization*

(1) *Overseas Investment is the Driving Force of GBP Internationalization*

England accumulated a large amount of wealth through trade surplus, and accompanied by military actions, England's overseas investment gradually reached across the world, and became an important driving force of GBP internationalization. England's overseas investment can be divided into two phases: The first phase is before the European free trade network was formally established. England's overseas investment was mostly conducted in European countries. Many investments were conducted by the means of government loans in the fields of railway, steel and coals. The second phase starts from the 1880s. England's overseas investment in this phase was focused on British colonies such as America, and its overseas investment aggregate gradually rose to the top of the world. By the beginning of World War I, England's overseas investment aggregate has surpassed 4 billion pounds, which accounted for 1/4 of British national wealth, and more than half of the overseas investment aggregate of major developed countries. The annual income of England's overseas investment increased from 385 million pounds at the end of the 19th century to 516 million pounds in the beginning of the 20th century.

(2) *Negative Effects of Overseas Investment*

It should be noted that England's overseas investments brought about some negative effects while obtaining high profits. Since

England's industrial revolution started early, the equipment in some old industrial departments was already worn, and new technologies were not sufficiently put to use. When large amount of capital was directed overseas, the domestic technical equipment was not updated and renewed timely. The emerging capitalist countries such as America and Germany swiftly developed their industries with new technologies, and quickly surpassed England in emerging industries. During the 40 years before World War I, England gradually lost its monopoly position in global industries. In 1872, England's economic aggregate was surpassed by America, but its comprehensive national strength was still the first in the world. By the beginning of World War I, England was still ranked the first in world trade, and London was still the financial center of the world, but England's position as a "world factory" has been lost. The two world wars greatly diminished England's comprehensive strength, and England's political and economic position in the world was completely surpassed by America.

4.1.4 *Financial Cooperation Basis of GBP Internationalization*

(1) *GBP's Dominant Position Brought About by Financial Internationalization*

In 1694, England became the first country in the world to establish a central bank system. In 1816, the British government issued the *Gold Standard System Act*, and first implemented the gold standard system. The *Act* stipulated that 1 pound was equivalent to 7.32238 grams of gold, and pound and gold could be freely exchanged. In 1826, the British government issued the *Banking Law* and encouraged establishment of joint-stock banks. Since then, England had been vigorously promoting cross-border loans of GBP. In 1844, the British government issued the *Banking Franchise Act*. It established the convertibility of GBP as a major responsibility of the central bank, and authorized the central bank to cooperate with central banks of various countries in currency exchange. In the beginning of the 19th century, London became the financial center of the world. England created a GBP area across different countries and districts, including Canada, Australia, New Zealand, Fiji and South Africa. The establishment and improvement of the British financial system and international financial market greatly accelerated GBP internationalization.

(2) *The Important Function of the British Central Bank*

The British central bank played an important role in GBP internationalization. The British central bank maintained a low gold reserve, and by taking advantage of its currency issuing power and currency policies, it influenced GBP's market interest rate and liquidity, flexibly adjusted international balance of payment, created a positive expectation for GBP, and strengthened GBP's position as an international currency. Through financial cooperation such as currency exchange, the British central bank effectively solved multiple credit crises of GBP, such as devaluation and payment. For example, in 1825, 1836 and 1839, payment crisis occurred multiple times in the British government, and through gold and silver exchange and loan cooperation, the British central bank gained urgent liquidity support from central banks of other countries, such as France. The effective cooperation between central banks and other financial institutions of England and other countries boosted the enthusiasm of overseas non-residents in using GBP and increased the GBP reserve of foreign countries. Finally, GBP replaced gold and became an international currency with functions of valuation, payment and reserves.

4.1.5 *The Role of Government in GBP Internationalization*

The British government played an important role in the process of GBP internationalization.

(1) *Political and Economic Basis*

The British government seized the historical opportunity of the first industrial revolution and developed England into a leading country whose political and economic strength was ranked the first in the world. England's political and economic position was the solid foundation of GBP internationalization.

(2) *Free Trade*

The British government strongly advocates manchesterism and exported England's advantageous products abroad. As a result, a free trade system centering on England was established, free trade has become a major driving force for GBP internationalization, and GBP has become the major currency for valuation and settlement in global trade.

(3) *Financial System*

The British government has set up an advanced system of financial institutions and directed national wealth to other countries in the form of capital. As a result, GBP's global influence was increased, and GBP's capacity of transaction and value increment were strengthened.

(4) *The Role of the Central Bank*

The British government stipulated GBP internationalization as a major function of the central bank, and conducted effective cooperation with central banks of other countries. By means of currency exchange, the British central bank pushed forward GBP's use across governments, strengthened GBP's reserve function, created a system for free convertibility of GBP on the basis of maintaining stable currency value, and enhanced convertibility of GBP across the world.

4.2 The US Dollars

4.2.1 *Overview of USD Internationalization*

(1) *Comprehensive National Strength was the Foundation of USD Internationalization*

By the beginning of World War II, GBP still maintained a strong currency inertia and was the most important leading currency in the world. USD internationalization started in the year 1879, when America implemented the gold standard system, and the stability and convertibility of USD were initially confirmed. In 1913, the USA established the Federal Reserve System, simply called Federal Reserve, which was serving as the central bank of the USA. The Federal Reserve provided an assurance for the internationalization of USD. In 1944, the Bretton Woods System was established. Since then, USD has been hooked with gold, and the currencies of member nations of IMF have maintained a fixed exchange rate with USD. USD was confirmed as the core of global currency system on the institutional level. It was internationalized in the real sense, and became a special international currency dominating all other currencies. America accumulated the most wealth in the world during the two world wars, and at the peak time, it owned 70% of the world's gold reserve and became the largest and the strongest economy in the world. The success of USD in replacing GBP and becoming an internationalized currency was partly due to the times and opportunities, but the root cause was that America had surpassed all other developed countries in economic aggregate, international trade, foreign investment and financial cooperation. Therefore, the internationalization of USD was the inevitable choice of history.

(2) *Weakening of USD's Position as an Absolutely Leading Currency*

The period from successful internationalization of USD to the present date could be divided into two phases — the phases of gold standard system and dollar standard system. In 1973, America abandoned the "Bretton Woods System", which had been in force for 30 years, after two dollar crises. In 1976, IMF and various countries reached a consensus to create a new international currency system which would replace the "Bretton Woods System". The times of dollar standard system formally arrived and continued till today. After the collapse of "Bretton Woods System", the currencies of major countries were unhooked from USD, and the legitimacy of floating exchange rate was confirmed. Although the USD was still the leading international currency, it lost its force to monopolize the foreign reserves of various countries. The USD's international position was obviously weakened. Additionally, the dollar standard system posed a significant risk to the international currency system. Issuance of USD is no longer restricted by the USA's gold reserve, and it is completely dependent on the will of the Federal Reserve. Through dollar output, the USA could tie its own economy closely to the world economy. Currently, USD is still the most important international currency in the world and is widely used in international trade and investment. Important commodities such as petroleum and gold are still valuated in USD, and the percentage of USD in global official foreign exchange reserve has always been maintained above 60%.

4.2.2 *Foreign Trade Basis of USD Internationalization*

(1) *Currency Dependency in International Trade*

In the second half of the 19th century, America accelerated its industrialization on the basis of its various advantages. With a rapidly growing economy, America replaced England as the largest industrialized country in the world. In 1913, the industrial output of USA accounted for about 36% of world industrial output. In the 1940s, the percentage rose to 50%. Along with the success of industrialization, America's foreign trade was developing rapidly. Its percentage in world trade rose from 8% in 1870 to 11% in 1913. In the period before World War I, America had already become the topmost industrial country, but the use of USD in international trade was still far behind GBP. In 1913, GBP accounted for 38% in the foreign exchanges held by 35 major countries, but USD accounted for less than 5%.

(2) *Historical Opportunities Put an End to Currency Inertia*

War trade greatly stimulated world requirements for American products. During World War I, America stayed far from the major battlefields due to its unique geographical location. While rapidly developing its own economy, America made a huge business from arms and ammunition, and its international trade was taken to a higher level. In 1915, America became the largest trade export country in the world. In 1919, America made a profit of 4.9 billion dollars in international trade, and the profit in the year 1920 was 3.5 billion dollars. During

World War II, America's export trade volume increased from 3.31 billion dollars in 1937 to 9.9 billion dollars in 1945. In a sharp contrast, England's export trade volume in the same period decreased significantly from 26.3 billion dollars to 1.82 billion dollars. In 1947, 23 countries signed the *General Agreement on Tariffs and Trade (GATT)*, which strengthened USD's position of authority in international trade. In 1948, the USA's total export volume was already twice of England, which was ranked the second, and accounted for 21.9% of the world value. During World War II and in the construction period after the war, the valuation and payment functions of USD in international trade were greatly strengthened, and the USD's international position was significantly raised.

4.2.3 *Overseas Investment Basis of USD Internationalization*

(1) *The Key Role of Overseas Investment*

During World War I, major European countries such as England, France and Germany had to put an end to the gold standard system. America did not join in the war; instead, it provided large-scale credit and loans for England, France and other countries to purchase war materials. America became an international loan provider, and the US dollars could still be freely exchanged with gold. The USD had turned into a strong currency. In 1919, America's overseas investment reached top in the world, with an overseas net asset of 12.562 billion dollars. During World War II, America's overseas direct investment increased rapidly, with a private capital output increasing from 11.3 billion dollars in 1940 to 13.7 billion in 1945. Additionally, America provided about 38 billion dollars' credit loans for the Allies. The number was 3 times of that in World War I, and effectively increased USD's overseas liquidity. In July 1947, when World War II had ended, the USA formally started the "Marshall Plan", by which the USA provided a series of donations, funding and loans for Europe, with an amount totaling 13.15 billion dollars. The amount was equivalent to 1.2% of the USA's GDP from 1948–1951, among which donations accounted for up to 88%, and the rest were loans. Under the driving force of "Marshall Plan", the USA acquired lots of export shares for export of commodity, currency and labor to West European countries, and the USD became the major settlement currency in the international trade of West Europe.

(2) *"Marshall Plan" Achieved Remarkable Effect*

The plan's implementation had taken 4 years, in a complex political and economic background. It aimed to stabilize West Europe's politics and economy in order to prevent Soviet Union's expansion to Europe. Meanwhile, it could consume the domestic surplus capacity, and adjust the malformed war-time economic structure. In terms of economy and trade, trade barriers and protectionism still existed in West Europe, and there were certain obstacles in exchanges of capital, industry, talents and technologies with the USA. In terms of currency, West European countries were left weak after the war, and there was a huge "dollar shortage". Due to foreign exchange control of various countries, the "Bretton International Currency and Financial System" could not work properly. During the "Marshall Plan", the GNP of West Europe increased by 32%, from 120 billion dollars to 159 billion dollars. Their industrial output increased by 40%, and USD reserves increased significantly. A new international system and order was gradually established. The new order centered on protecting the USA's investment security and facilitating economic integration of the USA and West Europe. In a word, by analyzing in terms of economy and currency, the "Marshall Plan" strengthened the USA's core position in the western world's politics and economy, transferred and released the USA's surplus capacity, adjusted and updated America's domestic industrial structure, revived Western European countries' economic strength, and further strengthened the USD's global position.

4.2.4 *Financial Cooperation Basis of USD Internationalization*

(1) *A Solid Foundation of Financial Cooperation*

USD internationalization has a solid foundation of financial cooperation. Firstly, the USA adopted the gold standard system in the beginning stage of the "dollar strategy". The USD had a stable currency value, therefore its convertibility was guaranteed. Secondly, the Federal Reserve played a significant role by adopting appropriate internationalization measures. During the 10 years since the founding of Federal Reserve in 1914, the USD became the official foreign exchange reserve currency of various countries. Thirdly, America strongly supports global development of the financial industry. America's financial market was well developed, and reached a first-class standard in its breadth, depth, degree of openness and infrastructure. Fourthly, America seized the historical opportunities of the two world wars and post-war re-construction of various countries. It rapidly developed domestic economy, exported financial assets valuated in USD in a large scale, and effectively increased the USD's overseas liquidity. Fifthly, the USA led the construction of the international currency system and global financial system, and established the USD as a leading international currency on system levels including international exchange rate arrangement, currency reserves and balance of payment mechanisms.

(2) *Breakthroughs in Trade and Financial Valuation and Settlement*

In the 1920s, the USD first challenged GBP's international position by financial cooperation. And the most important step was to vigorously develop trade acceptance with USD as the unit of settlement in international trade, under the strong support of the Federal Reserve. New York gradually became an international financial center in parallel with London, and the use of USD in trade credit loans exceeded GBP. The position of USD as an international reserve currency was gradually established, and the percentage of USD in official foreign exchange reserves of various countries first surpassed GBP in 1954. In the "Bretton Woods System", financial cooperation demonstrated its important support for USD internationalization, and finally established USD as the absolute authority in international currencies. Even after the collapse of "Bretton Woods System", financial cooperation was still playing a key and decisive role. Since America had a solid basis of financial cooperation with various countries, and had a highly open and developed capital market, the official foreign exchange reserves of various countries were mostly held in the form of USD bonds, and a large proportion of global private reserves was USD securities. By December 2016, the balance of international bonds and bills valuated in USD accounted for a percentage as high as 43.73% in the world, and the percentage of USD in official foreign exchange reserves of the world was as high as 63.96%; while RMB's share was only 1.07%. By December 2016, statistical data of SWIFT indicated that USD was ranked the first in the use of global payment currencies, and its use in global transactions accounted for 42.09%, while RMB's share in global payment was only 2.45%. Till today, USD is still an absolutely leading currency in the world.

4.2.5 *The Government's Role in USD Internationalization*

USD internationalization was started in 1879 and achieved a success half a century later, in 1944. Although historical opportunities played a role, the success of USD was mostly attributed to the US government's correct strategic thinking, active measures and long-term persistent efforts.

(1) *USD Internationalization was Pushed Forward with Strong Determination*

The US government set up the "international currency committee" in the beginning of the 1920s, conducted an exploratory research on currency and the banking system, and published some well-known academic works on currency and banking industry. In 1913, the Federal Reserve was adopted by the United States Congress as a permanent measure, and pushing forward USD internationalization was one of its important responsibilities. After the founding of the Federal Reserve, the US government started encouraging financial institutions to actively establish overseas branches in order to provide convenience for international trade, investment and the use of USD.

(2) *The USD Financial Market was Developed Vigorously to Facilitate USD's Inclusion as an International Reserve Currency*

When America became the first trading power of the world, the Federal Reserve encouraged the American banking industry to issue dollar exchange acceptances, and guaranteed the liquidity and interest stability of the acceptances as the final purchaser. Therefore, the Federal Reserve greatly enhanced the attraction of financial assets valuated in USD. In 1914–1924, the USD's share in international trade settlement and foreign exchange reserves first exceeded GBP, and the scale of bonds circulated in New York also exceeded London.

(3) *USD Internationalization was Facilitated by Setting Up International Rules*

The "Bretton Woods System" and GATT led by the US government facilitated free global trade and free flow of capital and foreign exchanges and strengthened the USD's authority among international currencies.

(4) *The US Government Actively Interfered with the USD Exchange Market*

By setting up the Exchange Stabilization Fund (ESF), and conducting currency swap and warehousing, the government maintained balance of supply and demand of USD as well as currency value stability, and tried to overcome the Triffin Dilemma.

(5) *Different Measures were Adopted to Strengthen USD's Core Position in International Trade and the Financial Field*

For example, the US government used USD in financial assistance schemes such as "Marshall Plan", to persuade international organizations such as OPEC, to use USD as the currency for valuation and settlement in trade of large commodities, and to curb the internationalization of JPY and EUR.

4.3 Japanese Yen

4.3.1 *Overview of JPY Internationalization*

(1) *JPY Internationalization was "a Flash in the Pan"*

The biggest characteristic of JPY internationalization was its decline after "a flash in the pan". Its lessons deserve our introspection. After World War II, Japanese economy revived and developed at a rapid speed. In 1955–1973, the annual average actual GDP growth rate of Japan was 9.24%. In 1974–1990, Japan's annual average actual GDP growth rate was 3.81%. However, more than 10 years after 1991, Japan's annual average actual GDP growth rate was only 1.25%. In 1968, Japan's GDP ranked second in the world, and gradually replaced the USA as the largest lending country and creditor country in the world. At the end of the 1980s, the top 10 commercial banks were all Japanese banks. JPY emerged as a strong currency, and maintained stability through two dollar crises, therefore the international financial market gradually increased demand for JPY. When the "Bretton Woods System" collapsed in 1973, USD's position as the "currency anchor" in the international currency system was shaken, and many countries chose Mark and JPY as substitutions to avoid risks. Thus, it was a great opportunity for JPY internationalization. Regretfully, the Japanese government hesitated in JPY internationalization at that time and did not include it as a goal of government work. In 1980, Japan comprehensively modified the *Law for Management of Foreign Exchange and Foreign Trade*, and JPY's internationalization slowly started. In 1984, the "JPY — USD Committee" founded by Japan and USA issued the *Report of JPY — USD Committee*. In 1985, the Japanese government issued the announcement *Current Situation and Outlook on Financial Liberalization and JPY Internationalization*, and started JPY internationalization process through economic and financial liberalization, and JPY internationalization entered a fast development phase.

(2) *Bubble Economy Put an End to JPY Internationalization*

In 1985, Japan signed the Plaza Accord. JPY kept rising, and bubble economy started, sowing the seeds of an economic crisis. In 1990,

Japanese stock market crashed, with a fall exceeding 40%, and most companies, banks and security companies suffered huge loss. Soon afterwards, Japanese real estate price fell sharply, with a drop exceeding 46%. The bursting of stock market and real estate bubbles caused an economic decline lasting over 10 years, and JPY internationalization was seriously frustrated. In 1999–2003, Japanese government put forward an "Asian currency" proposal. Instead of transforming JPY into a global currency, Japan tried to transform JPY into the regional currency of Asia. However, with the change of political and economic situation of the world, the political and economic foundation for JPY internationalization no longer existed, and the best opportunities of pushing forward JPY internationalization had passed. Additionally, America was curbing JPY internationalization. Japan lost the best opportunity and was finally unable to achieve the desired target. In 2013, JPY's share in global trade settlement fell from 14% at peak times to 4%, and its share in the foreign exchange market fell from 27% to 19%. The proportion of JPY-valuated bonds in the global bond market fell from 17.3% to 2.5%, and the proportion of JPY in global foreign exchange reserves fell from 8.7% to 3.1%.

4.3.2 *Foreign Trade Basis of JPY Internationalization*

(1) *Important Restricting Factors of JPY Internationalization*

The important factor restricting JPY internationalization was the late development of JPY's valuation and settlement functions in international trade. After World War II, Japan established the "rise by trade" strategy, and formulated its foreign trade policies in the framework of GATT and the World Trade Organization. The country emphasized its trade connections with the USA and vigorously developed petrochemistry, steel, non-ferrous metals and machinery. By focusing on heavy industries, Japan became the largest country of export in the world. In the 1980s, Japan changed its strategy from "rise by trade" to "rise by technology" and "expand domestic demand" in order to avoid trade frictions with America and European countries. The government directed large companies in the fields of electrical machinery and automobile to replace trade with overseas direct investment, and transferred many energy-consuming, resource-consuming and environment-damaging industries into developing countries. In this way, Japan gradually increased its volume of trade with Asian countries. In 1970–2004, JPY's share in export and import trade settlement developed from 0% to 40% and 24%, respectively, and had not made major breakthroughs in the long term since. The valuation and settlement proportion of JPY in international trade was always significantly lower than international currencies such as the USD, EUR and GBP. For example, Japanese export accounted for about 10% in the world in 1993, but JPY's valuation proportion in international trade was less than 5%. Meanwhile, the US export was almost completely valuated in USD, and 80% of German export was valuated in its domestic currency. The valuation and settlement functions in international trade are the foundation of a currency's internationalization process. The disadvantages of JPY in valuation and settlement functions are the major cause of the frustration of JPY's internationalization.

(2) *The Causes of Late Development of JPY's Valuation and Settlement Functions in International Trade*

There are multiple causes for the late development of JPY's valuation and settlement functions. Firstly, Japan had an unbalanced foreign trade structure and is highly dependent on USD in valuation and settlement. Japan has a narrow territory and lacks resources. The imported goods were mostly bulk commodities such as raw materials and resources, but the valuation and settlement of bulk commodities were mostly monopolized by USD. In terms of export, Japanese products were mostly sold to Europe and America, and their valuation and settlement were mostly conducted in USD. Secondly, currency transaction of JPY in Southeast Asian countries didn't make a qualitative change in its scale. Since the 1980s, Japan started transferring large quantities of intermediate products and components to Southeast Asian countries for processing, and JPY's valuation and settlement increased significantly. However, since the finished products of Southeast Asian countries were mainly exported to America and European countries, and most currencies of Southeast Asian countries were using USD as their reference, JPY could not replace USD as the leading currency in valuation and settlement. Thirdly, USD inertia and competitive pressure were also obstacles. Due to

USD's inertia as an international currency, and the sharp rises and falls of JPY value, Japanese companies were pressured to choose USD in valuation and settlement while exporting products with small differences and heavy competitive pressure.

4.3.3 *Overseas Investment Basis of JPY Internationalization*

(1) *Accumulated Risks in Overseas Investment had Shaken the Foundation of JPY Internationalization*

Japan's overseas investment started in the 1960s and focused on resource development and labor-intensive industries. The investments returned lots of overseas resources to Japan, provided relief to Japanese economy's "bottleneck", and laid a foundation for JPY internationalization. In the 70s, while continuing to expand overseas investment in the resource industry, Japan increased its investment in overseas manufacturing and business, effectively avoided trade frictions, opened up the overseas market, and created a regional cooperation space for JPY internationalization. However, along with the large-scale relocation of manufacturing industry to foreign countries, the same phenomenon in England in the old days — industrial hollowing-out — occurred in Japan, too. In the middle of the 80s, the Japanese government significantly increased JPY's value and loosened financial control under the pressure of the USA. As a result, large amount of capital of Japanese companies flowed into the USA to purchase real estates and financial assets, which increased the investment risks and caused the bursting of Japanese "bubble economy" in the 90s. And JPY internationalization process was therefore terminated.

(2) *An Overly Hasty Financial Liberalization Attempt is Only Harmful for JPY Internationalization*

Overseas investments of Japanese companies and the "stepping out" of Japanese financial industry are closely combined and facilitate each other. They were quite successful in the starting phase and the middle of development, and greatly relieved the conflict between foreign and domestic markets and the two kinds of resources. However, Japanese government neglected the transformation, the upgrades and long-term development of domestic real economy, surrendered to the pressure of the US government and western developed countries to liberalize Japanese finance and increase JPY value, and did not timely correct Japanese companies' irrational investment behavior — excessive expansion overseas and blindly investing in real estates and high-risk financial assets. The Japanese government made a big mistake in macro-management and did not solve the economic crisis in a proper way. As a result, Japanese economy was frustrated with no hope of recovery, and JPY internationalization failed. Japan's exchange rate liberalization and capital account opening had already completed, but JPY internationalization failed. The phenomenon indicates that a currency's internationalization should be supported by a stable exchange rate, and is not necessarily dependent on capital account opening.

4.3.4 *Financial Cooperation Basis of JPY Internationalization*

(1) *JPY Internationalization and Japan's Financial Liberalization were Started at the Same Time*

JPY internationalization was conducted along with marketization and liberalization reforms of Japanese financial system. From World War II to the end of the 70s, Japan had the strictest financial system control among industrialized countries. In 1984, Japan's Ministry of the Treasury clearly stipulated in *Current Situation and Outlook on Financial Liberalization and JPY Internationalization* that all citizens could conduct foreign exchange and futures trade without restriction of real trade, companies could freely exchange foreign currencies and JPY, and bring capital raised in European JPY market back to Japan. The decision signified the full start of Japan's financial reforms centering on JPY internationalization. In 1986, Japan set up the Tokyo offshore financial market and removed restrictions on the outflow of foreign capital. In 1996, Japan implemented the "financial system reform plan", loosened control in banking, security and insurance, and achieved integration of domestic and international markets. In 1997, Japan started pushing forward currency financial assistance and cooperation in surrounding countries such as South Korea, Philippines, Thailand and Indonesia. In 2000, Japan passed the *Chiang Mai Initiative*, which set up a currency cooperation framework in East Asian districts. Along with internationalization reforms of the Japanese financial system, JPY's internationalization made a fast breakthrough. JPY assets' proportion in international financial market rose from about 3% in 1980 to 12.4% in 1995, and newly issued offshore bonds valued in JPY rose from 5% in 1980 to over 17%.

(2) *Main Content of Financial Cooperation*

Financial cooperation in JPY internationalization was mainly conducted in five ways: (1) Accelerate opening of the domestic financial market. Japan's currency market, stock market and bond market were all on the way of internationalization, marketization and liberalization. (2) Strengthen construction of JPY offshore financial market. Japan vigorously developed the European JPY offshore market, and isolated and protected the domestic financial system through the offshore market. In 1986, Japan set up the Tokyo offshore market, and effectively facilitated JPY's use in global financial transactions. (3) Complete marketization reforms of the interest rate. Japan had been adopting interest rate control before 1979. In 1979–1994, Japan completed marketization reform of the interest rate on the principle of "from large to small amounts, and from loan interest rate to deposit interest rate". (4) Complete capital account opening. Japan achieved free exchange of current account in 1964, and basically achieved capital account convertibility in 1980. In 1985–1986, Japan removed control on capital flow of residents and non-residents, and completed capital account opening. (5) Attempt to conduct JPY's regional cooperation. Japan tried to transform JPY into the "Asian currency", but failed in both internationalization and regionalization due to economic decline and USD inertia. It could be summarized that the soft spot of JPY internationalization is valuation and settlement in international trade, but JPY internationalization achieved certain effect in its use as an investment and reserve currency.

4.3.5 *Government Role in JPY Internationalization*

The attitude and role of Japanese government in JPY internationalization could be described in three phases.

(1) *The 1960s to 1970s*

The Japanese government was worried that JPY internationalization will disrupt domestic financial policies, therefore they held a negative attitude toward JPY internationalization. During the period, Japan applied strict approval system on capital flow based on the *Law for Management of Foreign Exchange and Foreign Trade* issued in 1945, and the *Law on Foreign Capital* issued in 1950, and avoided the issue of JPY internationalization.

(2) *From the 1980s to the Asian Financial Crisis in 1997*

Under the continuous request of the US government to open the market, the Japanese government considered that as an economic great power, Japan should make steady effort to achieve JPY internationalization and financial market liberalization, and comprehensively modified the *Law for Management of Foreign Exchange and Foreign Trade*, and issued important documents including *Current Situation and Outlook on Financial Liberalization and JPY Internationalization*. During this period of time, Japan held a positive attitude toward JPY internationalization and considered the USD's leading position as its working objective.

(3) *From Asian Financial Crisis in 1997 Till Today*

The Japanese government realized the high risk of following USD and being overly dependent on USD. Particularly after the birth of EUR in 1999, Japanese government started actively transforming

JPY into a regional currency in Asia and tried to realize the goal of wide use of JPY in Asia. In 1998, the Japanese government founded the JPY Internationalization Committee, and on this basis, it set up the JPY Internationalization Research Seminar in 1999 and published a series of research report and concrete measures to push forward JPY internationalization. In 1999, Japan put forward the "Asian currency" concept. In 2000, the Japanese government set up a regional currency cooperation framework in East Asia through Chiang Mai meeting. In 2002 and 2003, JPY International Research Seminar issued two announcements, to indicate that by microscopic study of valuation currency choice in cross-border trade of companies, they considered that the objective of JPY internationalization was hard to achieve, and Japanese economic decline and USD inertia had put an end to JPY internationalization, respectively. In recent years, the Japanese government is still pushing forward currency swap arrangement with ASEAN countries in order to maintain JPY's influence in Asia.

4.4 The Euro

4.4.1 *Overview of Euro Internationalization*

(1) *Practice Guided by Theory*

In the 1970s to 1990s, German's economic aggregate was among top three in the world. Mark was an important international reserve currency and the core currency in Europe. Mark's position as an "anchor currency" in the European currency system formed in 1979 was the key premise for the start of euro. In 1999, euro was formally issued, and was managed by the European central bank system comprising the European Central Bank and the central banks of Eurozone countries. In 2002, euro was formally put in circulation and included into the international financial market. Currently, euro has replaced the original currencies of 28 countries (districts) in Europe, and has become the only legal currency in Eurozone and the second international currency. The birth of euro was partly attributed to the "optimal currency area theory" of the father of euro — American economist Robert A. Mundell. According to the theory, Western European countries were similar to each other in levels of economic development, and had high factor mobility between countries. Therefore, they could form a currency zone, in which the member states could maintain a fixed exchange rate for their currencies, or use a uniform currency. The statesmen of European countries transformed the theory into reality. Euro became the first non-sovereign state currency in world currency history and was successfully internationalized.

(2) *Regional Cooperation Basis of Euro's Birth*

Euro was the product of European economic integration. After World War II, European economy started from scratch, and the decision-makers chose the revival route of "unifying Europe". In 1951–1957, six countries in Europe signed the *European Coal and Steel Community Treaty*, *Treaty for Establishing the European Economic Community*, and *Treaty for Establishing European Atomic Energy Community*, which signified the start of European economic integration. In 1965, European Coal and Steel Community, European Economic Community and European Atomic Energy Community combined into the European Community, which was a major pillar for the founding of the European Union (EU) in 1993. Under the direction of the European Union, euro internationalization experienced three phases — system preparation, initial use and comprehensive circulation. In 1994–1998, the *Green Book on the Specific Plans of Introducing Single Currency* was issued, and the single currency was named "euro". A timetable and phased tasks were formulated, European Central Bank was formally founded, and various systems were prepared. In 1999–2002, euro was formally launched, and Eurozone countries used euro as their official valuation and settlement currency. The capital market of various countries started pricing and trading in euro. Since 2002, euro has been replacing the original currencies of Eurozone countries and has been in complete circulation. It has gradually become the second leading currency in the world.

4.4.2 *Foreign Trade Basis of Euro Internationalization*

(1) *Active Trading within the Region was the Basis of Euro Internationalization*

After World War II, German economic revived. With a remarkable export scale, Germany's foreign trade surplus was on the rise. In 1980–1991, Germany's export proportion was among top two in the world. With a reasonable trade structure, the high-end manufacturing products accounted for more than half of the export volume and laid the foreign trade foundation for the internationalization of Mark. Along with the progress of European economic integration, the customs union of member states of the European Community was established and strengthened. Industrial and agricultural products had an obvious competitive advantage in the region, and the trade among member states was quite active. The intra-trade volume of the European Union rose sharply from US$10.3 billion dollars in 1960 to US$122.9 billion dollars in 1973. And before the birth of euro in 1999, it reached US$870.2 billion dollars. After the birth of euro, Eurozone countries closely cooperated with each other, adopted effective measures to increase the proportion of euro settlement in international trade, and directed European transnational corporations to settle in euro in international trade and mergers and acquisitions outside of Europe. In 2008, the intra-trade volume of the Eurozone increased to 2.0092 trillion dollars.

(2) *Euro Facilitates Regional Trade Cooperation*

From the perspective of international trade, the launch of euro brought about huge benefits for Eurozone countries. The sharp rise of trade volume between Eurozone countries also strengthened euro's valuation and settlement functions. After the circulation of euro, the internal market of the Eurozone enlarged, the economic and trade environment was further optimized, unstable factors were greatly reduced, trade fluctuations were effectively controlled, and the growth of trade became faster and more stable. During the 10 years before circulation of euro, the annual average growth rate of intra-trade volume of Eurozone was about 2.9%; while during the 10 years following circulation of euro, the annual average growth rate reached nearly 9.7%, and the proportion in global trade volume was basically maintained at 15–30%. In 1990–1998, the growth rates of Eurozone intra-trade and foreign trade almost kept the same pace, with an annual average increase at about 16.01% and 17.12%. The growth speed of intra-trade slightly fell behind foreign trade. During the 10 years following euro circulation, significant trade effect of currency integration was achieved, and the euro's regionalization function was strengthened. The growth speed of intra-trade in Eurozone obviously exceeded foreign trade, and they were about 25.66% and 21.27%, respectively.

4.4.3 *Overseas Investment Basis of Euro Internationalization*

(1) *Germany's Overseas Investment and Cooperation Brought About the Capital Flow Effect*

By actively conducting overseas investment, Germany and other Eurozone countries produced a capital flow effect, facilitated output of goods and labor, and created an international cooperation basis with highly integrated economy for internationalization of Mark and euro. Germany's overseas investment started in the beginning of the 1950s, and with a slow growth of scale, it accumulated to 74 billion Marks by 1980. Since the 80s, with a growing capital liquidity, global industry relocation was accelerated, and Germany's overseas investment increased rapidly. By 1999, Germany's overseas investment reached 405.4 billion euros (1 euro was equivalent to about 1.9558 Marks), and Germany became one of the largest capital net output nations. Germany's overseas investment mainly involved large corporations and large projects. The 100 largest enterprises in Germany had an overseas investment accounting for 2/3 of the investment aggregate, and the 100 largest projects accounted for 38.7%. In terms of industrial distribution, the manufacturing industry (chemical, automobile, electrical appliance and machinery) ranked the top with a total overseas investment of 155.2 billion euros, accounting for 38.3% of Germany's overseas investment aggregate. The financial and insurance industries had an overseas investment of 136.2 billion euros, accounting for 33.6%. Foreign trade wholesaling and commercial retail had an investment of 55.2 billion euros, accounting for 13.6%. And the service industry (real estate, rentals and company services) had an investment of 41.7 billion euros, accounting for 10.3%.

(2) *Investment and Cooperation in the Eurozone Laid the Foundation for Euro Regionalization*

Germany's investment in EU countries always maintained the first place in amount, which facilitated the high dependency and mutual infiltration of Eurozone national economies, and laid the foundation for euro regionalization. By 1999, Germany's investment in EU countries was the highest and reached 180.3 billion euros, accounting for 44.5% of Germany's overseas direct investment. Germany's investment in England, Belgium and Luxembourg was focused on the financial industry; and its investment in France, Austria and Spain were focused on industry and trade. Meanwhile, 60.3% of direct investment of foreign countries in Germany was from EU countries which reached 135.1 billion euros. By 1999, Germany's largest destination country for overseas investment was America, except EU countries. Germany's investment in America was 129 billion euros in total, accounting for 31.8% of overseas direct investment of the country and was focused on the manufacturing and financial industries. Meanwhile, 25% of direct investment of foreign countries in Germany was from America, with an amount of 51.6 billion euros. Additionally, by 1999, Germany invested 20 billion euros in EU candidates, especially Hungary, Poland and Czech, accounting for 4.9% of its overseas direct investment. In the middle of the 1980s, Mark and JPY were both pressured by the USA to increase values, but in contrast to Japan's bubble economy, Germany relieved its pressure by regional cooperation in European investment and financing. Through the European currency linkage mechanism, Germany transferred investment capital to other European currencies and maintained stability of Mark value. As a result, it laid the currency foundation for the birth and internationalization of euro, and enabled euro, which centered on Mark, to achieve an advantageous position in parallel with USD.

4.4.4 *Financial Cooperation Basis of Euro Internationalization*

(1) *Financial Cooperation Facilitated Euro Internationalization*

By strengthening financial cooperation, Germany achieved Mark internationalization, and laid a solid foundation for the birth of euro. Before 1954, Germany applied strict control on foreign exchanges. With the rapid recovery of domestic economy and the development of foreign trade, Germany simplified non-residents' account opening procedures at domestic foreign exchange banks, gradually loosened control on overseas investors, separated the free currency zone and non-free currency zone and established a new cross-border payment system. In 1959, Germany achieved free convertibility of Mark and basically removed foreign exchange control. As a result, the capital of domestic citizens and overseas capital could flow freely. Since then, stability of Mark value had always been the core objective of currency policies of German central bank, and with a high international liquidity, Mark became a reserve asset accepted by many countries. In 1950, 16 European countries set up the European Payment Union in order to solve problems in currency settlement and free convertibility between different countries. In 1979, 8 member states of the European Community set up the European currency system according to the proposal of Germany and France. The currency system focused on German Mark and fixed the exchange rates between 8 countries in order to resist USD floating. It signified that the cooperation between European countries had taken a giant step toward currency integration and created an environment of stable currencies for the birth of euro.

(2) *The Unique Financial Market of the Eurozone*

In 1997, the EU set up the European central bank system consisting of European Central Bank and the central banks of member states. Eurozone countries meeting relevant standards started using euro and fixed the exchange rate between domestic currency and euro. A transition period of 3 years was established from euro start in 1999 to formal circulation in 2002. Eurozone countries authorized European Central Bank to implement uniform currency policies and take over foreign exchange reserves in order to maintain stability of euro value. Compared with the USA, Eurozone countries also had a financial market with quite favorable width, depth and liquidity, and they had a high degree of financial cooperation and development. Both Frankfurt and Luxembourg were world-class financial centers and created conditions for euros to rapidly develop into an international reserve currency and foreign exchange transaction currency. In terms foreign exchange reserve function, German Mark's proportion in the foreign exchange reserve of various countries rose from 0.1% in 1965 to 18% in 1989. And euro's proportion rose from 13.5% in 1999 to 18.5% in 2003. In terms of transaction function, international creditor's rights valuated in German Mark in 1970 had a proportion of 31.78%, secondary to the USD. In 2000, the proportion of international creditor's rights valuated in euro rose from 30.1% in 2000 to 40.5% in 2008, which surpassed USD.

4.4.5 *Role of Governments in Euro Internationalization*

Euro was the result of European governments' effort in pushing forward currency internationalization together. It was an international currency since the beginning, and soon developed into a globally leading currency only secondary to USD. (1) Euro internationalization was inseparable from active works of the governments of major European countries. Internationalization of German Mark was a precondition for euro internationalization. To facilitate Mark internationalization, German government gradually loosened financial and foreign exchange control, and withstood Mark's appreciation pressure by conducting foreign exchange operation and collecting capital in-flow tax. German tried to build Frankfurt into an international financial center, and by taking advantage of trade contacts and currency and financial cooperation in Europe, it successfully facilitated Mark internationalization. (2) Euro internationalization is attributed to the economic union of various European governments. Since the dollar crisis in the 1970s, governments of European countries has been actively establishing regional economic and currency cooperation mechanisms to prevent currency risks and taking the initiative of regional economy and currencies. The successive foundation of European Coal and Steel Community, European Economic Community, European Atomic Energy Community, European Community and European Union laid the organizational foundation for European economic integration. (3) European Central Bank was founded to unify and coordinate currency policies. The establishment of European Payment Union in 1950 and the European currency system in 1979 signified the start of European currency integration. In 1969, the government heads of member countries of the European Community first established the objective of setting up an "European economic and currency union", and proposed to set up the European Central Bank to unify and coordinate currency policies. In 1998, through cooperation of the governments of Eurozone countries, European Central Bank was finally established and became the strongest supranational financial institution in Europe. It enabled the Eurozone to adopt unified currency policies and foreign exchange policies, and provided assurance for euro to play a bigger role in international currency and financial system.

4.5 Referential Significance of Currency Internationalization Experience for RMB Internationalization

4.5.1 *The Government Leads RMB Internationalization by Conducting Top-Level Designs*

Based on the internationalization experience of major international currencies, our government should lead RMB internationalization during BRI construction by conducting and continuously optimizing top-level designs. We should strengthen policy communication with countries along "Belt and Road", improve RMB financial infrastructure and steadily push forward capital account convertibility. With the cooperation of companies, we should push forward cross-border use of RMB in countries along BRI in order to provide convenience for trade and investment, and promote RMB as an international reserve currency.

4.5.2 *Strengthen Economic Cooperation with Countries Along the Belt and Road Initiative Route*

An important reason for the failure of JPY internationalization was that Japan was overly dependent on the USA and neglected cooperation with Asian countries in the early stage. It was too late when Japan realized the issue and put forward the "Asian currency" concept. The success of euro internationalization was attributed to the success of European economic integration. When there is a high factor mobility between different countries, currency internationalization could be achieved without extra efforts. China is a great world trade nation and is closely united with many countries in economy and trade. Along with healthy adjustment of domestic economic structure, Chinese industries are advancing towards the high end of global value chain. As a result, China is able to transfer advantageous capacity to countries along BRI and expand trade cooperation. Therefore, China should learn from the experiences of international currencies, and actively set up economic cooperation framework together with relevant countries, and when necessary, set up multi-lateral institutions facilitating economic integration in order to create more favorable regional cooperation conditions for RMB internationalization.

4.5.3 *Strengthen Central Bank Cooperation of Countries Along the Belt and Road Initiative Route*

Internationalization of GBP, USD, JPY and EUR are all inseparable from the effort of the domestic central bank and close cooperation of central banks of various countries. Therefore, the key to pushing forward RMB internationalization through BRI is to create an RMB-centered regional currency cooperation system with participation of central banks of countries along "Belt and Road". Countries along BRI have a solid foundation for political and economic cooperation with China, and they expect high for and are highly dependent on China's investment, trade and capital. China should seize the favorable opportunity to set up central bank cooperation organizations for countries along "Belt and Road", establish a regional currency cooperation system focused on central banks of those countries, facilitate investment, financing and trade cooperation, and accelerate the process of RMB internationalization.

4.5.4 *Strengthen RMB Exchange Flexibility*

According to the historical experience of the competition between USD, EUR and JPY, strengthening RMB exchange flexibility while basically maintaining stability will help maintain RMB's position in global currency system and strengthen international investors' confidence in RMB's future price. It is the precondition for smooth progress of RMB internationalization. As China is more deeply integrated into the world, factors and mechanisms affecting RMB exchange rate are becoming more complex. Stability of RMB exchange rate is certainly a problem while pushing forward RMB internationalization in countries along "Belt and Road". We should keep improving statistical approaches such as RMB internationalization index and RMB exchange rate index in "Belt and Road", follow up on exchange rate variations of RMB and the currencies of countries along "Belt and Road", pay attention to the overall variation trend of RMB exchange rate relative to the currencies of those countries, and take effective and timely measures to maintain stability of RMB exchange rate.

4.5.5 *Gradually Achieve RMB's Capital Account Convertibility*

According to internationalization experiences of major currencies, a managed capital account convertibility will help reduce the impact of large-scale flow-in and flow-out of international capital, maintain stability of economy and finance, and take the initiative of economic development. According to IMF standard, the capital account is divided into 7 categories, 11 items and 40 sub-items. Latest evaluation indicates that there are 10 freely convertible items under RMB capital account, accounting for 1/4. 27 items are partly convertible, and only 3 are completely non-convertible. Along with the progress of regional economy integration of countries along "Belt and Road", RMB capital account should be convertible on a larger scale to strengthen RMB's function in investment, trade and value reserve. In BRI construction, we should prevent financial risk transfer of relevant countries, and should not blindly accelerate capital account convertibility. We must steadily push forward RMB capital account convertibility in a managed fashion.

4.5.6 *Facilitate RMB Investment and Trade*

Countries along the BRI route are mostly developing countries, and many countries still do not have branches of our country's financial institutions. RMB and the currencies of those countries could only be exchanged through USD and EUR. Therefore, the transactions have a high cost and exchange rate risk, and there is strong currency dependency. Even if the companies have RMB demand in their investment and trade, they are still compelled to choose USD or EUR due to inconvenience of exchange with RMB. Chinese financial institutions, especially the large Chinese banks with a high degree of internationalization could provide comprehensive financial services such as cross-border clearing, settlement, intermediate business and investment and financing. Therefore, while pushing forward RMB internationalization during BRI construction, it is imperative for our country to accelerate financial institutions' layout in countries along the BRI route and satisfy the financial needs of Chinese companies and employees in those countries. Our financial institutions should create financial products and businesses centering on RMB internationalization, and provide more convenient RMB financial services for investment and trade cooperation.

4.5.7 *Push Forward RMB Valuation and Settlement for Bulk Commodities*

According to the internationalization experience of USD, RMB valuation and settlement for bulk commodities will not only help our country acquire pricing power of bulk commodities, but accelerate the process of RMB internationalization. During BRI construction, our country should conduct bulk commodity cooperation with relevant countries by using RMB as the major valuation and settlement currency, and push forward RMB valuation and settlement for domestic crude oil futures. We should also rapidly develop international trade of RMB-valuated commodities such as iron ore, and provide necessary support of RMB financial derivatives for bulk commodity trade.

4.5.8 *Strengthen Reserve Function through Currency Swaps*

Internationalization of GBP and other currencies have benefited from currency swaps. People's Bank of China has signed bilateral domestic currency swap agreements with central banks of more than 21 countries and districts along "Belt and Road", with a total scale exceeding one trillion yuan. The currency swap agreements could not only help countries support each other in liquidity, but facilitate direct investment and financial asset investment with RMB as the currency for bilateral trade settlement and valuation, and on this basis, increase RMB reserve of countries along "Belt and Road". In recent years, many countries along BRI are suffering the lack of USD liquidity, therefore they have a strong demand for our country's liquidity support. It is advised to hold discussions with relevant countries on enlargement of the applicable scope of currency swap, and meanwhile, facilitate direct exchange of RMB with the currencies of those countries, and direct them to use RMB as a currency for investment and international reserves.

4.5.9 *Improve RMB Financial Infrastructure*

Based on the internationalization experience of major international currencies, our country should accelerate construction of financial infrastructure including overseas RMB clearing centers, improve

RMB registration, trusteeship and transaction systems, improve the functions of payment and clearing systems, extend the quoting, dealing, clearing and transaction information distribution functions of the RMB transaction system to financial institutions of countries along the BRI route, and gradually establish an RMB global payment system supporting clearing of multiple currencies. By learning from the experience of the USA's Clearing House Interbank Payment System (CHIPS), our country should adopt the commercial operation model, further improve the Cross-border Interbank Payment System (CIPS), and perform final clearing with the China National Advanced Payment System (CNAPS). We should increase clearing efficiency, reduce clearing cost, comprehensively monitor RMB's domestic and overseas transactions, and provide necessary financial infrastructure for RMB internationalization during BRI construction.

4.5.10 *Strengthen Construction of RMB Offshore Centers*

It can be concluded from the internationalization experience of major currencies that along with the construction of "Belt and Road", the demand for RMB offshore market and RMB financial products related to trade and investment will become prominent. For example, companies can conduct RMB cross-border trade financing with fixed-income financial assets such as RMB fixed deposit or bonds in the offshore market, and the banks can develop RMB funds, RMB-valuated derivatives and RMB foreign exchange products in the offshore market to meet the investment demand of global customers and attract banking and non-banking institutional investors and individual investors. Therefore, China should build diversified RMB offshore centers in countries along the BRI route which meet certain conditions, and in addition to traditional cross-border businesses such as international settlement, foreign exchange trade, bond issuance, international clearing and international credit and loans, China should rapidly develop RMB investment and financing products, and push forward RMB internationalization through trade, investment valuation and financial product innovation.

Chapter

5

Belt and Road Initiative and Financial Innovation

Finance is a country's core competitive force, therefore we should strengthen financial innovation in Belt and Road Initiative (BRI) construction. The Belt and Road Summit for International Cooperation and the National Conference on Financial Work in 2017 emphasized the need to strengthen BRI financial innovation, encourage green and inclusive finance development, facilitate financial cooperation with domestic currencies and steadily push forward RMB internationalization. In BRI construction, we should learn from international experience, gradually fit into the equator principles, develop green finance, set up an enlending platform, promote inclusive finance, advocate financial cooperation with domestic currencies and steadily push forward RMB internationalization. In addition, we need to share our green and inclusive development concepts and practices, solve problems of construction capital and foreign exchange risks in BRI construction, gain the support of the governments, corporations and the public of relevant countries, lead innovations with green, inclusive

and domestic currency finances, and push forward RMB internationalization in BRI construction.

5.1 Belt and Road Initiative and Financial Innovation

5.1.1 *Belt and Road Initiative is the New Leading Power Pushing Forward Globalization*

The industrial revolutions greatly pushed forward the historical
wheel of globalization. Especially, due to the arrival of the internet age, integrated development of global economy has become
the inevitable trend. But in recent years, "de-globalization" incidents occur now and then. Major countries quit the *Paris
Agreement*, terrorism takes place here and there, regional conflicts
expanded, and trade protectionism is on the rise. According to
history, "de-globalization" is always going against the current of
the times and is temporary. It takes place with higher probability
during sluggish growth of global economy, but always ends with
a re-structured world political and economic pattern. And it often
causes the birth of new leading powers pushing forward globalization. China's BRI is following the peaceful development concept
of "discussion, co-development and sharing". With regional integration as its foundation, BRI focuses on facility connection,
financing, trade connection, policy connection and popular connection. It will cultivate a new growth point for world economy
and push forward globalization on a higher level.

5.1.2 *Financial Innovation is an Assurance for the Success of the Belt and Road Initiative*

Financial innovation is an important assurance for sustainable
development and final success of BRI construction. In the BRI
Summit for International Cooperation and the National Conference
on Financial Work in 2017, President Xi emphasized that our country should strengthen BRI financial innovation, encourage development of green finance and inclusive finance, and push forward

financial cooperation with domestic currencies. By vigorously developing green finance and inclusive finance in BRI construction, our country could share the green and inclusive development concepts and practices, and gain the understanding and support of governments, corporations and the public of relevant countries. It is not only an important means in BRI to build a community of common interests, responsibilities and destinies, but the core content of developing countries, especially emerging economies to lead global economy and take part in global governance. Building a green and inclusive BRI will require huge amount of capital. In the current global credit and currency system, it is quite risky in terms of exchange rate to use foreign exchanges such as the USD, therefore we should encourage countries along BRI to conduct financial cooperation with domestic currencies, and strengthen construction of currency stability system and credit system in regions along the BRI route.

5.2 Scope Definition and Correlation Structure

5.2.1 *Scope Definition of Green Finance*

Green finance refers to economic activities conducted to support environmental improvement, tackle climate change and facilitate saving and effective use of resources. In other words, green finance is the financial service provided for project management, project operation and risk management in fields of environmental protection, energy saving, clean energy, green transport and green architecture. Financial institutions of various countries are actively developing green finance in recent years. The Equator Principles (EPs) — a set of voluntary industrial rules implemented by nearly 100 banks across the world — have become the reference standard, industry practice and development direction of international project financing. The principles require relevant parties to analyze and evaluate influences on nature, environment and the region, and take measures to protect the ecological system and community environment in their project financing activities.

5.2.2 *Scope of Inclusive Finance*

Inclusive finance refers to a financial system which widely provides reasonable, convenient and secure financial services for the general class of people and groups. The concept of inclusive finance was first put forward by the United Nations in 2005, and has turned into an important financial field with high attention of various countries, especially the developing countries. Inclusive finance was developed on the basis of small-credit and micro-finance, and its progress has always reflected the concept of financial innovation. So far, China's inclusive finance has combined many innovative factors such as internet finance, mobile payment and sharing economy, and could provide Chinese wisdom for financial innovation along the BRI route.

5.2.3 *Scope of Domestic Currency Finance*

Domestic currency finance means to conduct investment and financing cooperation with the domestic currency, in order to push forward BRI construction. According to estimates of the Development Research Center of the State Council, infrastructure investment demand of BRI alone will reach 10.6 trillion USD in the next five years. Capacity and trade cooperation will require even more capital. According to history, the USA vigorously promoted the use of dollars in "Marshall Plan". As a result, the USA increased its share of goods and services for export to Western Europe, and transformed USD into the major settlement currency in trade with Western European countries. A new international system and order which facilitated economic integration between the USA and Western Europe was thus established. Since China is an economic great power whose GDP and trade are ranked the second in the world, realizing RMB internationalization on a larger scale is fair for China. As to capital receiving countries, they could save exchange costs, reduce exchange rate risks, and attract more international capital. Additionally, in the global credit currency system, financial cooperation with domestic currencies will help maintain financial system stability in BRI regions and even the entire world, and increase convenience and security in global trade and investment.

5.2.4 *Structure of Correlation Between Green Finance, Inclusive Finance and Domestic Currency Finance*

Triangle is the most stable structure in the world. Green finance, inclusive finance and domestic currency finance could form a solid triangle which supports and leads the BRI financial innovation system. Green finance guides future development; inclusive finance promotes financing, and domestic currency finance serves practical needs. I worked in development-oriented financial business in multiple countries along the BRI route and have a rich experience of cooperation with Chinese financial institutions and major local banks. I have realized the prominent problem of "three more, three less" in BRI financial cooperation.

Firstly, our country supported cooperation of many major projects with traditional credit and loans, but made few breakthroughs in top-level design leading international credit standards. Therefore, our country could formulate green financial credit polices on which different countries can easily reach a consensus during BRI construction, and lead the trend of global financial cooperation.

Secondly, most participants are Chinese financial institutions, but the financial institutions of countries along BRI and international financial institutions are not sufficiently involved. Setting up branches in countries along BRI is a time-consuming task for Chinese financial institutions, and they have difficulties integrating into the local society, therefore this method cannot solve financing problem from the root. Our country could strengthen BRI inclusive financial cooperation mechanism, facilitate cooperation between Chinese and foreign financial institutions, and boost enthusiasm of the financial institutions on the condition of mutual benefit.

Thirdly, the financial institutions of China and countries along BRI are overly dependent on USD and EUR, and the Chinese financial institutions have few RMB financial products. Our country could encourage Chinese financial institutions to create green and inclusive financial products valuated in RMB based on the actual situation of BRI construction, and provide policy assurance for RMB internationalization in the investment and financing fields in order to satisfy the huge capital demand of BRI construction.

5.3 Challenges Faced by Countries Along the Belt and Road Initiative Route

5.3.1 *Severe Problems in Sustainable Development*

Sustainable development is not only the consensus of various countries, but an important issue they are facing together. Countries along the BRI route are facing severer challenges in the aspect of sustainable development. According to the research of Chinese Academy of Sciences (2017), most countries along the BRI route are developing their economy in the extensive pattern, and their ecological environments are weak. Most countries are in a dry or half-dry environment with a low forest coverage rate. Their unit GDP energy consumption, wood and material consumption, and carbon dioxide emissions are 50% higher than the world average level. Their unit GDP steel, cement, non-ferrous metals, water and ozone depletion are twice or more than twice of the world average level. China is also located along the BRI route. The extensive development in the beginning of the reform and opening-up process caused serious pollution, and China paid a great price in repairing the environment. Even till now, China is still troubled by pollution in the air, water and soil, and sustainable use of natural resources is facing a great challenge. The green development concept of BRI has won the hearts of all. It meets the common interests of countries along "Belt and Road", and will be supported by the governments, corporations and the public. Therefore, we should vigorously promote green finance in BRI construction.

5.3.2 *Limited Popularization of Financial Services*

Countries along the BRI route are mostly under-developed in economy and lack sufficient financial services. In those countries, micro, small and medium companies are often having difficulties in financing. Bank loans require complex procedures, and credit funds often have a high interest rate. The loan interest rate of Egypt even reached 10–20%. Due to lack of capital support, the medium-small-micro companies are weak in the capacity of self-improvement, and their products lack competitive force in the market. The vicious cycle of industrial structure seriously affected the real economy development of relevant countries. Our country is one of the largest capital output countries in the world, and strengthening financing cooperation with countries along the BRI route has strong significance in terms of inclusive finance. While putting risks under control, such financing cooperation could help with economic diplomacy with mutual benefit, help Chinese companies to step out of border, and facilitate investment and trade cooperation in the BRI framework. Additionally, since the countries along the BRI route are under-developed in mobile payment, and financial services are only popularized on a limited scale, internet economy and internet finance have a huge market space in those countries. China is a world leader in e-commerce, mobile payment and internet finance, therefore China has a lot to achieve in countries along "Belt and Road" and will effectively facilitate inclusive finance development and RMB internationalization.

5.3.3 *Risks in USD Reserve System*

After two dollar crises in the 1970s, America officially abandoned the "Bretton Woods System", which was in force for 30 years. USD was unhooked from gold, and a new age of credit currency system arrived. America was no longer restricted in dollar issuance. When the Federal Reserve increases the interest rate, dollar becomes stronger, and world economy sags. When dollar is weakened, global economy booms. In a certain extent, USD has become a "rogue currency". By quantitative easing and tightening, the USD "robbed" developing countries and emerging economies again and again, and the countries along the BRI route suffered the most. Countries in the world urgently need diversified foreign exchange reserves to prevent financial risks, and RMB stood out as the fifth currency included into the SDR basket, providing a high-quality choice for countries along the BRI route. According to the currency substitution theory, once a currency has become a globally leading currency, it will have strong inertia of use. Therefore, "de-dollarization" during the BRI construction will be a long process, and financial cooperation with domestic currencies is facing a big challenge.

5.4 Experience Analysis and Reference

5.4.1 *Green Finance: The Equator Principles*

The Equator Principles were established in October 2002, under the initiative of International Finance Corporation, a subsidiary of World Bank and ABN Amro Holding NV by multiple major world financial institutions, including the Citibank, based on the policies and directions of International Finance Corporation and World Bank. The Principles are a set of non-mandatory financial industry standards that aim to judge, evaluate and manage the environmental and social risks in project financing, and are considered as the action guidelines in global green finance. By 2015, there were 82 financial institutions of 36 countries announcing to accept the Equator Principles, and those financial institutions are uniformly called equator financial institutions, most of which are multi-national banks. Their project financing businesses account for more than 80% in the world. The Industrial Bank is the only bank in China which announced to adopt the Equator Principles (Tang Bin, Zhao Jie and Xue Chengrong, 2009). China Banking Regulatory Commission (2017) encourages domestic financial institutions such as China Development Bank to hold the green credit concept, refer to global good practices such as the Equator Principles in the process of loan issuance, strictly adhere to laws and regulations in the environmental protection and industrial fields, sufficiently evaluate the project's environmental and social risks, and make loan decisions based on the evaluation results.

The Equator Principles include 10 core articles, having listed the special terms and conditions for equator financial institutions to make investment decisions. Those are the preconditions for loan issuance. The first article is the classification basis of project risks, i.e. equator financial institutions should classify loan projects in compliance with the environmental and social screening criteria of International Finance Corporation (see Table 5.1). The second article requires social and environmental evaluation (SEA) on Class-A and Class-B projects, and provides specific requirements on evaluation. The third article stipulated the main content of social and environmental evaluation report. The fourth article requires the borrower to prepare an

Table 5.1 Loan Project Classification Standard of Equator Principles

Class Definitions in Equator Principles	Influence on the Society and Environment
Class-A project: The projects which may cause diverse, irreversible or unprecedented major negative influence on society or environment	1. Major influence on local community (such as land expropriation, involuntary migration, aborigines, etc.) 2. Major influence on biodiversity and natural habitat 3. Major influence on cultural heritage 4. Diverse material influence (not as serious in single aspect, but could be listed as Class-A when accumulated)
Class-B project: The projects which may cause certain extent of negative influence on society or environment, but items of influence are small in quantity, basically only cover the local district, are reversible to a large extent, and can be easily improved with relief measures.	1. Potential influence not as serious as in Class-A projects 2. Potential negative influence only covering the local district, and pollution can be prevented and controlled with appropriate measures
Class-C project: The projects that only cause the lowest degree of influence or has no influence on society or environment. Apart from screening, no additional measures need to be taken for Class-C projects.	Lowest degree of influence or no influence on society and environment

Source: The Equator Principles.

Action Plan (AP) for Class-A and Class-B projects, and establish a social and environmental management system (SEM) to implement the plan. The fifth article provides the system for public opinion seeking and information disclosure. The sixth article stipulates the appealing mechanism. Local groups can choose to appeal, and help the borrower learn of the project's influence on the society and environment and take necessary measures. The seventh article stipulates the independent review service. For Class-A project (including Class-B project in appropriate situations), equator financial institutions should hire independent social and environmental experts to comprehensively review the *Evaluation Report, Action Plan* and opinion documents. The eighth article requires the borrower to make a commitment in the financing documents. The borrower should promise to comply with the laws, regulations and permissions on the society and environment of the host country, follow the AP during project construction and operation, and regularly submit the project report to the equator financial institution. The ninth article stipulates the independent inspection and report system. During the term of the loan, the equator financial institution should hire or request the borrower to hire independent social and environmental experts to verify all information for all Class-A projects and some Class-B projects. The tenth article stipulated the reporting system of equator financial institutions. Each year, the equator financial institutions should disclose to the public their performance and experience in implementation of Equator Principles.

5.4.2 *Inclusive Finance: Enlending Platforms*

Sub-loans are mostly international financing loans. The banks signed loan agreements with foreign parties as debtors to borrow funds, and then re-lend the funds to domestic companies as creditors. Countries along the BRI route are mostly developing countries with small economic volumes. Loans for medium-small companies in China could be called as large loans in those countries. Currently, Chinese financial institutions mostly provide loans for certain projects in countries along "Belt and Road". Due diligence and credit approval often take a long time, and the objective of BRI financing cannot be effectively achieved. Setting up branches in those countries is even more time-consuming. And even if the branches have been established, their capacity of offering loans and other financial services is quite limited. Therefore, Chinese financial institutions provide credit for the financial institutions of countries along the BRI route, construct enlending platforms and push forward inclusive finance. The above are good measures to achieve the BRI financing objective, and a reflection of BRI financial innovation. In this way, our country could provide reasonable, convenient and security financial services for the medium-small companies, the general class of people and groups in countries along the BRI route.

China Development Bank has a rich experience in building international enlending platforms. For example, China Development Bank has issued sub-loans exceeding 2 billion USD to Central Bank of Egypt, National Bank of Egypt and Banque Misr to be used in fields including electricity, energy, traffic, medium-small companies and people's livelihood. Additionally, China Development Bank is responsible for issuing 250 billion yuan's special RMB loan for BRI project, in which 50 billion yuan will be used in the financial cooperation field. In September 2017, China Development Bank and SAI-Bank signed a special loan agreement in the amount of 260 million yuan, as the first lending of RMB loans in Egypt to support micro, small and medium companies with Chinese ownership. The enlending cooperative banks of the host country are often major banks which are high-quality customers of the Chinese financial institutions and have good credit ratings. Those banks can obtain sub-loans on a preferential rate. The customers of the enlending cooperative banks are often small in size, and their credit ratings often do not meet the customer standard of Chinese financial institutions. If they seek loans directly with Chinese financial institutions, they are either unqualified or obtain the loan at a high price. Chinese financial institutions added conditions of Chinese ownership in enlending cooperation with major banks of the host country. The banks are required to use the sub-loans for projects and companies related to China. In this way, we have reduced the operational cost of Chinese financial institutions, prevented and controlled credit risks, facilitated capacity and real economy cooperation between China and foreign countries, and pushed forward BRI inclusive finance development.

5.4.3 *Domestic Currency Finance: "Marshall Plan"*

In July 1947, America launched the "Marshall Plan" and started a series of donating, funding and loaning activities to help Europe. It was the plan of the USA to provide assistance for economy and reconstruction of Western European countries destroyed after World War II. During the period, Western European countries received different kinds of assistance from America, including finance, technologies and equipment, with a total amount of 13.15 billion USD (see Table 5.2). Donations accounted for 88% of the total assistance, and the remaining were loans. Implementation of "Marshall Plan" took four years in total. The plan had a complex political and economic background. It aimed to stabilize Western European politics and economy to prevent Soviet Union's expansion to Europe, and also assimilate domestic surplus production capacity and adjust the malformed war-time economic structure.

Wide use of USD in Europe was attributed to the profound influence of "Marshall Plan" on the development of European countries and world political and economic pattern. "Marshall Plan" has long been considered as an important factor which facilitated integration between Europe and the USA. It weakened or eliminated the tariff

Table 5.2   Assistance Received by Western European Countries in "Marshall Plan"

(Unit: 100 Million USD)

Country	1948/49	1949/50	1950/51	Total Amount
Austria	2.32	1.66	0.7	4.88
Belgium and Luxembourg	1.95	2.22	3.6	7.77
Denmark	1.03	0.87	1.95	3.85
France	10.85	6.91	5.2	22.96
Germany	5.1	4.38	5	14.48
Greece	1.75	1.56	0.45	3.66
Iceland	0.06	0.22	0.15	0.43
Ireland	0.88	0.45	—	1.33
Italy	5.94	4.05	2.05	12.04
Netherlands	4.71	3.02	3.55	11.28
Norway	0.82	0.9	2	3.72
Portugal	—	—	0.7	0.7
Sweden	0.39	0.48	2.6	3.47
Switzerland	—	—	2.5	2.5
Turkey	0.28	0.59	0.5	1.37
England	13.16	9.21	10.6	32.97

Source: Online information such as Wikipedia.

and trade barriers which had been existing between Western European countries and the USA in history, and closely united Western European countries and the USA in economy. Under the driving force of "Marshall Plan", America obtained large amount of shares for commodity, currency and labor export to Western European countries, and the USD became the major settlement currency in international trade of those countries. As a result, a new world system and order facilitating economic integration between America and Western Europe was gradually established.

5.5 Suggestions on Financial Innovation in Belt and Road Initiative

5.5.1 *Guide Future Development with Green Finance*

In constructing the green financial system, China could make full use of its advantages as a late starter. By learning from advanced rules of the world, China could optimize its financial system and mechanism, share results and experience with developing countries, and lead financial innovation in BRI construction. We should provide guidance in the front end of investment and financing, always follow the green standard in the financing of important projects, and allocate capital and other resources preferentially to the green industry.

(1) *Advocate the Green Finance Concept*

In BRI financial innovation, we should advocate green finance development concept, strengthen policy support for green finance, strengthen institution and mechanism construction of green finance, accelerate green finance legislation, actively connect to the social and environmental protection systems of relevant countries, and direct social capital to important green industry projects which people care most about.

(2) *Gradually Align with Equator Principles*

The Equator Principles have become a set of mature environmental protection credit rules commonly used in the world, but they are non-mandatory rules which provide encouragement and guidance. Chinese financial institutions should consider the actual situations of relevant countries, always advocate green finance, apply different standards for different nations, fields and projects, gradually align with Equator Principles and finally become a leader in global financial innovation.

(3) *Highly Value Information Disclosure*

The relationship between two countries depends on the intimacy of their people. Information disclosure is part of self-supervision, and an act to propagate positive energy. Chinese financial institutions should highly value regular information disclosure to the outside world, strengthen communication with governments, non-government organizations, borrowers, news media and the general public of countries along the BRI route, lead positive public opinions in communication, advocate the green finance concept and promote popular connections.

5.5.2 *Facilitate Financing with Inclusive Finance*

Most countries along BRI are developing countries and emerging economies. The covered areas include both cities and villages, and the covered fields include infrastructure construction, industrial transfer and medium-small-micro company cooperation. Many financial demands highly overlap with inclusive finance. Therefore, vigorously developing inclusive finance is part of BRI construction and the core content of financial innovation.

(1) *Properly Understand the Essential Meaning of Inclusive Finance*

Inclusive finance was once regarded as public welfare projects, or even assistance responsibilities. With the rapid development of Chinese economy and finance, more and more inclusive financial products have achieved marketized operation. The essential meanings of inclusive finance — fairness, extensiveness, convenience and availability — were finally recognized, and align with the objectives of BRI construction — integration, interconnection and sharing.

(2) *Institutionalize the Construction of Enlending Platforms*

Innovation comes from the front-line. The successful enlending experience of Chinese financial institutions such as China Development Bank in countries along BRI indicates that the construction of enlending platforms could effectively solve the problem of lack of branches, control risks, allocate capital to real economy and finally achieve the BRI financing objectives. Our country should always learn from practical experience, institutionalize the construction of international enlending platforms, and create an inclusive financial operation model that can be reproduced and promoted.

(3) *Support Internationalization of Mobile Payment and Internet Finance Industry*

As a world leader in mobile payment and internet finance industry, our country has accumulated rich operation and supervision experience in cross-border e-commerce, tourism and micro-payment, provided large quantities of marketized inclusive financial products, and are widely recognized in society in this field. Our domestic operation has provided valuable experience for inclusive financial cooperation with countries along the BRI route. Our country should strongly support internationalization of mobile payment and internet finance industry, and push forward BRI inclusive financial innovations.

5.5.3 *Serve Practical Needs with Domestic Currency Finance*

In BRI construction, settlement with bilateral domestic currencies in place of the currency of a third country will help achieve a win-win situation. China is already the second largest economy and trading country in the world, therefore RMB internationalization is not only fair for China, but a convenient choice for counties united with China closely in trade and investment. It helps countries along the BRI route, especially Chinese and foreign companies, to reduce currency exchange cost, prevent exchange rate risks and attract more investment.

(1) *Conduct Top-Level Designs for RMB Internationalization*

To push forward RMB internationalization in BRI construction, we need to conduct top-level designs, construct economic and financial cooperation frameworks in relevant countries, strengthen RMB exchange rate flexibility, push forward managed capital account convertibility, promote RMB valuation and settlement in bulk commodity trade and cross-border e-commerce, strengthen RMB's transaction and reserve functions with currency exchange, improve RMB financial infrastructure, and accelerate construction of RMB offshore centers.

(2) *Implement RMB Special Loans for Belt and Road Initiative*

Conducting overseas investment and assistance with the domestic currency was the common road to success of internationalization of GBP, USD, JPY and EUR. Implementing RMB special loans will not only solve the financing gaps in BRI construction, but encourage relevant countries to improve their RMB payment systems, direct domestic and foreign private capital to BRI construction, enlarge overseas RMB capital pool and liquidity, and create a "siphonic effect" of investment.

(3) *Make Innovations in Green and Inclusive Financial Products Valuated in RMB*

With the deepening of BRI construction, demands for RMB financial products related to trade and investment are becoming more prominent. In addition to traditional cross-border financial products such as international settlement, foreign exchange trade, bond issuance, international clearing and international credit, we should facilitate development of green and inclusive financial products valuated in RMB, and build a multi-level development model of RMB internationalization, including the driving forces of trade, investment valuation and financial product innovation.

Selection of Capital Account Opening Pathways

The meaning of RMB internationalization is to gradually achieve free convertibility of RMB, especially the basically free convertibility of the capital account. In this way, the overseas government, institutions and individuals will have the will and possibility to increase their holding of RMB assets. Complete free convertibility of the capital account is not the precondition of RMB internationalization, but long-term control of the capital account will certainly influence RMB internationalization process or cause a "bottleneck" restriction. As reported in the Party's 19th National Congress, our country should create a new pattern of full-openness by focusing on Belt and Road Initiative (BRI) construction. In this framework, this chapter reviews the history of capital account opening of our country, discussed the internal rules, current situation and objectives of capital account opening, and provided policy suggestion for the selection of pathways: Push forward RMB internationalization through BRI construction, enhance capacity of the financial industry to serve the real economy, achieve interest rate marketization, adhere to the managed floating exchange rate system, encourage innovation of financial products valuated in RMB, and construct a macro-prudential management system of capital account.

6.1 New Requirements in the New Pattern of Full-Openness of Our Country for Financial Opening

6.1.1 *Belt and Road Initiative Construction is the Key Point in the New Pattern of Full-Openness in the New Age*

As clearly pointed out in the report of the 19th National Congress, BRI construction is an important task in the new age. We should value both "allowing in" and "going out", follow the principle of "discussion, co-development and sharing", strengthen innovation cooperation and create a new pattern of full-openness which connect the domestic and the overseas, the west and the east. The new age assigned an important mission to BRI construction, and the initiative will play an important role in facilitating international capacity cooperation, creating a trade, investment, financing, production and service network, and cultivating new advantages in international economic cooperation and competition. Meng Gang (2017) indicated that BRI is a road of globalization, cooperation, public interest, greenness and financial innovation. In terms of pushing forward RMB internationalization, the "communications and connections" in BRI construction and RMB internationalization facilitate each other and go hand-in-hand. Financing helps broaden the use of RMB; facility connection activates the huge demand for RMB; trade connection solidifies the foundation of RMB internationalization; policy communication helps provide an assurance for RMB internationalization; and popular connection helps create a favorable atmosphere. Capital account opening is the internal demand of RMB internationalization. With the progress of BRI construction and RMB internationalization, the capital account will surely achieve a larger-scale of openness.

6.1.2   *New Requirements for Financial Industry Opening of Our Country in the New Age*

The report of the Party's 19th National Congress declared the latest strategy for financial opening of our country: "Deepen financial system reforms, strengthen capacity of the finance to serve real economy, increase proportion of direct financing, facilitate healthy development of multi-level capital market, improve the dual-pillar regulation and control framework of currency policies and macro-prudential policies, deepen marketization reforms of the interest rate and exchange rate, improve the financial supervision system, and as a bottom line, prevent systematic financial risks." The above is the guiding principle for financial opening of our country in the new age. Finance is a core competitive force of a country, and wide opening of a country could facilitate optimization and growth of finance through competition. Capital account opening is an important part of financial opening, therefore it should be considered in the new pattern of full-openness of our country. Zhou Xiaochuan (2017) provided a further explanation of the financial opening of our country in the new age. He indicated that China should accelerate financial reforms and opening, and actively prevent systematic financial risks in order to achieve opening in three aspects: (1) Opening of trade and investment; (2) Actively push forward reforms of RMB exchange formation mechanism; (3) Reduce foreign exchange control and steadily push forward RMB internationalization. In this way, we can provide convenience for foreign economic activities and achieve capital account convertibility in an orderly fashion.

6.2   Scope of Capital Account Opening

Capital account opening means loosening transaction control under capital and financial accounts in the balance of international payments. Balance of international payments is a financial record of the dynamics of trade, non-trade, capital, investment and reserve assets during economic cooperation with other countries. In essence, it is an income and expense table reflecting all of a country's economic exchanges with other countries during a certain period. Before 1993, the balance of international payments only contained the two basic accounts — the current account and capital account. In 1993, the *Manual for Balance of International Payments* defined capital account as the capital and financial account. The capital account opening widely discussed today, refers to the opening of capital and financial accounts. In the balance of international payments, current account is the main account, reflecting transfer of actual resources through trade, service and voluntary assignments between a country and other countries, including cargo, service, profit and current transfers. Large-scale speculation generally does not occur in foreign exchange flow under this account. Capital and financial account is the second type of account in the balance of international payments. It reflects long-term or short-term capital flow between a country and other countries, including capital transfer, non-production and non-financial transactions, direct investment, security investment, other investments, and reserve assets. Foreign exchange flow under this account reflects the profit-seeking, mobile, and speculative natures of capital.

6.3 Current Situation of Capital Account Opening of Our Country

6.3.1 *History of Capital Account Opening of Our Country*

The opening of RMB current account and capital account was gradually achieved by exploration during our country's reform and opening-up process. In 1986, the State Council issued the *Regulation on Encouraging Direct Investment of Foreign Businesses*, and allowed foreign businesses to directly invest in China. In 1993, the Third Plenary Session of the 14th Central Committee of the CCP clearly stated in *Decision of the CPC Central Committee on Several Problems in Establishing the Socialist Market Economy Mechanism*: "Reform foreign exchange management mechanism, set up a managed floating exchange rate system with market supply and demand as its basis and a uniform and standardized foreign exchange market, and gradually transform RMB into a convertible currency." In December 1996, our country accepted relevant regulations of the clauses 8.2, 8.3 and 8.4

of the International Monetary Fund, and achieved RMB's free convertibility under current account. In 2003, the Third Plenary Session of the 16th Central Committee of the CCP clearly stated in the *Decision of CPC Central Committee on Several Problems in Improving the Socialist Market Economy Mechanism*: "While effectively preventing risks, loosen restrictions on cross-border capital transactions with selection and procedures, and gradually achieve capital account convertibility." In 2005 and 2010, the objective of "gradually achieving capital account convertibility" was successively included into the nation's 11th Five-Year Plan and 12th Five-Year Plan. In 2013, *Decision of the CPC Central Committee on Several Problems in Comprehensively Deepening Reforms* put forward the policy intention of "accelerating the implementation of RMB capital account convertibility". After shocks of the stock market and offshore RMB market in 2015, our country paid more attention to risk control and the principle of prudence in its financial opening policies. In 2017, the national financial work conference emphasized: "Our country should increase financial opening, deepen reforms of RMB exchange formation mechanism, stably push forward RMB internationalization, and steadily achieve capital account convertibility."

6.3.2 *Current Situation of Capital Account Opening of Our Country*

IMF has a clear definition for current account convertibility, i.e. Article 8 in the above-mentioned IMF agreement, but did not issue a strict definition for capital account convertibility. Since IMF does not have a uniform standard to judge the degree of capital account opening, various countries can make free choices in their own judgment, and their standards of recognizing capital account opening degree might be different from IMF standards. So far, according to data of People's Bank of China and State Administration of Foreign Exchange, among the 7 categories, 11 items and 40 sub-items of the capital account of our country, 7 are completely convertible, 27 are partly convertible and 6 are completely non-convertible (see Table 6.1). And 85% of capital account transactions achieved convertibility in different

Table 6.1   Current Situation of Capital Account Opening of Our Country (February 2016)

7 Categories	11 Items	40 Sub-items	Current Situation	Remarks
I. Capital and currency market tools	1. Capital market securities	Stocks and other securities with a sharing nature		
		1. Domestic trading by non-residents	Partly convertible	Qualified institutional investors
		2. Domestic issuance to non-residents	Non-convertible	No explicit permission by law
		3. Overseas trading by residents	Partly convertible	Qualified institutional investors
		4. Overseas issuance to residents	Convertible	
		Bonds and other debt securities		
		5. Domestic trading by non-residents	Basically convertible	Inter-bank bond market is fully open to overseas institutional investors
		6. Domestic issuance to non-residents	Partly convertible	Entry criteria and entity restrictions
		7. Overseas trading by residents	Partly convertible	Qualified institutional investors
		8. Overseas issuance to residents	Basically convertible	Registration management
	2. Currency market tools	9. Domestic trading by non-residents	Partly convertible	Qualified institutional investors
		10. Domestic issuance to non-residents	Non-convertible	No explicit permission by law

	11. Overseas trading by residents	Partly convertible	Qualified institutional investors
	12. Overseas issuance to residents	Convertible	Qualified institutional investors
3. Collective investment securities	13. Domestic trading by non-residents	Partly convertible	Qualified institutional investors
	14. Domestic issuance to non-residents	Partly convertible	Mutual recognition by mainland and Hong Kong funds
	15. Overseas trading by residents	Partly convertible	Qualified institutional investors
	16. Overseas issuance to residents	Partly convertible	Mutual recognition by mainland and Hong Kong funds
II. Derivative tools and other tools			
4. Derivative tools and other tools	17. Domestic trading by non-residents	Partly convertible	Products for investment include stock index futures, special goods futures, and foreign exchange derivatives
	18. Domestic issuance to non-residents	Non-convertible	No explicit permission by law
	19. Overseas trading by residents	Partly convertible	Qualified institutional investors and companies meeting supervision requirements

(Continued)

Table 6.1 (*Continued*)

7 Categories	11 Items	40 Sub-items	Current Situation	Remarks
III. Credits and loans	5. Commercial credit	20. Overseas issuance to residents	Non-convertible	No explicit permission by law
		21. Provided by residents for non-residents	Basically convertible	Balance management and registration management
		22. Provided by non-residents for residents	Partly convertible	Strict approval conditions and restrictions apply for Chinese companies to borrow foreign debt
	6. Financial credit	23. Provided by residents for non-residents	Basically convertible	Balance and registration management
		24. Provided by non-residents for residents	Partly convertible	Strict approval conditions and restrictions apply for Chinese companies to borrow foreign debt
	7. Guarantee, assurance and spare financing	25. Provided by residents for non-residents	Basically convertible	Registration management after provision
		26. Provided by non-residents for residents	Basically convertible	Limited amount management

Category	Item	Sub-item	Convertibility	Notes
IV. Direct investment	8. Direct investment	27. Overseas direct investment	Basically convertible	Restrictions of industry and department
		28. Domestic direct investment	Basically convertible	Approval of commercial department is required
V. Direct investment for liquidation	9. Direct investment for liquidation	29. Direct investment for liquidation	Convertible	
VI. Real estate transaction	10. Real estate transaction	30. Overseas purchase by residents	Basically convertible	Requirements are the same as those in direct investment
		31. Domestic purchase by non-residents	Partly convertible	Commercial presence and self-occupation principle
		32. Domestic selling by non-residents	Convertible	
VII. Individual capital transactions	11. Transfer of individual capital	33. Provided by residents for non-residents	Non-convertible	No explicit permission by law
		34. Provided by non-residents for residents	Non-convertible	No explicit permission by law
		35. Provided by residents for non-residents	Partly convertible	Limitations of remittance amount

(*Continued*)

Table 6.1 (*Continued*)

7 Categories	11 Items	40 Sub-items	Current Situation	Remarks
		36. Provided by non-residents for residents	Partly convertible	Limitations of remittance amount
		37. Settlement of overseas debt of foreign immigrants	—	No explicit stipulation by law
		38. Transfer abroad by immigrants	Partly convertible	Transfer of large amount of wealth requires approval
		39. Transfer to China by immigrants	—	No explicit stipulation by law
		40. Transfer of lottery and prize income	—	No explicit stipulation by law

Source: People's Bank of China, and State Administration of Foreign Exchange. The author re-organized the statistics of Ba Shusong and Zheng Zilong (2016).

degrees. However, according to IMF's statistics in the latest *Annual Report for Exchange Rate Arrangement and Remittance Restriction*, our country basically does not apply restrictions in only the commercial credit and direct investment and clearing item under exchange settlement and credit and loans; but applies different degrees of restrictions in other capital account transactions. Obviously, our country's capital account opening means opening with partial restrictions or control. It is different from IMF's standard of recognition.

6.4 Pathway Selections in Capital Account Opening of Our Country

6.4.1 *Intrinsic Rules of Capital Account Opening of Our Country*

According to history, our country has clear goals in achieving capital account opening, but it is careful and prudent in pushing forward this process, and always makes policy adjustments based on actual situations. China is following the intrinsic rule of "first the imperative, and last the risky", and "first flow-in and then flow-out, first long-term and then short-term, first direct investment and then security investment, first institution and then individuals", and pushing forward capital account opening carefully with plans and procedures. The research group of the Financial Survey and Statistics Department of People's Bank of China (2012) put forward concrete goals for capital account opening of our country, and made short-term, medium-term and long-term plans for the 10 years in future. In the short-term plan (1–3 years), the country will loosen control on direct investment with a real transaction background and encourage companies to "step out". In the medium-term plan (3–5 years), the country will loosen control on commercial credit with a real trading background and facilitate RMB internationalization. And in the long-term plan (5–10 years), the country will strengthen construction of the financial market, first open up in-flow and then out-flow, and prudently and successively open up real estate, stock and bond trading, and gradually replace quantity control with price management. Accomplishing the above "three steps" will signify basic opening-up of the capital account of our country. Individual capital transaction, financial institution credit unrelated to capital transaction, currency market tools, collective investment securities, guarantees and assurances, and other capital account sub-items can be opened up when the opportunities come. Foreign exchange liberalization has little connections with capital transaction and could be opened up at last. Short-term foreign debt involves high possibility of speculation, therefore it could maintain a closed state in the long run.

6.4.2 *Objectives of Capital Account Opening of Our Country*

The 31st international currency and financial committee meeting was held in 2015. In the meeting, Mr. Zhou Xiaochuan first mentioned that the objective of RMB capital account opening is "managed convertibility"; in other words, even if the capital account is opened up, the government will still manage capital account transactions based on the situation. According to convention, 100% convertibility of the capital account is called complete free convertibility. Many medium-income market economy countries define capital account opening as 70–80% convertible of currency in order to reach the western market economy standard or join relevant international organizations. But actually the degrees of capital account convertibility of some of the countries are far behind China. Therefore, as long as IMF or other international organizations do not interfere or make a judgment, our country should follow the principle of benefiting economic development and overall opening-up process during financial opening, especially capital account opening. By considering ourselves as an emerging market economy country in transformation, we should establish goals meeting our country's interests, and should not tie up ourselves and set goals which are too high and unpractical. Our country has complex national conditions with unbalanced regional economic development, and we have unique political and economic systems such as "One Nation, Two Systems". From the angle of macro-prudential policies, our country should appropriately control hot money and overly speculative capital flow, and such control should not be considered as lack of openness of capital account.

6.5 Policy Suggestions for Selection of Capital Account Opening Paths of Our Country in the New Age

6.5.1 *Push Forward RMB Internationalization Through Belt and Road Initiative Construction*

The capital account opening process of our country should serve BRI construction. By focusing on both "coming in" and "going out", and deepening two-way investment cooperation, we should be able to facilitate free flow of capital and other factors, create an RMB-centered regional currency cooperation system with wide participation of relevant countries, optimize investment, financing and trade cooperation environment of countries along the BRI route, and push forward efficient allocation of capital and deep integration of global market. In the current global credit currency system, depending on extra-territorial currencies such as USD in BRI construction is both risky and unsustainable. We must push forward financial cooperation with domestic currencies centering on RMB, and strengthen construction of currency stability system and credit system in BRI region. BRI covers 65 countries across Asia, Africa and Europe and 63% of world population. The countries have different resource endowment, strong economic complementation capacity, and a huge potential for development. As estimated, the investment demand of BRI infrastructure construction alone will reach 10.6 trillion USD in the next 5 years. RMB internationalization starts from trade settlement, but it can be predicted that investment in the future will become an important driving force of RMB internationalization. BRI construction could facilitate RMB's output under capital account, and back-flow under current account through cross-border trade. Our country is the largest trading country and second largest economy in the world, and pushing forward RMB internationalization during BRI construction is fair and beneficial for both our country and the world.

6.5.2 *Enhance the Capacity of Finance to Serve the Real Economy*

As an important part of financial opening-up, the objectives, procedures and processes of capital account opening should focus on enhancing the capacity of finance to serve the real economy. Serving real economy is the basis of the financial industry and an important measure to prevent financial risks. According to our country's history of capital account opening, both active reforms and passive adjustments has been determined based on actual needs of real economy development. Along with rapid development of economy and substantial increase of comprehensive strength, our country is able to control the situation, strengthen prospective top-level design, and realize capital account opening goals with plans and procedures. According to the report of the 19th National Congress, our country should focus on BRI construction and create a new pattern of full-openness, and it is the guiding principle to push forward our real economy simultaneously in international and domestic markets. Currently, during BRI construction and the process of RMB internationalization, capital account opening should be conducted based on the needs of real economy development, and should aim to provide convenience for RMB's use in cross-border investment and trade, strengthen RMB's functions of valuation, settlement, payment, investment and reserves, develop RMB financial assets with innovation, push forward construction of RMB's onshore and offshore financial centers, improve financial infrastructure for RMB cross-border payment, and overcome shortcomings of finance in serving real economy. In a global environment with loud voices calling for capital account opening, our country should keep calm and avoid hasty movements which could impact stable development of domestic economy. We should improve the dual-pillar regulation and control framework consisting of currency policies and macro-prudential policies, always ensure stable development of domestic economy, and guarantee real effect of supply-side structural reforms. While conducting overseas investment, we must prevent domestic industry from hollowing, and steadily push forward managed capital account opening.

6.5.3 *Achieve Marketization of the Interest Rate*

Marketization of interest rate is an objective reflection of price signals and plays the role of directing reasonable flow of capital and resources. The theoretical circle holds different opinions on the sequence of interest rate marketization, exchange rate liberalization and capital account opening. Representative person of the progressive school Mckinnon (1991) thinks that developing countries should push forward economic reforms in the sequence of macro-economic stability, domestic financial liberalization, exchange rate liberalization and capital account opening. The representative person of the radical school — founder of the shock therapy, Sachs (1994), thinks that a sequence is not required, and capital account opening can be pushed forward together with marketization of interest rate and exchange rate, or achieved prior to other items. Representative person of the comprehensive school, Johnston (1998), thinks that capital account opening should be pushed forward in coordination with interest rate and exchange rate reforms, and the three items have no absolute sequence. Meng Gang (2017) thinks that if our country first completely opens the capital account while interest rate is under control, many negative effects will emerge, such as capital flight and currency substitution, and the effectiveness of our currency policies will be significantly influenced. Significant increase of capital in-flow or out-flow will cause sharp fluctuation of the exchange rate. It should be pointed out that financial risks are spread out with a fast speed, strong elusiveness, high infectivity and great harms in a background of economic globalization. The currency policies of developed countries are centering on their own interests and have a strong overflow effect. Therefore, countries with an open capital account will easily suffer significant impact. The international financial crisis, which just passed, has provided us with an important enlightenment that countries with effective capital control suffer the least impact. Therefore, our country should take full advantage of the market economy reform model led by the government, control domestic problems, and prevent international risks, and we can accept the opinions of both the progressive school and comprehensive school, and push forward interest rate marketization, exchange rate liberalization and capital account opening in a coordinated fashion. But in sequence, we must follow the "first in, and then out" principle. We should first complete interest rate marketization, adhere to a managed floating exchange rate system, and finally achieve managed capital account opening.

6.5.4 *Adhere to a Managed Floating Exchange Rate System*

Since our country adopted the "managed floating exchange rate system" on July 21, 2005, the real exchange rate of RMB has basically been in a reasonable and balanced range, and has made great contributions to facilitating stable working of macro-economy and the process of RMB internationalization. According to international experience, a stable currency value is crucial for healthy development of economy and determination of the currency's international status. Through currency swap and other methods, the British government conducted effective financial cooperation with central banks of other countries, maintained currency value stability of GBP and greatly accelerated GBP's internationalization. To maintain USD's international position, the US government strove to overcome the "Triffin Dilemma", and worked toward the objective of maintaining supply-demand balance and currency value stability of USD. The currency policies of German central bank focused on maintaining currency stability of Mark, and by regional cooperation on European investment and financing, German relieved the pressure of exchange rate fluctuations, and finally established euro's international position. Although Japan completed exchange rate liberalization and capital account opening at an early time, drastic fluctuation of JPY value caused frustration of JPY internationalization, and Japan's economy started a downward trend for 10 years. According to history, our country should maintain stability of the RMB exchange rate in a reasonable and balanced range, manage RMB value expectations, monitor cross-border capital speculations, and prevent sharp fluctuation of RMB exchange rate. Currently, in our country's overseas assets, reserve assets with low rate of return, such as US national debt, have the largest proportion, and direct investment and equity investment with a higher rate of return have a smaller proportion. In terms of exterior liabilities, direct investment with a higher interest rate has the highest proportion. The above structure of overseas assets and debts is obviously unfavorable for maintaining a stable RMB exchange rate. By taking advantage of the opportunity of BRI construction, our country should increase capital output in the form of direct investment through marketable operation, improve the structure of international balance of payments, increase rate of return of external assets and maintain relative stability of RMB exchange rate.

6.5.5 *Encourage Innovation of Financial Products Valuated in RMB*

Along with BRI construction, demand for RMB financial products related to trade and investment became prominent. To enhance the capacity of finance to serve real economy development, capital account opening should be helpful for Chinese companies' expansion overseas and RMB internationalization, and should encourage creation of financial products valuated in RMB and widely accepted in international financial market. Currently, among the sub-items of capital account opening of our country, credit and direct investments have the highest degree of openness; security investment is in the middle; and individual capital transactions are the least open items. According to the consensus of the academic circle, individual capital transaction items can be opened after our country's market economy system becomes more mature in future. Security investment items, especially the derivatives, have a low degree of openness. They are the "short slabs" of our country's financial system, and reflect our distance from the financially developed countries. To open up the capital account in the new age, our country should encourage Chinese financial institutions to develop RMB-valuated funds, derivatives and foreign exchange products by taking advantage of the opportunity of BRI construction, creating a multi-level development model for RMB internationalization including the driving forces of trade, investment and financial product innovation, and meeting the RMB demands of global customers. Additionally, in order to direct global capital to BRI construction, we should gradually lower threshold of domestic Chinese companies to borrow foreign debt, and strive to lift the strict approval management and policy restrictions on unified foreign debt management department, entity qualification approval, long-term and short-term borrowing model, diversity of capital use, and specific repayment requirements, and motivate and restrict Chinese companies' international investment and financing with market mechanism.

6.5.6 *Construct a Macro-Prudential Management System of Capital Account*

According to the consensus of the academic and industrial circles, macro-prudential policies are a great cure for systematic financial risks. On the G20 Leaders' Summit in November 2010, various countries reached a consensus on the definition of macro-prudential policies: Macro-prudential policies refer to the policies which prevent systematic financial risks with prudential tools and protect real economy from impact. On this basis, International Monetary Fund (IMF), Financial Stability Board (FSB) and Bank for International Settlements (BIS) jointly issued the *Factors of Effective Macro-Prudential Policies: International Experience and Lessons* in August 2016. The document re-stated the importance of macro-prudential policies from the angle of reducing frequency and impact of financial risks. To avoid systematic financial risks caused by capital account opening, our country should improve the dual-pillar regulation and control framework of currency policies and macro-prudential policies, establish a macro-prudential management system for capital account, and make the best use of macro-prudential regulation and control tools. For example, by following the procedure of "monitor → analysis → warning → intervention" (Lin Hongshan *et al.*, 2017), our country could integrate and update the business system of supervision departments and financial institutions, strengthen the capacity of big data analysis, establish cross-border capital flow monitoring and analysis system, lock on abnormal cross-border capital fluctuation more precisely, and effectively implement the warning and intervention functions. Additionally, based on IMF's policy suggestions (Ge Qi, 2017), tools involving cross-border capital flow management can be divided into two categories: One is traditional capital control in which capital flow management is carried out based on the cross-border financial trader's place of residence. It applies to transactions between residents and non-residents, such as taxation against stock and creditor's rights investment of non-residents. The second is macro-prudential policies based on the currency instead of the place of residence, such as taxation against banks' foreign-currency non-deposit liabilities. In conclusion, our country should establish a macro-prudential management framework for capital account, make the best use of prudential regulation tools, and provide more comprehensive policy assurance to prevent cross-border capital flow risks.

Chapter

7

Overseas RMB Offshore Financial Markets

This chapter clarifies the meaning, development and classification of offshore financial market. According to this chapter, developing RMB offshore financial market during BRI construction can facilitate RMB internationalization, and help set up BRI cooperation platforms, lead global financial innovation and increase our country's right of speech in global financial system governance. From the angles of geographical quartering, core objectives and determinants, this chapter puts forward multi-level development concept, analyzes major challenges and provides suggestions on policy communication and legal connections.

7.1 Introduction

BRI construction is our country's key task in creating a new pattern of full-openness. The Party's 19th National Congress was successfully held in 2017, and the incorporation of BRI into the Party constitution signified the Party Central Committee's determination and confidence to build new international cooperation relationships and create a world community through BRI construction. Developing RMB offshore financial market in BRI construction will help direct social capital into BRI construction, create a "siphonic effect" of investment, solve financing gaps, expand overseas RMB capital pond and liquidity, improve RMB payment system and steadily push forward RMB internationalization. Currently, BRI construction is advancing along a spiral path of "top-level design → implementation → improvement → comprehensive deepening". In this new age, how to develop RMB offshore financial market during BRI construction, and facilitate financial cooperation with domestic currencies on the basis of "discussion, co-development and sharing" has become an important topic of top-level design.

7.2 The Meaning, Development and Classification of Offshore Financial Market

7.2.1 *Basic Meaning of Offshore Financial Market*

(1) *Traditional Definition of Offshore Financial Market*

Offshore financial market was originally a USD market formed in London at the end of the 1950s, therefore it was initially called external financial market, euro currency market and euro dollar market. In the traditional concept, offshore financial market is the site of financial transactions and financing with certain currency outside of the currency's issuing country. "Offshore" indicates that the transaction or financing with certain currency is conducted outside of the currency's issuing country. For example, in the European dollar market and Asian dollar market, USD is transacted outside of the issuing country — the USA. The transaction entities of offshore financial market are classified into institutions and individuals, and the institutions mainly include banks, non-bank financial institutions, corporations, government departments and international organizations. Banks are the principal participating entity in offshore financial market, and inter-bank transactions take up a percentage over 80% in the offshore financial market. Financial services provided by banks in the offshore financial market mainly include deposit taking, loan issuance, bond issuance, callable loans, and provision of exchanges, bills and other financial derivatives.

(2) *Modern Definition of Offshore Financial Market*

Along with financial innovative development of various countries, "offshore" is no longer limited to overseas presence. And overseas presence is no longer the standard to distinguish between offshore and onshore. Offshore finance refers to financial activities conducted by non-residents, and it is different from onshore finance in applicable laws. For example, transaction between a resident and a non-resident is a foreign-related financial business of onshore finance, and belongs to the category of traditional international financial business. In the modern sense, offshore financial market refers to an international financial market in which non-residents conduct financial transactions with the domestic currency outside of the domestic financial system. The offshore financial market could be located within or outside of the currency issuing country. Non-residency means the specific financial transaction is executed by a financial institution in a jurisdiction on behalf of the customer in another jurisdiction. In 1999, the *Modern Finance Dictionary* of our country defined offshore financial market as the site on which international financial businesses are conducted between non-residents. In 2000, IMF defined offshore financial market as: the financial market where offshore financial activities (financial service provided by banks or other financial institutions mainly for non-residents) take place.

7.2.2 *Development History of Offshore Financial Market*

After World War II, interventionism represented by keynesianism prevailed. The financial industry was under strict supervision. To get rid of restrictions, the European dollar market in London started developing. According to Wu Nianlu's research (1981), offshore finance initially referred to Eurodollar, i.e. the interest-bearing dollar deposit of overseas American banks (including overseas branches of

American banks), which are not supervised by American financial departments. Along with the growth of European dollar market, the geography of offshore financial market expanded to Asia, South America and Oceania. The currencies of single offshore financial market developed in a diversified pattern. The offshore financial markets of major international currencies, such as the euro offshore financial market in London and Luxembourg, the JPY offshore financial market in Tokyo, and the RMB offshore financial market in Hong Kong, apart from USD, increased in number. Overseas RMB offshore financial market refers to the offshore financial market established in other countries or districts with RMB as the major transaction currency.

7.2.3 *Functional Classification of Offshore Financial Market*

Currently, based on supervision and functions, offshore financial markets in the world can be classified into three types: The first is onshore-offshore integrated type. For example, in London and Hong Kong, onshore and offshore finances are a whole, and both residents and non-residents can conduct financial businesses with various currencies. The second is onshore-offshore separated type. For example, New York, Tokyo and Singapore separated offshore and onshore businesses by bank account instead of territory, and bank accounts of different types cannot be confused. The third is tax avoidance type. For example, in Cayman and Bermuda, bank accounts are often opened with the purpose of tax avoidance. Those markets mainly play the role of account keeping centers. In terms of currency, offshore financial markets can be classified into the dollar, euro, JPY, GBP and RMB markets. In terms of industry, offshore financial market can be classified into offshore banking, securities and insurance. Among them, deposit, loans and trade financing take up the largest proportion in offshore financial market transactions. Issuance and trade of medium-term and long-term bonds are the main part of offshore security businesses. Cross-border investment insurance, life insurance, reinsurance and subsidiary insurance are the main content of offshore insurance business.

7.3 Importance of Developing Overseas RMB Offshore Financial Market

7.3.1 *Push Forward RMB Internationalization*

In 2009, China started RMB settlement in cross-border trade. RMB capital started large-scale output overseas, and RMB internationalization formally set sail. Since China is a leader of global economy, RMB's use on a larger scale is fair for China. For capital receiving countries, they could reduce exchange risks, save exchange cost, and build more channels for international capital income. America accomplished distribution of Eurodollars through "Marshall Plan", and Japan facilitated JPY internationalization through "surplus circulation". Both achievements were inseparable from the great contribution of offshore financial market. Developing multi-level overseas RMB offshore financial market in BRI construction will help set up an RMB capital use platform, capital management platform, clearing and settlement platform and risk management platform (E Zhihuan, 2016), and will make great contribution to RMB internationalization.

7.3.2 *Set Up a Cooperation Platform for BRI Construction*

Financing is crucial in BRI construction, and is the key to the success of facility connection, trade connection, policy communication, and popular connection. In recent years, USD's strong back-flow caused a global currency crisis, and the developing countries along BRI and emerging market economies suffered the most. In this background, as a strong currency with stable value and a currency included in IMF's SDR basket, RMB has the possibility of supporting BRI construction with the means of domestic currency cooperation. Developing RMB offshore financial market in BRI construction could help relevant countries strengthen financial cooperation with domestic currencies centering on RMB, enable China to break through the USD zone from angles of political and economic security, and help developing countries reduce the huge impact of foreign exchange crisis on economy; furthermore, the offshore financial market is an important strategic cooperation platform supporting BRI construction.

7.3.3 *Lead Global Financial Innovation While Supporting Economic Development*

Financial innovation is an important assurance for the success of BRI construction. The BRI Summit for International Cooperation and the National Conference on Financial Work in 2017 have emphasized the extreme importance of greenness, inclusiveness and financial innovation of domestic currencies. According to Meng Gang's research (2017), China has been actively pushing forward application and popularization of green finance in BRI international project financing in recent years, and China's inclusive finance has combined many innovative elements such as internet finance, mobile payment and sharing economy, and could effectively provide Chinese wisdom for BRI financial innovation. RMB capital could solve the huge capital demand in BRI construction. Overseas RMB offshore financial market provided a platform for mechanism and product innovation in green finance, inclusive finance and financial cooperation with domestic currencies, and it is the cutting-edge incubator of BRI financial innovation.

7.3.4 *Increase Our Country's Right of Speech in Global Financial Governance System*

According to Wang Honggang's research (2017), there are serious defects in existing global financial governance system, and our country should push forward optimization of global governance system by expanding BRI cooperation, and help solve the unbalance of rights and obligations of leading currencies. The core of BRI construction is to direct social capital to serve real economy development of relevant countries, provide new momentum for world economy recovery, and re-balance the global financial governance system. Developing overseas RMB offshore financial market in BRI construction could help solve inefficiencies of world financial market, direct social capital to support major projects, increase RMB's position in international currency system, reduce impact of policy overflow effect of western countries on the economy of developing countries, and prevent regional financial risks.

7.4 Proposals for Developing Overseas RMB Offshore Financial Market

7.4.1 *Geographical Quartering*

Meng Gang (2017) referred to the geographical trichotomy of international financial centers put forward by Geoffrey G. Jones, and proposed geographical quartering in developing RMB offshore financial market system: global RMB offshore financial market — regional RMB offshore financial market — sub-regional RMB offshore financial market — RMB offshore financial market of important countries. The sub-regional RMB offshore financial market and RMB offshore financial market of important countries are focused on RMB financial cooperation between China and the host country or surrounding countries. Regional offshore financial market is focused on providing RMB financial service for the entire district. And the global offshore financial market is focused on providing RMB financial service on a global scale. While pushing forward in-depth cooperation with countries along "Belt and Road", geographical quartering is a practical method which can help our country create an RMB international circle by uniting with developing countries and emerging economies, and break through the global financial governance system led by the western world.

7.4.2 *Core Objectives of Developing Overseas RMB Offshore Financial Market*

Belt and Road Initiative construction is in a development stage in which RMB internationalization is pushed forward by investment and trade, therefore the overseas RMB offshore financial market should be able to serve real economy. Additionally, from the angle of innovative development of modern financial industry, the scale of global investment and financing and international capital flow have exceeded international trade scale, and the offshore financial market is striving to provide diversified financial service. Therefore, the core objective of developing overseas RMB offshore market is to cultivate the internal impetus to lead global financial development and innovation. The offshore market should be able to provide basic financial services for goods and service trade, such as payment, settlement, credit and credit guarantee valuated in RMB, and also provide diversified financial services such as financial investment products and financial derivatives. The above is also an important standard to determine if the overseas RMB offshore market has good vitality and the capacity of sustainable development.

7.4.3 *The Determinants of Developing Overseas RMB Offshore Financial Market*

When RMB stepped out of the border in 2009, China's financial service was in the beginning of its rise, RMB demands overseas were still in the process of cultivation, and cross-border RMB financial infrastructure was weak, therefore an independent RMB offshore market could not be established easily, and we mostly relied upon mature global or regional financial centers such as Hong Kong, Singapore and London to develop RMB offshore businesses. Along with growth of China's economic strength, development of Chinese financial institutions, increase of innovation capacity of RMB financial products, and maturing of cross-border RMB financial infrastructure, China gained the comprehensive strength to actively develop overseas RMB offshore market in BRI construction. Determinants of overseas RMB offshore market development include: China's strong political and economic position in the world, the policies and laws of the host country, complete cross-border financial infrastructure, sufficient market requirements, innovative financial products and active participation of important systematic or national financial institutions.

7.5 Challenges in Developing Overseas RMB Offshore Financial Market

7.5.1 *Belt and Road Initiative is Affected by Global Political and Economic Inertial Trend*

In the world scope, current global financial market is deeply affected by western politics and economy. Developed countries such as

America persisted in maintaining their economic and financial hegemony. "Thucydides's trap" became a common topic. IMF-centered reforms of global financial governance system could not achieve effects quickly, and the position and right of speech of developing countries and emerging economies still need improvement. BRI construction has more important missions in the new age. It will help the countries re-construct international cooperation relationships, create a regional network of trade, investment, financing, production and services, and cultivate a new pattern of global economic cooperation and competition. Developing overseas RMB offshore financial market in BRI construction will require China and relevant countries to integrate development strategies and create a new pattern of cooperation. It is a breakthrough in the current global financial governance system, and we should take precautions against influence and interference of oppositions within and outside of the territory.

7.5.2 *Deepening is Required for Top-Level Design of BRI Financial Cooperation*

The key to achieving a success in developing overseas RMB offshore financial market is to strengthen top-level designs of BRI financial cooperation, construct a financial cooperation framework across relevant countries, make innovations in RMB financial products, and improve RMB financial infrastructure. Especially, we should make plans regarding domestic and overseas financial cooperation. I have work experience in multiple countries along the BRI route, and learned that the problem of "three more and three less" is still prominent in BRI financial cooperation. Firstly, our country emphasizes support of major projects in BRI through traditional credit and loans, but made few breakthroughs in top-level designs leading international credit standards. Secondly, most participants are Chinese financial institutions, but our country lacks top-level designs regarding how to strengthen cooperation with financial institutions of countries along BRI and international financial institutions. Thirdly, our financial products are highly dependent on USD and EUR, while RMB financial products are still lacking.

7.5.3 *Mutual Influence Between Onshore and Offshore Financial Markets Cannot Be Neglected*

Developing BRI overseas RMB offshore financial market while the capital account is not fully opened is a challenging task, because both the domestic and foreign financial markets should be taken care of. Along with gradual increase of use of RMB in the overseas offshore financial market, any kind of financial incidence in the onshore and offshore financial markets could produce a chain reaction. Take "8.11 exchange reform" as an example. According to research of Chen Zhi and He Jingjing (2016), after "8.11" exchange reform, global speculation capital stirred up three rounds of RMB short selling, and RMB exchange rate fell continuously. As a result, our country's foreign exchange reserve had a substantial fluctuation. During the period from June 2015 to September 2016, overseas institutions reduced holding of 1.29 trillion yuan's RMB financial capital, including stocks, bonds, loans and deposit (Bian Weihong, 2017). The incident caused great influence to RMB liquidity in the overseas offshore financial market.

7.6 Policy Suggestions

7.6.1 *Provide Necessary Assurance Through Policy Communication and Legal Connections*

The offshore financial market in the modern sense has different characteristics including a complete legal system, a high degree of internationalization, low cost of financing, preferential tax policies, market transaction freedom, strict protection of customer privacy and other legal rights and interests, therefore it should be protected on the policy and legal levels. Overseas RMB offshore market should be first constructed in relevant countries with smooth policy communications. If the target country has a strong will of cooperation, and has the policy and legal basis for building an RMB offshore financial market, work efficiency could then be improved, and unnecessary resistance could be avoided. In terms of policy communication and legal connection, construction of the RMB offshore financial market in Hong Kong was a successful example worth promotion. According to history, Chinese

Table 7.1 The 8 Policies for Hong Kong RMB Offshore Financial Businesses in the Starting Phase

Policy	Relevant Laws Issued Afterwards	Issuing Department
1 Cross-border RMB direct investment	*Notice on Relevant Issues in Cross-border RMB Direct Investment*	Ministry of Commerce People's Bank of China
2 Expand RMB settlement area for cross-border trade	*Notice on Expanding RMB Settlement Area for Cross-border Trade*	People's Bank of China and other 5 ministries and commissions
3 Encourage qualified overseas institutions to invest in inter-bank bond market	*Notice on Relevant Matters in Trials of Three Types of Institutions Including Overseas RMB Clearing Bank Using RMB to Invest in Inter-Bank Bond Market*	People's Bank of China
4 Increase numbers of domestic financial institutions which issue RMB bonds in Hong Kong	*Announcement of NDRC dated January 11, 2012*	National Development and Reform Commission
5 Conduct trials of RMB capital increase of foreign banks	—	—
6 Allow qualified overseas institutions to invest in domestic security market	*Notice on Relevant Matters in Implementing "Methods for Trials of Fund Management Companies, Security Companies and Qualified Overseas Institutional Investors Investing in Domestic Security"*	People's Bank of China
7 Issue RMB bonds in Hong Kong in the long term and expand scale of issuance	—	—
8 Encourage Hong Kong to develop offshore RMB products with innovation	—	—

Source: Arranged as per relevant materials.

government actively developed the 8 policies for Hong Kong RMB offshore financial businesses in 2011 (see Table 7.1). The 8 policies were considered as an assurance for comprehensively building Hong Kong RMB offshore financial market, and can serve as a reference for developing overseas RMB offshore financial markets in BRI construction.

7.6.2 *Set up RMB Clearing Banks and Conduct Currency Swaps*

Currently, the RMB offshore financial market has not been developed systematically, but it has a good foundation for development. The countries and districts where RMB clearing banks have already been established have a good foundation for RMB cooperation as well as favorable policies and laws (see Table 7.2). They actively cooperate with China in investment, trade and finance, and could be considered as important locations for developing overseas RMB offshore financial market. In those countries and districts, Hong Kong, Taiwan, London, New York, Paris, Seoul, Singapore and Luxembourg have already become major overseas RMB offshore financial markets. Our country could first establish RMB clearing banks in countries and districts where RMB market has been initially formed, and then gradually set up the overseas RMB offshore financial market. Additionally, our country has signed currency swap agreements with countries along the BRI route. Apart from providing

Table 7.2 Countries and Districts with Existing RMB Clearing Banks (up to December 2017)

Countries and Districts	Clearing Bank
Hong Kong, Macao, Taiwan, Kazakhstan, Germany, France, Hungary, Australia, Philippines, Cambodia, Malaysia, America, South Africa, Zambia	Bank of China
Luxembourg, Singapore, Laos, Cambodia, Qatar, Thailand, Canada, Argentina, Russia	Industrial and Commercial Bank of China
England, Switzerland, Chile	China Construction Bank
South Korea	Bank of Communications

Source: Website of People's Bank of China.

Table 7.3 Bilateral Domestic Currency Swap Agreements Signed by China (up to December 2016)

S/N	Date of Signature	Country/District	Scale (100 Million Yuan)	Period of Validity
1	2009-3-11	Belarus	200	3 years
2	2009-3-23	Indonesia	1,000	3 years
3	2009-4-2	Argentina	700	3 years
4	2010-6-9	Iceland	35	3 years
5	2011-4-18	New Zealand	250	3 years
6	2011-4-19	Uzbekistan	7	3 years
7	2011-6-13	Kazakhstan	70	3 years
8	2011-10-26	South Korea (renewal)	3,600	3 years
9	2011-11-22	Hong Kong (renewal)	4,000	3 years
10	2011-12-22	Thailand	700	3 years
11	2011-12-23	Pakistan	100	3 years
12	2012-2-8	Malaysia	1,800	3 years
13	2012-2-21	Turkey	100	3 years
14	2012-3-20	Mongolia	100	3 years
15	2012-3-22	Australia	2,000	3 years
16	2012-6-26	Ukraine	150	3 years
17	2013-3-7	Singapore	3,000	3 years
18	2013-3-26	Brazil	1,900	3 years
19	2013-9-9	Hungary	100	3 years
20	2013-9-12	Albania	20	3 years
21	2013-10-10	European Central Bank	3,500	3 years
22	2014-7-21	Switzerland	1,500	3 years
23	2014-9-16	Sri Lanka	100	3 years
24	2014-10-13	Russia	1,500	3 years
25	2014-11-8	Canada	2,000	3 years
26	2015-3-18	Suriname	10	3 years
27	2015-3-25	Armenia	10	3 years
28	2015-4-10	South Africa	300	3 years
29	2015-5-10	Belarus	70	3 years

(*Continued*)

Table 7.3 (*Continued*)

S/N	Date of Signature	Country/District	Scale (100 Million Yuan)	Period of Validity
30	2015-5-15	Ukraine	150	3 years
31	2015-5-25	Chile	220	3 years
32	2015-9-3	Tajikistan	30	3 years
33	2015-9-26	Turkey	120	3 years
34	2015-9-27	Georgia	—	3 years
35	2015-10-22	England	3,500	3 years
36	2015-12-14	The UAE	350	3 years
37	2016-5-11	Morocco	100	3 years
38	2016-6-17	Serbia	15	3 years
39	2016-9-12	Hungary	100	3 years
40	2016-9-27	European Central Bank (renewal)	3,500	3 years
41	2016-12-6	Egypt	180	3 years
42	2016-12-21	Iceland	35	3 years

Source: Website of People's Bank of China.

liquidity support, currency swap could also facilitate RMB's use as a bilateral trade settlement currency and encourage relevant countries to use RMB in direct investment and financial asset investment, and include RMB as part of their official foreign exchange reserves (Table 7.3). Therefore, expanding scales of currency swap with countries along BRI will help provide necessary RMB financial products for overseas RMB offshore financial market.

7.6.3 *Financial Product Innovation Should Meet the Actual Needs of Local Market*

To construct multi-level RMB offshore financial markets, our country should implement the mechanism of "one policy for one country", and especially, conduct financial product innovation with clear objectives (Table 7.4). In developing countries with an under-developed financial market, we should mainly provide financial products

Table 7.4 Major Financial Products of Overseas RMB Offshore Financial Business

Business Category	Major Financial Products
Deposit business	RMB deposit, remittance, exchange and credit cards
	RMB certificate of deposit
	RMB structural deposit
Loan business	RMB trade and financing loan
	RMB circulating fund loan
	RMB syndicated loan
	RMB project financing loan
Security business	RMB sovereign bond
	RMB financial bond
	RMB corporate bond (issued by Chinese corporations)
	RMB corporate bond (issued by foreign corporations)
	RMB equity-type IPO
Capital transaction business	RMB foreign exchange swap transaction
	RMB inter-bank borrowing
	Deliverable RMB options
	Deliverable RMB exchange rate swap
	Deliverable RMB forward
	Deliverable RMB exchange rate swap options
Asset management business	RMB fund business
	RMB insurance business

Source: Arranged as per relevant materials.

including RMB cross-border settlement, deposit and loans, and should not neglect small amount of transactions. The key point is to have long-term goals and cultivate RMB demands. In countries with developed financial markets, we should focus on providing RMB bonds, financial derivatives and green financial products in addition to conventional financial products. By participating in and leading institutional arrangements of global financial products, we should make bigger breakthroughs in RMB transaction volume, and create RMB offshore financial markets with greater influence.

7.6.4 *Direct Chinese Financial Institutions to Conduct Business Cooperation*

In the construction of overseas RMB offshore financial market, our country should rely on institutional advantages and lead Chinese financial institutions to conduct business cooperation. For example, in the credit and loan field, we could learn from the "3 banks and 1 guarantee" cooperation mechanism successfully implemented by Chinese financial institutions in Egypt (Meng Gang, 2017). In June 2015, Chinese and Egyptian governments held the first meeting of China-Egypt capacity cooperation mechanism work team. China Development Bank, Exim Bank of China, Industrial and Commercial Bank of China and China Export & Credit Insurance Corporation decided to implement the "3 banks and 1 guarantee" mechanism in large capacity cooperation projects in Egypt. Later, Bank of China also actively joined the mechanism. On the principle of "uniform planning, risk sharing and resource integration", the mechanism dealt with the outside world in the name of a bank consortium, in order to unify the financing institutions, prices, management and services of Egypt. The mechanism was highly praised by our country's Ministry of Commerce and the NDRC as an innovative breakthrough of Chinese financial institutions in international capacity cooperation field. It could effectively prevent vicious competitions and help create a win-win situation for both China and the foreign country. RMB offshore financial market is inseparable from wide participation of Chinese financial institutions, therefore the government must provide proper directions and create cooperation mechanisms which could prevent vicious competition between the Chinese financial institutions.

7.6.5 *Accelerate Construction of RMB Financial Infrastructure*

To develop overseas RMB offshore market, our country should accelerate construction of cross-border RMB financial infrastructure, extend functions of RMB transaction system, including quoting, bargaining, clearing and transaction information distribution to the financial market of relevant countries, and create an RMB globalized payment system supporting clearing with multiple currencies. Currently, multi-channel parallel methods are adopted in RMB cross-border payment, such as the "RMB clearing bank" model which conducts cross-border RMB receipt and payment on behalf of the overseas banks, the "agent bank" model which establishes running accounts with other countries to provide cross-border RMB services, and the "NRA" model which sets up non-resident accounts in domestic banks. These methods mostly depend on the Society for Worldwide Inter-bank Financial Telecommunications (SWIFT), and pose a major systemic risk to China's economic and financial security. In October 2015, the first edition of cross-border inter-bank payment system (CIPS) was formally put to use. This brand new RMB cross-border payment system was developed in reference to internationally advanced cross-border clearing systems of USD and JPY. It increased clearing efficiency, facilitated supervision of RMB cross-border capital flow, and is an important update of RMB payment and clearing infrastructure of our country. While developing overseas RMB offshore market in BRI construction, we should accelerate improvement of the CIPS system; we especially need to develop an independent message system to achieve independent operation of our RMB international clearing system.

8

Petroleum RMB and RMB Internationalization

8.1 Introduction

Petroleum plays an important role in world industry and large commodity trade and is the product with the largest export volume among bulk resource commodities. For many years, changes in geopolitics and geo-economy had been closely related to petroleum price, and the petroleum valuation system had always been the point of attention of countries around the world. So far, the USD is still the major valuation currency in the spot market, futures market and derivatives market of petroleum. Such a valuation method basically separated petroleum's valuation rights, pricing rights and ownership. And the USD's issuing country — the USA, benefited immensely from the mechanism and strictly controlled the initiative of the global currency governance system. In recent years, along with the great changes in global political and economic situation, there are more obvious signs of unhooking of petroleum trade from USD in the international spot market, and the buyer's bargaining power increased substantially.

So far, China is the largest petroleum import country in the world, and China's dependency on foreign petroleum has exceeded 65%. According to data of China's General Administration of Customs, China imported 8.76 million barrels/day in May 2017, while America only imported 8.12 million barrels/day in the same period. The number was 15% higher than the same period of last year and 8% higher than April. Therefore, our country should take advantage of the opportunity of BRI construction, lead and participate in reconstruction of the global political and economic governance system, and push forward RMB's use by following the realistic pathway of "first settle, then valuate, and formulate rules at last" in various petroleum markets. We should strive to create a petroleum RMB system, and by means of currency substitution, increase our country's right of speech in the international crude oil market, and push forward RMB internationalization.

8.2 Formation of the Petro-Dollar System

8.2.1 *History of the Petro-Dollar System*

According to history, petro-dollar valuation system was basically formed in the 1970s. Before the 1970s, international oil trade was valuated and settled with multiple currencies. After World War II, the political powers of the Middle East were reshuffled, and the transnational corporations named "seven sisters" still controlled the mineral resources of the Middle East. Under the remaining effect of the colonial rule, oil trade was mainly valuated and settled in major international currencies such as GBP and USD. In 1971, the "Bretton Woods System" collapsed. The international currency system centering on USD was seriously damaged, and capital outflow from America was accelerated. The Organization of Petroleum Exporting Countries (OPEC), which represented the interests of major oil producing countries, even proposed to use a basket of currencies as the valuation and settlement currencies of oil trade. In 1973, the fourth Middle East War broke out. Due to its support for Israel, America was banned from importing oil from Arabic countries. The ban caused the first global oil crisis, and international oil price increased fourfold. In 1975, in order to relieve domestic conflict, ensure stable supply of oil, maintain USD's hegemonic position and attract capital back-flow,

America initiated in-depth contact with multiple oil production countries in the Arab world; it especially signed a so-called irrevocable secret agreement with Saudi Arabia, which had the greatest influence among OPEC members. Saudi Arabia agreed to use USD as the only valuation and settlement currency for oil export, and its oil income was used to invest in the financial market of developed countries. As a result, the global petro-dollar valuation system was formed.

8.2.2 *Benefits of Petro-Dollar for America*

The petro-dollar valuation system relieved the difficult situation of USD after the collapse of the "Bretton Woods System", strengthened the USD's position as a global reserve currency, and protected the USA from exchange rate fluctuations in oil trade. In the petro-dollar valuation system, countries across the world must rely upon USD in their oil trade. With oil as the engine, the USA tied up the trade of other bulk commodities to USD, maintained USD's international position in a monopolizing fashion, and kidnapped the world's actual demand for USD. In the petro-dollar valuation system, the USA is protected from the exchange rate fluctuation risks in oil trade. By printing banknotes, the USA provides convenience for various countries to purchase oil. It gained privileges from the USD as a global valuation, settlement, payment, investment and reserve currency. It not only obtained seigniorage income, but reduced deficits in international balance of payments. In sharp contrast with the USA, since countries around the world use USD instead of their domestic currencies to purchase oil, they are easily influenced by oil price fluctuations and the changes in exchange rate of their domestic currency to USD. They are subject to hedging risks with high cost and difficulties.

8.3 Disadvantages of the Petro-Dollar System

8.3.1 *Political and Economic Stability of Oil Export Countries is Dependent on the USA*

Many oil export countries in the world only have a singular economic structure. They rely on oil as their economic pillar. In the petro-dollar system, the political and economic stability of those countries is dependent on the USA. Firstly, the USA could threaten those countries by economic sanctions. For example, the USA sanctioned Russia by relying on the USD's international clearing system. By restricting or blocking financial transaction channels, the USA seriously hampered Russia's oil export. Secondly, the USD's liquidity and value stability have a great influence on those countries. The change of USD value and liquidity will greatly affect the above countries' economic stability. Thirdly, in recent years, the "America first" slogan is becoming more and more popular, and crude oil valuated in USD plunged into a lasting low price phase. The fiscal revenue and economic growth speed of major oil export countries dropped obviously, and chain reactions such as capital outflow, deficit worsening, currency devaluation, and financial market fluctuation occur successively. In 2017, the USA cut short the balance sheet, increased interest rate and reduced tax. The actions of the USA caused resonance in the global USD market, and more negative impacts on the oil export countries.

8.3.2 *The Petro-Dollar System is Unfavorable for World Economy Recovery*

After the financial crisis, new economic growth points might be found to help recover world economy, under the continuous effort of China and other emerging economies and developing countries. However, petro-dollar system is internally contradictory with the above recovery process. The singular petro-dollar system has always been a potential risk of global economy. Firstly, the USA's currency policies have a strong negative outflow effect. In the petro-dollar system, once the policies of the Federal Reserve are in conflict with global economic recovery, the petro-dollar surplus of oil export countries will be withdrawn from the emerging markets, and therefore cause a shortage of global liquidity and weaken the power of global economic recovery. Secondly, the USA's trade protectionism is on the rise. Currently, free trade and geo-cooperation are politicized, and the USA's interest is put in the first place. The petro-dollar system is supporting the USA's leading position in global financial governance system. Emerging markets such as China has made a great contribution to global economic recovery, but our rights of speech does not match our contributions. Our capacity to take part in global governance is restricted, and the power of global economic recovery is suppressed.

8.3.3 *The Petro-Dollar System Does Not Serve the Interests of Developing Countries such as China*

In the global credit currency system, petroleum guarantees the USD's convenience, liquidity and security. Due to the petro-dollar system, countries around the world have a strong demand for USD and US public debts. Since oil import countries purchase oil with USD, and oil export countries make investments with USD, the USD could gradually accumulate in the balance sheets of various countries, and flow back to the USA when the countries purchase the US public debts issued by the US government. Many countries in the world have accumulated large amount of USD, and by purchasing US public debts, they are lending the USD to the US government. The deposit and loan interest rates of most countries are hooked with the interest rate of national debt. Demands for USD enable the US government, corporations and citizens to borrow more money with a lower interest rate. Emerging economies such as China own a large amount of foreign exchange reserves by means of trade surplus. When we purchase the US public debts, which have a low rate of return, we are providing low-cost capital for the USA to use in national development. This is the well-known phenomenon of developing countries providing "subsidies" for developed countries.

8.4 Urgency of Constructing the Petroleum RMB System

8.4.1 *Lead RMB Internationalization with the Petroleum RMB System*

If the petroleum RMB system can be established, RMB will be used between third countries. To import and export oil, relevant countries will need to hold certain amount of RMB. The system will greatly enhance global RMB demands and capital pool stability. According to the USD's historical experience, petroleum RMB system will be the starting point of controlling bulk commodity pricing power in the world. On the basis of petroleum RMB, valuation and settlement functions of RMB for other bulk commodities such as ores, natural gas, coals and grains will develop rapidly, and further expand RMB's international demands. Additionally, when oil export countries have accumulated large amount of RMB through oil trade, they will make global investments with RMB. Such investments will lift RMB's value center, strengthen RMB's currency credit, solidify the confidence of global central banks to hold RMB assets, and facilitate RMB financial product innovation. The petroleum RMB system will help international financial market cast off dependency on USD products, create a new driving force for RMB internationalization, and further strengthen RMB internationalization with RMB capital.

8.4.2 *Reduce China's Oil Import Cost*

If RMB makes a breakthrough in the valuation system of global oil trade, it will reduce impact of international oil price fluctuation on many Chinese companies in the oil industry and reduce Chinese companies' foreign exchange transaction cost. As a result, our country will no longer accept international oil price passively, and will obtain a fairer market position and better prices in global oil trade. Establishing the petroleum RMB system means achieving RMB valuation and settlement of oil trade. The Asia Pacific market could provide a benchmark oil price similar to WTI and Brent, in order to establish a fair, transparent and marketized oil pricing mechanism. Our country could engage more deeply in the formation of international oil price, and reduce extra expenses caused by difference of oil formation mechanisms.

8.4.3 *Increase China's Oil Pricing Power*

The lack of international crude oil pricing power poses a great threat to the economic security of our country as a large country of crude oil consumption. Our country is a large country of oil production and consumption, but we are incapable of balancing international oil prices. Since we do not have our own crude oil futures market, we are in a very passive position in the international crude oil pricing system. The most prominent disadvantage is that our import oil price is controlled by other countries, and we are subject to the discriminatory policies of "Asia premium". China has become the largest country of oil consumption and import, but we only have "Chinese demand", and have no "Chinese price" in the weights affecting oil pricing. Since we do not have the pricing power in international crude oil market, we need to pay more cost of import exchange. In essence, we need to make a substantial breakthrough in RMB internationalization in order to gain the rights of speech in oil pricing. The historical experience of USD has shown us that RMB internationalization and oil pricing power facilitate and support each other. Increasing RMB's value of use and reserves in the international market will facilitate RMB pricing in spot oil trade, and will play a significant role in the security and sustainable development of the Chinese economy.

8.5 Countries Which Might Adopt Petroleum RMB at Present

8.5.1 *Venezuela is Increasingly Dependent on RMB*

In September 2017, the president of Venezuela Mr. Maduro indicated that Venezuela has started to use RMB in place of USD to valuate for oil. Venezuela published oil and fuel prices valuated in RMB. The Venezuelan government has ordered domestic oil traders to stop accepting or initiating USD payment. Since then, international payments of Venezuela has been using a basket of currencies, including RMB, JPY and EUR, which could be exchanged with the domestic currency Bolivar.

8.5.2 *Russia Strengthened Its Cooperation with China*

In the beginning of August 2008, China conducted trials of RMB trade settlement with Russia on the northeast border. In the 14th regular meeting of Chinese and Russian prime ministers in 2009,

China and Russia issued a joint declaration that both counties decided to expand settlement with domestic currencies in their trade. In 2010, the 15th regular meeting of Chinese and Russian prime ministers achieved an important result. Both countries decided to reduce use of USD in China-Russia bilateral trade, and instead, use the domestic currencies for settlement. At the end of 2010, rouble became the second currency of emerging countries after Malaysia ringgit, that could be freely listed and traded with RMB. In 2011, China and Russia decided to enlarge the scope of trials of using domestic currencies in bilateral trade settlement again. In 2015, the amount of RMB settlement between China and Russia increased by 250% and exceeded 120 billion yuan. RMB swap amount increased 11 times since the beginning of the year and reached 92 billion yuan RMB (about 14.2 billion USD). The RMB L/C transaction amount of the year increased 12 times. Vnesheconombank signed trade export loan agreements with a total amount of 14.7 billion yuan (about 160 billion rouble) with multiple large banks of China, and issued L/Cs valuated in RMB. The bank also obtained 12 billion yuan's RMB credit financing from China Development Bank.

8.5.3 *Saudi Arabia has the Possibility of Accepting Petroleum RMB*

According to news media, China has started to modify its crude oil trade agreement with Saudi Arabia in recent years. The modification includes plans for RMB payment in crude oil trade between China and Saudi Arabia. If Saudi Arabia refuses to accept China's plan to purchase crude oil with RMB, its position in China's crude oil market will be gradually marginalized. In the past few years, China has transferred many crude oil imports from Saudi Arabia to Russia and other oil producing countries. The proportion of Russia's crude oil export to China in China's total crude oil imports rose sharply from 5% to 15%. So far, China's crude oil imports from Russia, Iran, Iraq and Oman keep rising in proportion, while oil import from Saudi Arabia has been decreasing. If Saudi Arabia accepted RMB as the settlement currency in crude oil trade, the petro-dollar system initially advocated by America and Saudi Arabia will be challenged to some extent. However, Saudi Arabia needs to cast off its dependency on USD in order to maintain and increase its share in China's crude oil market.

8.5.4 *Petroleum RMB is Feasible in Iran and Nigeria*

Since Iran has been in a tense relationship with the USA, the country declared to adopt the petro-euro valuation mechanism as early as 1999. In March 2006, Iran set up an oil exchange which used euro as the trading and pricing currency. Nigeria is the second largest oil and natural gas export country in Africa. Crude oil export of the country is valuated and settled in USD. In 2009, Chinese companies obtained the mining right of Nigerian oil fields after many years' effort. In 2010, Nigeria and China signed a memorandum of understanding, with China agreeing to invest 23 billion USD to construct three oil refineries in Nigeria. In 2013, China provided a loan of 1.1 billion USD for Nigeria. As reported by news media, the condition for the loan was that Nigeria should increase oil export to China, from 20,000 barrels/day to 200,000 barrels/day in 2015. In February 2014, the central bank of Nigeria declared to increase RMB's share in foreign exchange reserves from 2% to 7%, and dump some USD.

8.6 Realistic Obstacles in Developing Petroleum RMB

8.6.1 *The USA's Position in World Oil Market Cannot be Easily Replaced*

Currently, the USA is still the only superpower in the world. In the geo-political and geo-economic perspective, the USA is controlling most areas of recoverable reserves of world oil, such as the Middle East, which has half of the world's recoverable reserves; and Latin America, which is rich in resources. In 2000, Iraq declared to settle oil trade in euro, but it was militarily stricken by the USA only two years later. In 2003, Iraq's oil trade was changed to USD settlement again. Obviously, the USA does not willingly accept challenges to its hegemonic position in the petro-dollar system. Additionally, in terms of oil refinery capacity, the USA is far more advanced than any other country in the world. Although the USA reduced its dependency on imported oil due to the shale revolution, its oil consumption is still the largest in the world. It can be predicted that the USA's position in the world oil market cannot be replaced in a long term in future.

8.6.2 *The USA is the Axis of Global Financial Governance System*

The current global financial governance system is basically led by the USA. In the financial perspective, the petro-dollar system has tied petro-dollar to financial products to a large extent. As the axis of global financial system, the USA is fully capable of controlling the situation. The global financial governance system is a powerful weapon of the USA to defend the petro-dollar system. New York is the largest financial center in the world, American financial institutions have absolute advantages in international clearing transactions, and the USD is in an absolute position in the international payment system, therefore the USA is able to effectively impose financial sanctions against other countries. Due to the USA's financial sanctions, Russia, Venezuela and Iran are under the pressure of American government and financial institutions; moreover, the governments, banks and companies of other countries are avoiding business contact with the sanctioned countries for fear of punishment.

8.6.3 *Willingness of Oil Producing Countries to Accept RMB Still Needs to be Strengthened*

Currently, apart from the USD, RMB does not even have absolute advantages in its competition with rouble, euro and JPY in oil trade. In 2016, China's oil imports from top 10 source countries accounted for 83.4% of the total imports. Russia, Saudi Arabia and Angola are the first echelon, accounting for 11.5–14%, respectively. Iraq, Oman and Iran are the second echelon, accounting for 8–10%, respectively. Venezuela, Brazil and Kuwait are the third echelon, accounting for 4–6%, respectively. And the UAE is at last, accounting for about 3.2%. In 2016, Russia was the largest source country for China's oil imports. However, Russia put forward the rouble internationalization plan as early as 2006, and was expected to transform rouble into a hard currency. Russia emphasizes on settlement with rouble in oil trade. Currently, part of the oil trades between Russia and China, and between Russia and Japan are settled in rouble. Additionally, Angola and Nigeria in Africa, Saudi Arabia, Iran, Iraq, Kuwait, Oman and the UAE in Middle East, and Venezuela and Brazil in Latin America mostly hope to settle oil trades with a basket of currencies, and do not have a strong will to use RMB.

8.6.4 *The Pricing Mechanism of Petroleum RMB Still Needs Improvement*

So far, the oil exchanges set up by China mostly conduct spot trading, and do not have the pricing mechanism for future trades. Although our country has been an important buyer in oil trade for a long time, we have been passively accepting oil prices and has not been able to influence the price through the pricing mechanism. Bulk commodities such as oil have obvious financial attributes, and their pricing mechanism was gradually formed after the USA dominated the oil market. The pricing power of oil is basically in the hands of New York Mercantile Exchange. China has already gained the comprehensive strength to lead the world, and is actively taking part in reconstruction of the world economic and financial system. In this manner, China is accelerating construction of an open oil futures market in order to occupy an advantageous position in oil trade. Although China plans to gradually open up crude oil futures valuated in RMB for global investors, exchanges and oil companies, no tangible result has been achieved yet, and China is still incapable of leading the pricing power mechanism of international oil market.

8.7   Policy Suggestions

8.7.1   *Increase China's Comprehensive Strength*

When England weakened in its comprehensive strength, GBP's position in the global currency system was replaced. Similarly, with the continuous weakening of the USA's global influence, the decline of petro-dollar system becomes a historical necessity. Therefore, China should be patient and focus on domestic economic development; we should especially develop technologies as the primary productive force, persist in supply-side structural reforms, and strive to create a new pattern of full-openness by pushing forward BRI construction. Meanwhile, we need to prevent hollowing of domestic industries, steadily increase China's political and economic strength in the world, and provide necessary assurance for the formation of petroleum RMB system.

8.7.2   *Use Petroleum RMB as the New Starting Point of RMB Internationalization*

The petro-dollar strengthened the USD's international currency position. It also provided a pathway reference for RMB internationalization. In the historical perspective, RMB internationalization started from cross-border trade. More specifically, it started from border trade, and with expansion, an RMB trade settlement system in the global scope will be gradually formed. Along with RMB's wide usage in international trade settlement, China's domestic financial market system is gradually maturing, and RMB has become freely convertible under the current account and 85% of the capital account. RMB is becoming a valuation currency for credit and investment assets in the international financial market, and a reserve currency of more countries. To become a more important leading currency in the international currency system, RMB needs to be hooked with bulk resource products, especially oil in valuation and settlement, as a new starting point for its stronger rise. Undoubtedly, petroleum RMB will open up a new path for RMB's rise as a strong currency: "valuation and settlement currency → investment currency → reserve currency → anchor currency".

8.7.3 *Design a Road Map for Petroleum RMB to Realize Its International Currency Functions*

In BRI construction, the impetus of RMB internationalization can be transformed from cross-border trade in manufacturing industry into capital output, reserve functions and valuation and settlement for bulk commodities. Petroleum RMB is at a core position in the new path of RMB internationalization. Once we have made an achievement in petroleum RMB, the entire process of RMB internationalization will become much easier. At present, signs of unhooking of oil from the USD already appeared in the spot oil market. Along with diversification of oil import channels, China's buyer bargaining capacity in the international market will also increase significantly. By taking advantage of this opportunity, and following the realistic pathway of "first settlement, then valuation, and at last pricing", our country could comprehensively increase its rights of speech in the international crude oil market, and design a road map for petroleum RMB to realize its international currency functions: Oil export counties accept RMB in oil trade — oil export countries use RMB in bilateral trade valuation and settlement — oil export countries use RMB as a reserve currency — oil export countries use RMB reserves to invest in RMB assets.

8.7.4 *Push Forward RMB Settlement in Spot Oil Trade*

In the four major methods of international oil trade — spot, futures, long-term contracts and share oil, spot purchase accounts for 70% of our country's oil imports. According to statistics of relevant scholars, a large proportion of our country's oil imports comes from countries along the BRI route. A conservative estimate reveals that if 1/4 of oil trades between China and countries along the BRI route are settled in RMB, then the scale of RMB settlement would get close to the RMB deposit scale of Singapore RMB offshore market. Therefore, our country could support BRI infrastructure construction and international capacity cooperation with RMB investment, and gradually promote RMB valuation and settlement in trade cooperation of BRI, especially RMB valuation and settlement in spot oil trade. Additionally, our country could make use of the recent cold relations between the USA and Russia, Iran and other Middle East countries, and promote RMB valuation and settlement in long-term oil purchase agreements with those countries.

8.7.5 *Set Up Oil Futures Exchanges and Launch RMB Crude Oil Futures*

At present, there is no benchmark oil price in the Asia Pacific region which can be compared with WTI and Brent. China's spot market can only passively follow the international oil price, and the oil price in Europe and America cannot realistically reflect the supply and demand of oil in China and the Asia Pacific region. For China, the urgent affair is to set up an oil futures exchange with RMB pricing, and launch crude oil futures contracts with RMB pricing and participation of international customers. In this way, we could provide an objective and fair reference coefficient for global oil pricing, reflect the fundamentals of the Chinese and Asia Pacific oil market more realistically and timely, reduce the admittance threshold of oil market, facilitate diversification of transaction entities, and help prevent and tackle the sharp fluctuations of global oil price. The futures market has the function of price discovery. China should improve its domestic oil price formation mechanism by referring to the exchange pricing model widely adopted by western developed countries including the USA, increase its rights of speech in the international oil market and push forward the formation of petroleum RMB valuation system. Only by allowing international investors to take part in the oil price formation process in China and Asia Pacific region can we comprehensively obtain the information of participants of global oil market, and develop a fairer and more transparent market price, which could be accepted by the international market.

Green Finance and RMB Internationalization

9.1 Green Finance

9.1.1 *Origin of the Green Finance Concept*

The academic circle studies the concept of "green finance" in different aspects. For example, According to Salazar (1998), green finance refers to innovative finance conducive to environmental protection. According to Cowan (1998), green finance is the product of disciplinary crossing between green economy and finance. In 2000, *American Heritage Dictionary* defined green finance as "environmental finance" or "sustainable finance", and considers green finance as an aim to achieve coordinated development of environment and economy with diversified financial tools. Labatt and White (2003) consider green finance as a financial tool aiming to improve environment quality. In our country, many scholars have also published research report on green finance. According to Wang Junhua (2000), green finance makes use of finance's function of social capital allocation to direct capital into the environmental protection field, in order to facilitate

Table 9.1　Comparison between Traditional Finance and Green Finance

	Traditional Finance	Green Finance
Operation objective	Profit maximization. For example, commercial banks operate business on the principle of security, liquidity and profitability	Manage environmental risks and opportunities, protect and improve natural environment, and facilitate sustainable development of economy
Policy support	The market needs government supervision, and policy-based finance requires policy support	Environmental pollution is a reflection of market failure, and green finance requires policy guidance
Financial products	Credit, bond, stock, futures, fund and insurance	Basic financial products are the same as traditional finance, but have green attributes

Source: Arranged based on online information.

coordinated development of economy and ecology. Li Xinyin (2006) emphasized that green finance should be closely connected to the development of the environmental protection industry.

Compared with traditional finance, green finance stresses natural environment protection and requires companies to bear environmental and social responsibilities (Table 9.1). For example, while conducting project financing, green finance requires the bank to evaluate the project's environmental impact, such as pollution treatment, resource usage efficiency and ecological effects.

9.1.2　*Theoretical Foundation of Green Finance*

Theoretical foundation of green finance includes two aspects: One is the "green" theoretical foundation formed by the sustainable development theory; the other comes from environmental economics, and is a theoretical basis with more "financial" characteristics.

(1)　*Green Finance and Sustainable Development Theory*

Sustainable development is already the consensus of the entire world, but it was reached in a series of processes. In the historically significant Brundtland Commission in 1987, sustainable development was provided with a new definition, which includes two aspects: "Sustainable development should meet the need of the contemporary people, but should not harm the next generation's capacity to meet their own need." In the United Nations Conference on Environment and Development held in Rio de Janeiro in 1992 (hereinafter referred to as the "UNCED"), the concept of sustainable development was described in more detail with 40 chapters of the *21st Century Agenda*. Compared with the UNCED, the "World Summit on Issues in Sustainable Development" held in Johannesburg in 2002 further clarified the three elements and their interactions in sustainable development theory on the basis of the concepts of economy, society and environment, as well as their relationships.

Economy, society and environment are the three elements constituting the sustainable development theory. Generally, people simply equate sustainable development with environmental protection, but actually, sustainable development refers to the interaction and coordinated relationship between economy, society and environment, and has a much richer meaning than natural environment protection. Different groups of people would view sustainable development from different angles. For example, industrialized countries would pay more attention to natural environment protection, while developing countries attach more importance to sustainable development of economy and society. The mainstream environmental protection organizations emphasize on the environment factor in sustainable development, while the industry and commerce circle pay more attention to fairness and openness of economic policies.

Development of green finance could effectively coordinate the three elements — economy, society and environment. It complies with the purpose of sustainable development and could help increase environmental, social and economic benefits in the following three aspects:

Firstly, green finance could push forward joint development of environment and economy.

Green finance is beneficial for both environmental protection and economic development. It internalizes the economic value of environmental damage and reflects the value in the financial evaluation and resource allocation fields. In this way, green finance optimizes the financial evaluation system, and by means of price and market, it assigns more priority to projects favorable for natural environment in financial resource allocation, and increase financing threshold for high-pollution projects, in order to facilitate joint development of economy and environment.

Secondly, green finance could facilitate industrial upgrade and transformation, and increase economic efficiency.

Supply-side structural reform requires our country to abandon outdated capacities and push forward industrial structure upgrade. While cutting capacities with conventional administrative measures, green finance could help us make use of green investment credit tools, set up admittance thresholds, and differentiate interest rates in order to restrict expansion of excess capacity, push forward development of new energies, facilitate industrial upgrade and transformation and increase economic efficiency.

Thirdly, green finance could improve social recognition of sustainable development concept.

Financial industry is an important part of the society. By developing green finance, financial institutions could improve social recognition of green development and sustainable development concept while fulfilling social responsibilities and increase the sense of social responsibility of enterprises and general people.

(2) *Green Finance and Environmental Economics Theory*

As pointed out in environmental economics theory, environmental problems have strong externality. On one hand, production and operation activities of companies cause pollution to the environment, but the companies do not pay compensations for the ecological damage to society and residents. As a result, social cost is far greater than private cost, and the polluting enterprises are not motivated to make improvement on the pollution. This is called negative externality of environmental problems. On the other hand, environmental improvement has obvious social benefits, which are far greater than private benefits. When there are too many beneficiaries and income source cannot be ascertained, environmental improvement enterprises have difficulties making a profit, therefore they are not motivated to engage in environmental protection. This is called positive externality of environmental problems. The positive and negative externality of environmental problems caused resource allocation to deviate from the optimal social standard. Therefore, relevant measures such as government control and market transactions should be taken to correct the market failure caused by externalities.

The first is government control — Pigovian tax theory: According to Pigou's opinion, the government should play a role in correcting externality. By raising tax or providing subsidies, the government could correct the private cost of relevant economic parties. By means of regulations and policies, the government could attach the social cost of environmental pollution to the companies' cost, and curb pollution emissions by increasing cost. For example, the government could collect tax from the polluting companies to increase the cost of pollution, and therefore curb pollution conducts and protect the natural environment. Additionally, the government could also adopt positive motivation measures. For example, it can formulate relevant policies to increase the income of green investment. The government may support green investment of both environmental protection companies and traditional companies in order to increase private benefit of green investment. Positive motivation includes various kinds of subsidies and tax reductions for green investment, such as providing subsidies for green products.

The second is market transaction — Coase Means: According to Coase Theorem, when property rights are clearly specified and sufficiently protected with a low cost of transaction, the economic entities can achieve optimal benefits by trading in rights of pollution emissions; meanwhile, external effects can be internalized through voluntary transactions between the parties. Coase Means could provide two choices for the polluting party — stopping pollution, or continuing pollution but purchasing rights of pollution from the polluted parties. The producers will make the corresponding choice by comparing the cost. The Coase Means are less likely subjected to government intervention. It reduces the government's administrative cost, avoids the possibility of power corruption, and reduces the negative impact of government failure or decision-making mistakes. A typical example in the field of green finance is the carbon finance market. The carbon finance market implements responsibility restraints based on United Nations climate change framework agreements (such as *Kyoto Protocol*) and the total quantity control mechanism of emissions of various countries.

9.1.3 *China's Green Finance: Definition and Policies*

In April 2015, the CPC Central Committee and the State Council issued the *Opinions of the CPC Central Committee and the State Council on Rapidly Pushing Forward Ecological Civilization Construction*, in which a top-level design was proposed. In September 2015, the *Overall Plan for System Reform of Ecological Civilization* was issued. The *Plan* proposed to establish a green financial system. In March 2016, the 13th Five-Year Plan of our country provided more specific green finance development policies and requested to vigorously develop green financial products such as green credit and green bonds.

In August 2016, after early-stage preparations, the 7 ministries and commissions headed by People's Bank of China formally issued the *Guidance for Constructing a Green Financial System*, which carried great significance in green finance development. In the *Guidance*, Chinese government provided a new definition for green finance: Green finance should be a healthy economic activity aiming to support environmental improvement, tackle climate change and facilitate reasonable usage of resources. Specifically, green finance provides high-quality financial services for projects, investment, financing and project operations involved in different fields including environmental protection, energy saving and green traveling. Although the concept of green finance was put forward in recent years, the State Environmental Protection Administration and "the central bank and three commissions" already provided specific requirements on environmental protection factors in financing and operation of financial institutions and companies, as early as 2001. Those requirements actually contain characteristics of green finance. The policy documents issued since 2001 are listed in Table 9.2. The green finance development plans of various districts are listed in Table 9.3.

Table 9.2 Some Important Policies on Green Finance

Title of Policy File	Date of Issue	Issuing Department	Main Content
Announcement for Environmental Auditing of Listed Companies	2001	SEPA, CSRC	Content and objectives of environmental auditing of listed companies
Announcement for Additional Environmental Auditing for Listed Companies or Stock Refinancing	2003	SEPA, CSRC	IPO of listed companies and refinancing should be approved by environmental protection departments
Suggestions on Environmental Information Disclosure of Listed Companies	2003	SEPA, CSRC	The specific content and methods of environmental information disclosure of listed companies
Opinions on Implementing Environmental Protection Policies and Regulations and Preventing Credit Risks	2007-7	SEPA, People's Bank of China, CBRC	Set up an information communication mechanism across environmental protection department, People's Bank of China, bank supervision department and financial institutions to prevent environmentally unqualified projects from being re-conducted by other means
Guidance on Works of Environmental Pollution Liability Insurance	2007-12	SEPA, CIRC	Select some industries, enterprises and districts with heavy pollution, frequent pollution incidents and easy damage assessment to conduct trials of environmental pollution liability insurance

(*Continued*)

Table 9.2 (*Continued*)

Title of Policy File	Date of Issue	Issuing Department	Main Content
Guidance on Strengthening Environmental Protection Supervision and Management of Listed Companies	2008-2	SEPA	When the companies apply for initial public offer or refinancing, environmental protection examination will be a mandatory requirement
Green Credit Guidance	2012-2	CBRC	Financial institutions in the banking industry are obliged to push forward green credit development. While advancing in the correct direction and focusing on key fields, the financial institutions should implement differentiated and dynamic credit grant policies, adopt the risk exposure management system, and establish relevant statistics systems
Guidance on Conducting Trials of Environmental Pollution Liability Insurance	2013-2	SEPA, CIRC	Push forward trials of environmental pollution liability insurance in industries with high environmental risks, such as heavy metal and petrochemical engineering
Green Bond Announcement	2015-12	People's Bank of China	Provide guidance and regulations for green finance bond in aspects of green industry project definition, investment direction of raised capital, capital management in period of existence, information disclosure and independent agency evaluation and certification

Source: Arranged as per internet information.

Table 9.3 Green Finance Development Plans of Various Districts (Guidance and Implementation Plans)

Date of Issue	District	Policy Document	Issuing Department
2016-3	Qingdao, Shandong	*Guidance on Enhancing Green Finance Services*	Qingdao banking bureau
2016-3	Datong, Shanxi	*Action Plan of 2016 to Facilitate Financial Revival*	Datong municipal government
2016-8	Qinghai	*Implementation Opinions on Developing Green Finance*	Xining Branch of People's Bank of China, the provincial financial office and Qinghai banking bureau
2016-9	Suzhou, Jiangsu	*Tentative Methods for Green Finance Performance Evaluation of Banking Financial Industries in Suzhou*	Suzhou Branch of People's Bank of China, financial office of Suzhou municipal government, Suzhou commission of economy and information technology, Suzhou environmental protection bureau
2016-11	Heilongjiang	*Guidance on Strengthening Financial Credit Work in Energy Saving and Environmental Protection Field in Heilongjiang Province*	People's government of Heilongjiang province
2016-11	Guizhou	*Opinions on Accelerating Green Finance Development*	People's government of Guizhou province
2016-11	Xiamen, Fujian	*Opinions on Encouraging Banking Financial Institutions in Xiamen to Develop Green Finance*	Xiamen municipal financial office, Xiamen banking bureau, Xiamen finance bureau, Xiamen branch of People's Bank of China

(Continued)

Table 9.3 (*Continued*)

Date of Issue	District	Policy Document	Issuing Department
2016-11	Guangdong	*Implementation Opinions on Strengthening Integration between Environmental Protection and Finance to Facilitate Green Development*	Guangdong environmental protection office, Guangzhou branch of People's Bank of China, and provincial financial office
2016-12	Anhui	*Plans for Implementing Green Finance System of Anhui Province*	Hefei branch of People's Bank of China, Anhui provincial financial office
2016-12	Beijing	*Financial Industry Development Plan During the 13th Five-Year Period in Beijing*	Beijing municipal bureau for financial works, Beijing NDRC
2017-3	Inner Mongolia	*Implementation Opinions on Constructing a Green Financial System*	People's government of Inner Mongolia
2017-5	Beijing	*Methods for Managing Capital Supporting Deep Integration and Innovative Development of Technologies and Finance in Zhongguancun National Exemplary Zone for Independent Innovation*	Zhongguancun management committee
2017-5	Yangzhou, Jiangsu	*Implementation Rules of Guidance on Constructing a Green Financial System*	Yangzhou branch of People's Bank of China
2016-3	Qingdao, Shandong	*Guidance on Enhancing Green Financial Services*	Qingdao banking bureau

Source: Arranged as per internet information.

9.1.4 *International Green Finance: Definition and Policies*

The latest and relatively complete definition of green finance can be found in the *G20 Green Finance Synthesis Report* issued in 2016: "Green finance is an investment and financing activity with environmental benefits, which could provide strong support for sustainable development. The environmental benefits of green finance covers many aspects, including reducing air, water and soil pollution, controlling emissions of greenhouse gases such as carbon dioxide, and increasing utilization rate of limited resources. At present, successful development of green finance requires us to internalize externality of the environment and improve financial institutions' awareness of environmental risks. With different methods and measures, we should create an investment atmosphere which is environmentally friendly and curbs pollution."

Globally, the practice of green finance started from the Super Fund Act issued by the USA in the beginning of the 1980s. The Act required companies to bear responsibilities for the environmental pollution caused by their operations and productions. As a result, more commercial banks were paying attention to and actively preventing credit risks caused by environmental pollution. The Act stirred up a wave of reforms. Afterwards, the governments of England and many other countries, and many international organizations conducted trials and explorations to improve the environment, and they accumulated some experiences in their effort.

(1) *The USA*

The USA has already established a complete green financial system. The green financial laws and regulations of the country effectively combined economic development and environmental protection. The green financial system could legally bind the American financial institutions, companies and markets, and encourage them to actively develop green finance. To ensure the leading position of the USA's green finance development in the world, the US government took a series of stimulating measures to motivate market entities to take part in green finance development. Those measures achieved real effects and facilitated the coordination between the USA's economic development and environmental protection.

The USA issued multiple laws and regulations successively to push forward and guarantee green finance development. In 1980, the US government issued the *Comprehensive Environmental Response, Compensation and Liability Act*, which clearly indicated that banks are also responsible for fixing environmental pollution caused by their customers. Additionally, the US government also formulated a series of policies to support healthy development of the green finance industry. In 1978, the US government issued the *Energy Tax Law*, which specified that during purchase of solar energy or wind energy equipment, 30% of the initial payment of 2,000 USD and 20% of the subsequent payment of 8,000 USD could be deducted from the income tax payable in the same year according to regulations. Meanwhile, the banks in the USA started a wave of technical reforms. By improving their IT systems, the banks accomplished data communication with social and environmental departments, and established a complete and highly efficient information communication mechanism.

(2) *The European Union*

The EU countries are also actively exploring and striving to develop green finance. In 1974, the first environment bank in the world settled in West Germany. In 1991, Poland also set up an environmental protection bank based on problems in environmental protection. In 1998, Lithuania announced the "NEFCO-APINI credit line", which greatly facilitated the development of financing for clean production projects upon its issuance. England has always been supportive for investment in energy saving equipment, and provided many preferential benefits including low-interest loans. In Sweden, the government provides credit upgrade and guarantee services for environmental protection projects. Construction of carbon emission trading market has made a success in Europe. The regional carbon market ranked the first in the world is the EU emission trading system, which covers

29 countries, 8 trading centers and 12,000 entities involved in industrial greenhouse gas emission. In the 30 billion USD's total amount of global carbon trade in 2006, European Union Allowance (EUA) had 24.4 billion USD, with a trading proportion up to 81.3%.

(3) *Japan*

Japan has established a complete green financial policy system, and has long been implementing motivational finance and tax polices for green economic development, including tax, subsidies, price and loan policies.

The Development Bank of Japan is a large state-owned bank with a registered capital over 10 billion USD. In 2004, the bank implemented an important decision — selecting and determining the investment target by means of environmental rating — meanwhile, the bank also strengthened cooperation with commercial banks, made the best use of its coordinating functions, and provided a good platform for green credit development. Commercial banks should make full use of the environmental rating system established by policy banks, conduct evaluations on loan applicants, and carry out supervision in order to prevent risks as far as possible and maximize efficiency of the use of investment.

Japanese commercial banks have made full use of the policy banks' environmental rating system to evaluate and supervise the loan targets. They avoided investment risks and significantly increased investment efficiency. For example, after learning of the significance of the Equator Principles, Mizuho Corporate Bank applied the Principles in its operation. As a result, the bank developed more and more customers, and achieved better performance. By adopting environmental protection technologies, the loaning enterprises enhanced their capacity to conduct clean production, and obtained some practical benefits; for example, such companies can obtain loans from banks on a preferential basis. In Japan, due to the driving force of interest mechanism, banks and companies could actively respond to and observe the Equator Principles. The above situation greatly facilitated the development of green credit business.

(4) *Regional Principles*

International organizations and financial institutions developed a series of principles to facilitate sustainable development of economy, society and environment. Some well-known principles include:

A. Principles for Responsible Investment (PRI)

The PRI initiative is a global initiative which encourages investors to apply the six principles of responsible investment in their practice. The purpose of PRI is to learn of the influence of sustainability on the investors and encourage contracting parties to include these principles in their investment decision and ownership practice. While implementing these principles, the contracting parties are making contributions to sustainable development of global financial system. By August 2017, more than 1,750 members from 50 countries had joined the PRI.

B. Equator Principles (EP)

The Equator Principles were established on the proposal of multiple commercial banks including ABN Amro Holding NV, Barclays and Citibank in 2002 and based on the policies and guidelines of International Finance Corporation (IFC) and the World Bank. The guidelines have become principles in the financial industry, and their purpose is to ascertain, evaluate and manage social and environmental risks which might occur in project financing activities. By 2016, there were 84 financial institutions which adopted the Equator Principles, including JPMorgan Chase & Co, Wells Fargo, HSBC, Standard Chartered and Citibank, distributed across 36 countries in the world.

C. Natural Capital Declaration

In the UN Conference on Sustainable Development in 2012, more than 40 financial institutions signed a financial initiative calling upon financial institutions to include considerations of natural capital into their products and services. The initiative also called upon public and private departments to strengthen cooperation, create necessary environments and conditions for natural capital to become an important economic, ecological and social asset, and finally help financial institutions fulfill their promises of sustainable development.

D. Carbon Disclosure Project (CDP)

The Carbon Disclosure Project was founded in 2000 as a charitable organization registered in the UK. As a global NGO, CDP collects climate change data from more than 1,550 companies around the world and establishes the most complete carbon emission database. Additionally, CDP also provides services for many international companies, and helps to collect climate change data in the supply chain system.

9.2 Push Forward RMB Internationalization with Green Finance — Multiple Approaches and Tools

9.2.1 *Green Credit*

(1) *Basic Concept of Green Credit*

At present, green credit has become an important tool of international banking industry to push forward sustainable development. Green credit means the banking financial institutions provide preferential interest rate and loan support for projects which could increase positive environment effects or reduce negative environment effects. The essence of green credit is to combine environment and social responsibilities with loans and management processes of commercial banks, facilitate green development of commercial banks, and cultivate a green credit culture.

Generally, green credit takes three forms: The first is to support environmental protection and energy saving projects through credit tools and push forward green development. The second is to add environment risk evaluation to loan approval and after-loan management processes. It takes measures such as loan suspension, loan delay or early recycling of loans against projects and companies which violated relevant laws and regulations on energy saving and environmental protection or might cause negative impact on the environment in order to facilitate green development. The third is to supervise borrowing companies and lead them to pay attention to and prevent environmental risks in their production by credit means. The borrowing companies should fulfill social responsibilities and reduce environment risks and operation risks.

(2) *Development of Green Credit*

Green credit originates in western countries. In the middle of the 1970s, Germany established the first policy-related environmental protection bank in the world. The work content of the bank was to provide preferential loans. At the end of the 1980s, the CERES company of the USA elaborated relevant concepts of Valdez Principles after analysis, and proposed to solve the earth's ecological environment problems. And on the basis of the Principles, CERES encouraged companies closely involved in earth's environmental problems to actively participate in environmental improvement. Currently, in the development of international financial market, green credit has become popularized into a general trend, and has gradually gained the wide attention of financial organizations of various countries.

The Chinese government has always been actively pushing forward green credit practice of the banking industry. In July 2007, the government issued the *Opinions on Implementing Environmental Protection Policies and Laws and Preventing Credit Risks*, which signified the establishment of green credit policy system in our country. In 2008, the environmental protection department of our country initialized business contact with the World Bank and signed a cooperation agreement. Together, they issued the *Guidelines for Environmental Protection with Green Credit* based on China's basic conditions and development phenomena. The "Guidelines" provided the basic standards and specifications of environmental protection in China, and serve as the basis for financial organizations to conduct green credit business. In 2012, the CBRC formally issued the *Green Credit Guidance* (hereinafter referred to as "*Guidance*"), which formally put forward the concept of green credit and provided a definition: While conducting green credit business, we must provide support for environmental protection economies such as green economy and low-carbon economy, reduce risk factors as far as possible, and enhance our environmental and social performance. The *Guidance* provides clear assessment requirements and plays a positive role in the development of green credit in China.

(3) *Green Credit: The Foundation of RMB Internationalization*

With the progress of RMB internationalization, green credit has become an important tool serving this objective. In the investment and financing risk management of international projects, some environmental and ecological risks, which are drawing relatively less attention might actually cause significant impact, in addition to conventional risks, such as nation, finance and operation risks. In the past, China's major projects would occur now and then, due to environmental and ecological impact. Therefore, the potential reputation risks and credit risks cannot be overlooked. Although green credit development does not push forward RMB internationalization directly, green credit is the basic condition for our financial institutions, especially banking financial institutions to conduct overseas business. As a precondition for pushing forward RMB internationalization with green finance, green credit carries great significance. Financial institutions should follow the *Green Credit Guidance*, observe the rules of green credit business, dutifully conduct project due diligence, effectively avoid environmental and social risks, improve credit policies, systems and process management, and lay a solid foundation for overseas expansion of financial business.

9.2.2 *Green Bonds*

(1) *Green Bonds: Basic Concept*

Green bonds are the bonds issued for green projects or the purpose of green investment. The core difference of green bonds from other bonds is that the raised capital of green bonds is focused on pushing forward and realizing green benefits. Green Bond Principles (GBP) are the guidelines formulated by relevant organizations and the international market consisting of bond issuers, investment organizations and underwriters, strictly in accordance with the basic requirements of green bonds. The objective of GBP is to increase information disclosure and facilitate sound development of the market. GBP (2017) classified green bonds into four categories based on the cash flow and repayment obligations.

Green bond market could provide the following benefits for green projects and investors: (1) Provide more financing options for green projects, but does not provide loans or equity financing; (2) Provide large amount of long-term financing; especially in districts where infrastructure is being constructed but available loans are limited; (3) Motivate the issuer to participate in green projects after achieving the "reputation benefit"; (4) Prevent risks more carefully and fulfill green disclosure obligations; (5) Provide more green projects for investors to help them achieve cyclic development.

(2) *International Development of Green Bonds*

Green bonds originate in the international market in 2007. During the 6 years from 2007 to 2012, the accumulated issuance of green bonds in the world was about 1 billion USD, and issuing entities are mostly multi-lateral developmental financial institutions and policy-related financial institutions, such as European Investment Bank, Work Bank and International Finance Corporation. In 2013–2014, the green bond market increased rapidly. The issuers including policy-related banks, public undertakings and enterprises issued green bonds totaling to about 31 billion USD. The amount of issue was 42.2 billion USD in 2015 and 86 billion USD in 2016. However, in the huge amount of issue of the global bond market, which was several trillion USD, green bond market accounted for less than 5%. The above data means the green bond market has a great potential for development.

Green bonds mainly support the sustainable investment projects in the fields of transport, energy, construction and industry. The issuers include multi-lateral developmental banks, local governments, municipal departments, companies and financial institutions.

(3) *Green Bonds: An Important Carrier Pushing Forward RMB Internationalization*

In 2015, People's Bank of China issued the No.39 announcement and promoted the green financial bonds. According to analysis, green financial bonds are a kind of negotiable securities issued by directors of financial organizations in the financial bond market, strictly in accordance with the legal requirements. The raised capital will be used to support development of green projects. Since then, China's green bond market started its rapid development. In 2016, our country's domestic and overseas green bond issuance reached a total amount of 230 billion yuan, which accounted for 40% of the world total and ranked the first in the world.

According to the interim report of 2017 published by China-UK green finance work team, from the beginning of 2016 to the middle of 2017, our country issued green bonds exceeding 324 billion yuan (about 48 billion USD). At present, the proportion of green bonds in our country's bond market is gradually rising. It has reached 2%, which is much higher than 0.2% — the proportion of the international market.

While green bonds has been rapidly developing in China, green RMB bonds also made the first breakthrough in the overseas market. See Table 9.4.

Table 9.4 Green RMB Bonds Issued Overseas or by Overseas Institutions

Date of Issue	Issuer	Amount of Issue (100 Million Yuan)	Period (Years)	Facial Rate of Return	Place of Issue
2014-6	International Finance Corporation (IFC)	5	3	2%	London Stock Exchange
2015-10-13	Agricultural Bank of China	6	2	4.15%	London Stock Exchange
2016-7	New York Branch of Bank of China	15	2	3.60%	Hong Kong Stock Exchange
2016-7	BRICS New Development Bank	30	5	3.07%	China Inter-bank Bond Market

Source: China financial information network of Xinhua News Agency.

As more RMB green bonds will be issued in other countries, and more foreign institutions will issue green bonds in our country in future, RMB will be more extensively circulated in the international market by using the carrier of green bonds. Therefore, the green bonds are an important part of RMB internationalization. In consideration of the wide space of green bond market and the high proportion of China's green bonds in the world, RMB green bonds will have a wider space of development overseas and push forward RMB internationalization more strongly.

9.2.3 *Carbon Finance*

Carbon finance is the total sum of trading in greenhouse gas emission rights and various financial businesses and trading. The foundation of carbon finance system is the international agreements and domestic policies related to greenhouse gas reduction. In the policies and systems, emission reduction is considered as tradable goods, and companies and financial institutions take part in the market and help achieve green and sustainable development. In 2011, the global carbon market had a transaction amount of 176 billion USD, and by 2013, the transaction volume reached 10.4 billion tons. Afterwards, the global carbon market was in a weak, dull state in a background of sagging macro-economy. However, the transaction volume in 2015 still reached 6 billion tons, with an amount of 50 billion USD.

Our country's carbon finance has made initial development. Our country is the largest supplying country of Clean Development Mechanism (CDM) in the world. In recent years, our country has started promoting carbon emission rights trading in 7 trial provinces and cities, and will establish a uniform carbon emission rights trading market in 2017.

Selection of settlement currency for carbon trade plays a significant role in RMB internationalization. A currency's rights of binding to international bulk commodities, such as energies in valuation and settlement are a precondition for the currency to become an international currency. Petro-dollar is an example. In the present day of low carbon economy, carbon asset will play an important role in international currency market as the main subject of carbon trade. RMB internationalization is the necessary condition for China to achieve the great rejuvenation, and the core interest of China's financial internationalization. Along with the continuous growth of China's carbon trade market, RMB internationalization is facing new opportunities in the carbon finance field. Due to the large scale of carbon emissions in China, RMB will have its position in the global carbon finance system. China's carbon market will become the largest spot carbon market in the world. China should vigorously develop the carbon finance market, deepen international cooperation on carbon emission trade and increase RMB's proportion in carbon finance trade.

9.3 Obstacles and Solutions

9.3.1 *Obstacles*

(1) *Development of Green Finance is Facing Many Challenges*

Although green finance development has made some progress, it is still facing many challenges. The first is environmental externality. Environmental externality is the innate obstacle of green finance development. Positive externality of green investment is favorable for the society and environment, while polluting investment could damage social and public interest. It is called the negative externality of environment. Since positive externality of environmental problems increases environmental protection cost, and negative externality reduces pollution cost, there is difficulty in internalizing externality risks. As a result, we lack sufficient green investments, while polluting investments are excessive in quantity.

The second is the financing cycle. Green infrastructure projects mainly rely on bank credit financing to carry out construction, but ordinary commercial banks have short terms in the liability end, and have difficulty matching asset and liability terms. As a result, long-term green infrastructure projects have difficulty in financing. Term mismatch has become the challenge in green financial market development and will restrict the financing and construction of green financial projects.

The third is the lack of a clear definition of green finance. At present, our country lacks clear definitions and scopes for green financial products. Therefore, investors, companies and financial institutions have obstacles recognizing green investment opportunities. A consensus on the definition of green finance is the foundation for financial institutions to develop green financial products and for green companies to conduct industrial recognition. Without an appropriate definition, financial institutions will have difficulty allocating financial resources to green projects based on a uniform standard.

(2) *Green Finance and RMB's "Stepping Out" Process is Not Sufficiently Integrated*

In the previous chapters, we can find that green financial carriers such as green credit, green bonds and carbon finance are developing rapidly in recent years, but few results have been achieved to meet the condition of "green + RMB internationalization". In the beginning stage of green finance development, major green financial tools in the world are still valuated in USD and EUR, and RMB green finance has difficulties "introducing in" and "stepping out". Our country needs to reverse currency inertia by means of policy promotion, market construction and product innovation, and push forward the development of green financial products valuated in RMB.

There are also good news, however. For example, our country's green bond market is developing rapidly, with an issuance accounting for half of the world issuance. The situation serves as a good condition for increasing integration between green finance and RMB internationalization.

(3) *The Lack of Relevant Research and Policies is Unfavorable for Pushing Forward RMB Internationalization with Green Finance*

Firstly, different green standards should be connected. China's definition of greenness is different from the definition widely accepted in the world, and the above difference might cause deviations in green investment and financing. On one hand, investors may worry that they had invested in a project defined as non-green by their important customers, and such investment goes against their own green investment guidelines. On the other hand, the investors may worry that the green bonds issued by China do not meet the conditions to be included into relevant green indexes.

Secondly, green finance does not have sufficient impetus to attract private capital. Although our country issued various policies to encourage green finance development, there is still no policy that could essential benefit green finance in a differentiated way. For private capital, investments in green projects and ordinary projects are not essentially different. Companies and investors could not obtain additional benefits by participating in green finance; therefore, they lack the driving force to engage in green investment.

Thirdly, there are obstacles in information communication. The communication cost caused by non-smooth exchange of information between green investors and green projects is unfavorable for green finance development. Investors need to conduct investment after learning of the invested company's environmental information and effectively recognizing green companies. For example, some information is still lacking in China's green bond market. The lack of information related to the use of raised capital, post-issuance disclosure requirements and external inspections might restrict the investors' will and amount of purchase. The above situation caused certain obstacles for market investors to join the green bond market.

9.3.2 *Solutions*

(1) *Strengthen Support for Green Development*

The first is to strengthen promotion of the green finance concept. Our country should actively advocate the green development concept, strengthen policy support for green finance, complete the institution and mechanism construction of green finance, enlarge green finance's market participation, and direct social capital to invest in important green industry projects. Government agencies, market associations, financial institutions and other market organizations could all conduct the propaganda and promotional activities. While carrying out infrastructure construction of green financial market, our country should vigorously promote the concept of green investment and green operation among companies.

The second is organization construction and policy support. On the national level, our country already issued the *Guidance on Constructing a Green Financial System* to push forward green finance development. On the regional level, Guizhou province founded the green finance innovation and development work team headed by the provincial secretary. And Shenzhen founded the specialized committee for green finance. Development of green finance involves many departments and levels, and may affect the interests of vested interest groups. Therefore, it is necessary to establish special institutions on the organizational level, as Guizhou and Shenzhen did, and conduct top-level designs for green finance development under a strong leadership. Various districts should set up specialized institutions to push forward green finance development, issue detailed local policies, and push forward and supervise the development of green finance.

The third is to strengthen market construction. Our country should establish an interest subsidy system and guarantee system for green credit, set up regional green industry development funds, and direct more social resources into the green finance field. We should also encourage the development of green bond market, set up a more complete green bond labeling system and issuance auditing system, and increase levels of greenness of the green bonds. Meanwhile, our country should strengthen carbon financial market construction, conduct trials of carbon emission trading market in more areas, and encourage development of carbon trade between China and foreign countries.

(2) *Set Up Green Financial Institutions*

The first is to increase degree of greenness of financial institutions. The financial institutions should develop green finance on a strategic level, set up green financial development departments, establish green development strategies and system frameworks, and vigorously develop the green finance business. By using mature green financial products in an innovative way, and making innovations in green financial products, the financial institutions should provide high-quality service for the green economy.

The second is to integrate into the world system. By including green finance into our major objectives, we should adopt the green finance standards based on fields and items, gradually align ourselves with international and regional green financial rules such as UN Principles for Responsible Investment and the Equator Principles, and push forward international cooperation on green finance and cross-border green investment and financing.

(3) *Systematically Push Forward Green Finance Development to Facilitate RMB Internationalization*

The first is to facilitate diversification of RMB green financial products. Our country should accelerate development of green financial products valuated and settled in RMB, push forward construction of cross-border market mechanism of green bonds based on traditional cross-border financial products and green attributes, set up green industry development funds, strengthen exploration and development of overseas green credit, and provide richer choices for RMB green finance to "step out" by making active innovations and developing RMB green financial products.

The second is to formulate RMB green financial policies. Our country should conduct top-level designs, push forward construction of RMB green financial system, provide preferential treatment for RMB green financial market and products on the policy level, and increase the market's attention to green financial products. We should establish transaction standards and supervision mechanism of the green financial market to prevent financial risks. Green finance combined with the objective of RMB internationalization should be a key point in policy design and should be promoted vigorously.

The third is to deepen international cooperation on RMB green finance. Our country should actively integrate into the international green financial system, expand green financial cooperation platforms, and promote internationalization of RMB green financial products. By means of currency swap, product exchange and market connections, we can open up both the domestic and international market, attract foreign investors to invest in RMB green financial products, and deepen international cooperation on RMB green finance.

Overseas RMB Funds in France

10.1 Introduction

Chinese president Xi Jinping declared in the Belt and Road Summit for International Cooperation in May 2017: "China will strengthen capital support for "Belt and Road" construction, and will add 100 billion yuan to the Silk Road Fund. China will encourage financial institutions to conduct overseas RMB fund business, with an expected scale of 300 billion yuan." Prime minister Li Keqiang pointed out in the government work report in March 2016: "We should expand international capacity cooperation, set up overseas RMB cooperation funds, make use of bilateral capacity cooperation funds, strive to output our equipment, technologies, standards and services, and build a golden brand of 'Made in China'."

Setting up overseas RMB funds has great significance. Firstly, it is favorable for RMB internationalization. Overseas RMB funds could become an important channel of Chinese financial institutions and social capital to internationalize RMB and will greatly increase RMB's proportion of use in global trade, investment and financial activities. Secondly, it helps meet the financing demand of the Belt and Road Initiative (BRI) construction. According to initial statistics, infrastructure construction of BRI requires a total investment up to 6 trillion USD. It is unsustainable and risky to use USD or existing international currencies as the investment currencies. Overseas RMB funds could help solve the financing gap of BRI construction. Thirdly, it helps with China's international capacity cooperation. Overseas RMB funds could encourage domestic manufacturing companies to "step out". They could not only strengthen bilateral capacity cooperation, but also motivate Chinese companies and companies of developed countries, which have advanced production capacity to conduct capacity cooperation together in a third-party market.

European Union (EU) is China's largest trading partner and has close economic and trade relationships with China. The EU developed from European Community and has 28-member countries. Headquartered in Belgium's capital Brussels, the EU is a regional integrated organization which combined political and economic entities and has important influence in the world. Members of the EU have not necessarily joined the Eurozone, but all Eurozone countries are members of the EU. Currently there are 18 countries in the Eurozone in total. Europe is a geographical area, however, it includes about 50 countries and districts, including Russia.

This chapter uses Europe as its major scope of research and studies the feasibility of setting up overseas RMB funds in France.

10.2 Current Situation of RMB Internationalization in the EU

10.2.1 *RMB's Trade Settlement Function*

In 2015, the total RMB cross-border trade settlement across the world was 7.23 trillion yuan, with a year-on-year growth of 10.38%. The proportion of RMB settlement in the world in the same year was 3.38%, with a growth rate a little lower than 2014. RMB trade settlement was mainly conducted in Hong Kong, Taiwan, ASEAN and Russia, while the EU only accounted for a small percentage.

As an international payment currency, RMB accounted for up to 2.79% in August 2015, and first surpassed Japanese yen as the fourth largest payment currency in the world. However, in 2015, RMB exchange rate fluctuated sharply, and RMB's proportion in international payments reduced rapidly. By June 2016, it dropped by nearly 40%. According to the data of Society for Worldwide Inter-bank Financial Telecommunication (SWIFT), RMB accounted for only 1.6% in global payments by April 2017 and was ranked the sixth in parallel with Swiss Franc, second to USD, EUR, GBP, JPY and CAD.

10.2.2 *RMB's Financial Transaction Function*

By December 2016, European countries including England issued 282 RMB bonds in total, accounting for 16% of global RMB bonds. The above bonds raised 90 billion yuan, accounting for 9.7% of total raised funds of global RMB bonds.

10.2.3 *RMB's Reserve Function*

According to the data of State Administration of Foreign Exchange, foreign central banks were holding RMB capitals of 563.5 billion yuan (about 72 billion euros) by December 2016. Among the above capitals, European Central Bank was holding 500 million euros of RMB assets (Table 10.1). RMB only accounts for 1% in the EU's foreign exchange reserve, and is still in the start-up stage; while the USD assets account for up to 75%. Major currencies in the foreign exchange reserves of various countries are ranked in the following

Table 10.1   RMB Reserves of the Central Banks of EU Countries (Including the UK)

S/N	Name of Bank	Currency Value	Date of Inclusion	Source
1	Bank of England	5.8 billion RMB	2014	China Daily website
2	European Central Bank	Equivalent to 500 million euros	2017	European Central Bank website
3	Belgian Central Bank	Equivalent to 200 million euros	Unclear	Hexun.com
4	Swiss National Bank	Small amount, but unclear	Unclear	Finance.sina.com.cn

Source: Arranged as per internet information.

order: USD, EUR, JPY, GBP, CAD, AUD, CHF. And the proportion of RMB as a reserve currency is still small.

10.2.4 *Currency Swaps*

So far, 4 EU countries have signed currency swap agreements with People's Bank of China, and 8 EU currencies are directly convertible with RMB (Tables 10.2 and 10.3). There are 6 RMB clearing banks in the EU (Table 10.4).

Table 10.2 Currency Swaps between EU Countries (Including the UK) and China

S/N	Country	Date of Signature	Swap Scale	Period
1	The UK	2013.6.22	200 billion RMB/20 billion GBP	3 years
		2015.10.20 (renewal)	350 billion RMB/35 billion GBP (renewal)	
2	Hungary	2013.9.9	10 billion RMB/375 billion HUF	3 years
		2016.9.12 (renewal)	10 billion RMB/416 billion HUF (renewal)	
3	European Central Bank	2013.10.8	350 billion RMB/45 billion euros	3 years
		2016.9.27 (renewal)	350 billion RMB/45 billion euros (renewal)	
4	Switzerland	2014.7.21	150 billion RMB/21 billion CHF	3 years
		2017.7.21 (renewal)	150 billion RMB/21 billion CHF (renewal)	

Source: Arranged as per information on the website of People's Bank of China.

Table 10.3 Currencies of EU Countries (Including the UK) Directly Convertible with RMB

S/N	1	2	3	4	5	6	7	8
Currency	GBP	EUR	CHF	HUF	DKK	PLN	SEK	NOK
Date of achieving direct convertibility	2014.6.19	2014.9.30	2015.11.9		2016.12.12			

Source: Arranged as per information on the website of People's Bank of China.

Table 10.4 RMB Clearing Banks in EU Countries (Including the UK)

S/N	1	2	3	4	5	6
Location	London	Frankfurt	Paris	Luxembourg	Budapest	Zurich
Clearing Bank	China Construction Bank	Bank of China	Bank of China	Industrial and Commercial Bank of China	Bank of China	China Construction Bank
Date	2014	2014	2014	2014	2015	2015
Other				EU countries		

Source: Arranged as per information on the website of People's Bank of China.

10.2.5 *The EU's RMB Business Center*

London is one of the largest offshore financial centers in the world, and the RMB business center of the EU (Table 10.5). After the UK's exit from the EU, France, Germany and Luxembourg hoped to build an RMB offshore financial center which could take London's position in their own countries. This issue will be described in more detail in the following passages.

10.3 Offshore Financial Centers in Europe

10.3.1 *Existing Offshore Financial Centers in Europe*

(1) *Categories of Offshore Financial Centers in the World*

Categories of offshore financial centers in the world can be found in Table 10.6.

(2) *The Offshore Financial Center in London*

The London financial center belongs to the in-out mixing category, i.e. it does not distinguish between the offshore and onshore financial centers. Transactions can be conducted freely in the market, with no restrictions on capital in-flow and out-flow, and the GBP currency market is connected with major currency markets of Europe. The

Table 10.5   RMB Business in London

RMB Business	Basic Information	Source of Data
The largest offshore RMB foreign exchange transaction center	By March 2017, 36.3% of RMB foreign exchange transactions (excluding China mainland) were conducted through the UK. Hong Kong was the second (29.3%), the USA and France were the third (7.3%), and Singapore was the fourth (5%). In addition, London's RMB foreign exchange transactions had been steadily increasing in the past 5 years, and the quantity of RMB foreign exchange transactions in 2016 had exceeded 13 million	SWIF, March 2017
RMB use ranked the second in the world	In 2017, the UK surpassed Singapore as an overseas economy with the second largest RMB use, with a weight of 5%. Hong Kong's position as a super intermediary of RMB internationalization was strengthened, with a proportion of 76.26%	SWIFT, July 2017
Largest RMB clearing amount out of Asia	By February 2017, the UK's RMB clearing bank (China Construction Bank's London branch) had set up RMB accounts for 69 financial institutions. The total RMB clearing amount was near 14 trillion yuan, and the average daily clearing was 21.052 billion yuan. The average daily clearing quantity was 342 transactions, with a first-pass business rate of 95.82%. The RMB clearing amount in London remained as the largest out of Asia	Media report
An important participant of RMB bond market	London played an important role in overseas issuance of RMB bonds	Media report

(Continued)

Table 10.5 (*Continued*)

RMB Business	Basic Information	Source of Data
Ranked the fourth among the top 5 payment countries (and districts), with China being the fund receiving country	The proportion of RMB payment in all countries/districts is still low, and between 1–2%. The USD is still a major currency used in payments to China. In terms of amount, 98% of payments from the USA to China are using USD. The proportions of RMB payment in Hong Kong, the USA, South Korea, the UK and Taiwan are 17%, 8%, 5%, 5% and 4%, respectively. In payments to China, the UK demonstrated the lowest dependency on USD (79%) and the largest diversity in currency choices.	SWIFT, RMB special

Source: Arranged as per internet information.

Table 10.6 Categories of Offshore Financial Centers in the World

Model	Typical Center	Transaction Entity	Formation	Business Scope	Characteristics
In-out mixing	London, Hong Kong	Non-residents, residents, offshore financial institutions	Formed naturally	Medium-term and long-term capital loans	The offshore institutions were not founded in accordance with strict application procedures.
					They do not set up independent offshore and onshore accounts. No restrictions for capital inflow and outflow
In-out separated	IBF of the USA, JOM of Japan	Non-residents, residents, offshore financial institutions	Specially founded	Medium-term and long-term capital loans	Founding of the offshore institution requires authority approval.

(*Continued*)

Table 10.6   (*Continued*)

Model	Typical Center	Transaction Entity	Formation	Business Scope	Characteristics
					Offshore businesses can only be conducted in special accounts (IBF). Offshore and onshore businesses are separated. Offshore and onshore capital infiltration is not allowed
Infiltration	Jakarta, ACH of Singapore, Bangkok	Non-residents, residents, offshore financial institutions	Specially founded	Medium-term and long-term capital loans	Three cases: out-in and in-out types
Tax haven	The Cayman Islands, Bahamas and Bermuda	Non-residents, residents, offshore financial institutions	Specially founded	Only handling accounts, no actual transactions	Bookkeeping type (Paper Company, Shell Branch), Anglo-American legal system, low taxes, basically no financial control

Source: Arranged as per internet information.

London financial center has the largest foreign exchange market, gold market and financial derivative market in the world. The British financial market has adopted a dual-supervision model consisting of the Prudential Regulation Authority and Financial Conduct Authority, which conduct macro-prudential and micro-prudential supervisions, respectively. Meanwhile, the Bank of England has internally set up a currency policy committee, financial policy committee and prudential regulation committee.

10.3.2   *Influence of the UK's Exit from the EU on the Development of RMB Offshore Financial Centers*

Since the UK conducted the "Brexit" vote in June 2016, whether London could maintain its position as an international financial center became a question, uncertainties arose on the agreements between China and the UK on RMB internationalization, and London's position as a bridge tower of RMB internationalization irradiating to Europe was weakened. Major EU countries started their works on the European continent and tried to replace London as a financial center; they were especially paying attention to RMB businesses.

So far, the RMB offshore financial center in London has remained steady. The volumes of RMB foreign exchange transaction and clearing business in London are steadily increasing. In the fourth quarter of 2016, the daily average transaction amount of London offshore RMB was 56.31 billion GBP, with a 9.6% increase from the last quarter. In terms of clearing business, London's RMB clearing bank — London Branch of China Construction Bank completed an RMB clearing amount of 4.3 trillion yuan from July 2016 to February 2017, with a year-on-year growth of 14%. By the end of February 2017, 69 financial institutions opened RMB accounts in London Branch of China Construction Bank, and the RMB clearing amount in London was about 14 trillion yuan in total. The daily average clearing amount was 21.052 billion yuan, with a daily average quantity of 342 transactions and a first-pass business rate of 95.82%. London's total clearing amount was still the largest out of Asia.

10.3.3   *The EU Countries are Actively Pushing Forward Construction of RMB Offshore Financial Centers*

The continuous growth of China's economic strength changed the international capital flow pattern. Currently, apart from the UK, which already built an RMB offshore financial center, France, Germany and Luxembourg are also actively seeking RMB financial cooperation and trying to set up RMB offshore financial centers. While UK is exiting from the EU, it is important to take the lead and set up an RMB offshore financial center of the EU countries.

(1) *France*

A. Construction of an offshore RMB financial center in France

In recent years, France has been actively pushing forward construction of the RMB offshore center in Paris. Especially when the UK is exiting from the EU, France is taking great interest in founding an offshore RMB financial center. In March 2014, France obtained 80 billion yuan's RQFII quota for investment in China's domestic capital market. In December 2014, Paris Branch of People's Bank of China became France's RMB clearing bank. The incident signified the establishment of RMB payment system in France. In November 2016, Ma Kai, vice premier of China's State Council and Michel Sapin, minister of economy and finance of France pointed out together in the fourth China-France high-level economic and financial dialogue: They support the construction of an offshore RMB financial center in Paris and hope France will become a concentrated place for RMB businesses in the Eurozone.

B. Opinions of high-level authority

On July 24, 2016, France's financial minister Michel Sapin stated in the G20 meeting of financial ministers and central bank governors in Chengdu: France has been considering Paris as a potential RMB offshore transaction center over many years, and he believes Paris will be ranked the first in the candidate list after the UK exits from the EU. In December 2016, Christian Noyer, the honorary president of Banque de France visited China and stated that Paris would replace London as the new financial center of Europe. Mr. Noyer indicated that while the UK is exiting from the EU, France has set up a complete RMB payment and clearing system, and multiple RMB bonds have been successfully issued in France. France will replace the UK as an important country for RMB internationalization in Europe.

C. Paris capital market

The Paris capital market is ranked high among EU cities in terms of development level, therefore it could provide great help for expansion of RMB businesses. The largest corporate bond market of Europe is located in Paris. It accounts for 40% of market shares of the entire Europe, and surpassed the UK and Germany, which account for 27% and 10%, respectively. Moreover, the headquarter of Euronext, which is the largest stock exchange in Europe and the second largest derivative exchange in the world is located in Paris. Euronext has extensive contacts and cooperation with multiple Chinese financial institutions, such as state-owned banks including Bank of China, Agricultural Bank of China, Industrial and Commercial Bank of China and China Construction Bank, and transaction platforms such as Shenzhen Stock Exchange. Additionally, Paris has a developed banking industry. The Societe Generale and Credit Agricole, headquartered in Paris are ranked the second and third in Europe in terms of asset total, respectively. French banks are also famous for their strong executive force, because they are more closely led by investors than the banks of other countries. In Europe, the scale of asset management industry of Paris is only second to London.

D. Paris' financial services have irradiated to multiple African countries

14 countries in Africa used to be in the French franc zone. French banks have been developing in these countries over many years and are the main suppliers of local financial services. Currently, RMB deposit in Paris is ranked the second in Europe, and a large portion of it came from China-Africa transactions, therefore Paris will hope- fully become a transit location for RMB cross-border trades between China and Africa. Foreign exchange transaction is a highlight of the London RMB offshore center, RMB investment funds are the key item of development of Luxembourg, while RMB business related to trade financing is the strength of Paris.

(2) *Germany*

A. Construction of an offshore RMB financial center in Germany

Germany is China's third largest trade partner and the largest country for Chinese investment in Europe. Therefore, Frankfurt became a competitive city for building an RMB offshore financial center in the EU. Frankfurt has obvious advantages in its financial environment. The headquarters of European Central Bank, Bundesbank, Federal Financial Supervisory Authority of Germany, Deutsche Boerse AG, Deutsche Bank and Commerzbank AG are all located in Frankfurt. Among them, the Federal Financial Supervisory Authority is one of the few supervisory institutions in the EU which have experience in complex derivative trade management.

In March 2014, People's Bank of China declared to set up an RMB clearing bank in Frankfurt. In June of the same year, People's Bank of China appointed the Frankfurt Branch of Bank of China as the RMB clearing bank. The clearing bank could open RMB accounts for other banks and companies, and conduct euro and RMB businesses. Although China-Germany trade volume is twice of China-UK, and Germany's direct investment in China is 1.3 times of the UK's, RMB settlement in Frankfurt is still significantly lower than that in London; therefore, RMB businesses in Frankfurt still have great potentials.

B. China Europe International Exchange

In November 2015, the China Europe International Exchange (hereinafter referred to as CEINEX) headquartered in Frankfurt, Germany was formally put in operation. The investors included Shanghai Stock Exchange, Deutsche Borse Group and China Financial Futures Exchange, which held 40%, 40% and 20% of the shares of the joint venture company, respectively.

The emphasis of CEINEX at present is the cash bond market. The products include bonds and exchange-traded funds, and subsequently, CEINEX will launch D-shares, which will be issued by a company registered in China mainland and traded in Germany. The

ETF on the CEINEX platform tracked the quotations of the most important Chinese indexes. The RMB bonds traded in this exchange were all issued by blue-chip companies and large financial institutions. To participate in trading of products of CEINEX cash bond market, the investors need to obtain the membership of the Frankfurt Stock Exchange, which is a cash bond market under Deutsche Borse Group.

CEINEX provided a new channel of investing in China for global investors (Table 10.7). By April 2016, listed products of CEINEX had a total transaction amount of 337 million euros (approximately 2.4 billion RMB), with a daily average of 3 million euros (approximately 21.5 million RMB). Among the listed products, ETF products had a transaction amount of 333 million euros (approximately 2.378 billion RMB), accounting for 98% of the total transaction amount. It should be noted that RMB-valuated products have been accepted by the market. RMB-valuated products had a transaction amount of 218 million RMB, accounting for 9.1% of total transaction amount.

Table 10.7   An Overview of the Trading Products of CEINEX

S/N	Category	Product Name	ISIN
1	Exchange-traded funds	BOC International Shanghai Stock 50A-Share Index UCITS ETF	LU1306625283
2		Commerzbank CCB International RQFII Currency Market UCITS ETF	GB00BVJF7G73
3		Commerzbank CCB International RQFII Currency Market UCITS ETF	GB00BVJF7F66
4		CSOP FTSE China A50 UCITS ETF	DE000A1XES83
5		Deutsche Bank X-Trackers Shanghai and Shenzhen 300 UCITS ETF 1C	LU0779800910
6		Deutsche Bank X-Trackers Harvest Shanghai and Shenzhen 300 Index UCITS ETF (Direct Clone Fund)	LU0875160326

(Continued)

Table 10.7 (*Continued*)

S/N	Category	Product Name	ISIN
7		Deutsche Bank X-Trackers Harvest FTSE China A-H-Share 50 UCITS ETF (Direct Clone Fund)	LU1310477036
8		Deutsche Bank X-Trackers II Harvest Shanghai and Shenzhen China Sovereign Bond UCITS ETF (Direct Clone Fund)	LU1094612022
9		ETFS E Fund MSCI China A-Share UCITS ETF	DE000A1XEFE1
10		RMB/USD ETF	DE000A1EK0K5
11		USD/RMB ETF	DE000A1EK0L3
12		ICBCCS WisdomTree S&P China 500 UCITS ETF	LU1440654330
13		ComStage FTSE China A50 UCITS ETF	LU0947415054
14		BOC International Commerzbank Shanghai Stock 50A-Share Index UCITS ETF	LU1377632572
15	Bonds	KFW Bankengruppe RMB Medium-Term Note NTS.V.15 (18)	DE000A14J850
16	ETF derivative	Deutsche Bank X-Trackers Harvest Shanghai and Shenzhen 300 Index ETF Futures (listed on February 20, 2017 for transaction)	DE000A2BMKV2
17		Deutsche Bank Harvest Shanghai and Shenzhen 300 Index ETF Options	Undetermined

Source: Arranged as per website information of CEINEX.

(3) *Luxembourg*

A. Construction of an offshore RMB financial center in Luxembourg

Luxembourg is also a strong competitor for setting up RMB offshore centers. Luxembourg is only a small country, but it has an outstanding position in private banking and wealth management businesses in the Eurozone, and it is the second largest investment fund center, only second to the USA. So far, Bank of China, Industrial and Commercial Bank of China and China Construction Bank have already established European headquarters in Luxembourg. Meanwhile, Agricultural Bank of China is preparing to set up its European headquarter, and China Merchants Bank has decided to start company formation process in Luxembourg.

B. Luxembourg's RMB business has prominent characteristics

So far, Luxembourg has become one of the most important cross-border RMB business centers in the Eurozone. As the largest fund center second to the USA, the Europe's leading international bond listing platform and a first-class private banking center in the Eurozone, Luxembourg is rich in professional knowledge in the financial service field.

In the field of RMB dim sum bonds, Luxembourg is a place of issue of dim sum bonds that is the fourth largest in the world and the first largest in Europe. 43% of RMB-valuated bonds issued out of Asia are listed in Luxembourg. The percentage is higher than London and Dublin, which are 27% and 9%, respectively. Major investors of dim sum bonds come from Europe, accounting for 47% of all investors. In history, Luxembourg Stock Exchange (LuxSE) first issued China sovereign bonds in 1994. The first RMB bond of the European issuer (Volkswagen) was listed in LuxSE in 2011. In 2014, Chinese companies issued RMB bonds in the Eurozone for the first time, and the place of issue was Luxembourg.

In the field of RMB RQFII funds, Luxembourg is also far ahead compared to other European countries. By November 2015, RMB RQFII funds registered in Luxembourg have a scale of 632 million euros, accounting for 79.77% of the Europe's total registered amount 796 million euros. The scale in other countries: Ireland, 86 million euros; France, 41 million euros; and the UK, 37 million euros.

In the field of RMB investment funds, Luxembourg is the largest investment fund center in Europe and the second largest in the world, second to the USA. And it is managing assets exceeding 3 trillion euros. Almost all world-renowned companies in the asset management business have selected Luxembourg as their capital home, including some of the largest Chinese asset management companies, such as China Southern Fund Management, China AMC and Harvest Fund. By September 2015, investment funds registered in Luxembourg were holding 208.4 billion yuan's RMB-valuated assets.

10.4 RMB Clearing and Settlement System of EU Countries

10.4.1 *RMB Payment and Clearing System of EU Countries*

(1) *Traditional Model of Payment and Clearing System*

A. Domestic clearing system

The core of RMB payment infrastructure of our country is the China National Automatic Payment System (CNAPS) set up by People's Bank of China. The CNAPS mainly processes RMB inter-bank transfers based on various transactions of residents and companies, and inter-bank RMB payments based on inter-bank borrowing.

B. Offshore clearing system

A typical example of RMB offshore payment system is Hong Kong's CHATS. In this system, Bank of China (Hong Kong) operates as the RMB clearing bank to process RMB payment businesses in cross-border trade and international financial transactions, and it is connected with the central settlement system for bond tools in Hong Kong and CHATS system for foreign exchanges such as USD and EUR. Currently, RMB internationalization is mainly pushed forward through overseas clearing banks, i.e. the overseas branches of Chinese commercial banks perform the function of RMB capital clearing, and overseas financial institutions are connected to Chinese payment system through the overseas branches of Chinese banks.

C. Cross-border clearing system

In the RMB agent bank model, the overseas participating bank opens RMB accounts in the domestic agent bank, and the domestic agent bank is connected to CNAPS. In the RMB overseas clearing bank model, the overseas participating bank opens RMB accounts in the overseas RMB clearing bank, and the overseas RMB clearing bank is connected to CNAPS. In the overseas institution's RMB account model, the overseas company directly opens RMB accounts in domestic banks and accomplishes RMB cross-border settlement through CNAPS directly.

(2) *The Disadvantages of Traditional Payment and Clearing Model*

Traditionally, domestic and overseas banks transfer cross-border payment information via the SWIFT system, and complete final settlement via CNAPS. This model has a lot of disadvantages.

Firstly, CNAPS is overly dependent on SWIFT system in cross-border payments. SWIFT system is an infrastructure set up in the 1970s which adopts a unified standard, covers the entire globe and supports payment information transfer between cross-border agent banks. Although SWIFT is a joint institution founded by inter-bank industry associations, it is easily influenced by the politics of western countries and has certain security risks for users of non-western countries. Since the Ukraine crisis in 2014, the USA and Europe threatened to suspend Russia's right to use SWIFT.

Secondly, with an unreasonable operation time setting, the model cannot adapt to cross-timezone clearing. CNAPS has not covered all time zones; therefore, it can cause time vacancies when no payment can be made. This unfavorable condition is preventing CNAPS from becoming a global RMB payment infrastructure.

Thirdly, the system lacks enough security. After message conversion with SWIFT, China's supervisory department could not easily monitor RMB payment data. In addition, since the cross-border clearing business is directly connected with China's banking payment system, relevant risks cannot be effectively separated.

Therefore, our country should set up an independent cross-border payment system with proprietary IPR which could separate risks and cover all time zones, in order to deepen the process of RMB internationalization.

10.4.2 *Latest Progress of CIPS System*

The RMB's Cross-border Inter-bank Payment System (CIPS) is strongly supported by People's Bank of China, and aims to facilitate RMB's use in international payments. On October 8, 2015, CIPS (first phase) successfully came online. Methods of participation include direct participation and indirect participation. Direct participation means to open accounts in CIPS; while indirect participation means to open accounts in institutions connected with CIPS. In the first batch, direct participants include 19 domestic Chinese and foreign banks, and indirect participants include 176 institutions (Table 10.8).

Table 10.8   The 19 Direct Participants of CIPS in the First Batch

Bank Category	Participating Institutions
Chinese state-owned commercial banks (5)	Industrial and Commercial Bank of China, Agricultural Bank of China, Bank of China, China Construction Bank, Bank of Communications
Chinese joint-stock banks (6)	China Merchants Bank, Shanghai Pudong Development Bank, China Minsheng Bank, Industrial Bank, Ping An Bank, Hua Xia Bank
Foreign banks (8)	HSBC (China), Citibank (China), Standard Chartered (China), DBS Bank (China), Deutsche Bank (China), BNP Paribas (China), Australia & New Zealand Banking Group (China), Bank of East Asia (China)

Source: Arranged as per internet information.

Since CIPS system was put in operation, number of participants and volume of business has been steadily increasing. By July 2017, the number of direct participants of CIPS increased from 19 to 31, and the number of indirect participants reached 600, among which over 60% were overseas institutions, covering 6 continents and 78 countries and districts, including free trade zones (Table 10.9). Among the direct and indirect participants of CIPS, 9 participants are RMB

Table 10.9   Information of 31 Direct Participants of CIPS

S/N	English Name	CIPS Code	SWIFT BIC
1	Bank of China Ltd.	BKCHCNBJXXX	BKCHCNBJXXX
2	Agricultural Bank of China Limited	ABOCCNBJXXX	ABOCCNBJXXX
3	Industrial and Commercial Bank of China	ICBKCNBJXXX	ICBKCNBJXXX
4	China Construction Bank Corporation	PCBCCNBJXXX	PCBCCNBJXXX
5	Bank of Communications	COMMCNSHXXX	COMMCNSHXXX
6	Shanghai Pudong Development Bank	SPDBCNSHXXX	SPDBCNSHXXX
7	China Merchants Bank	CMBCCNBSXXX	CMBCCNBSXXX
8	Huaxia Bank	HXBKCNBJXXX	HXBKCNBJXXX
9	China Minsheng Banking Corporation, Limited	MSBCCNBJXXX	MSBCCNBJXXX
10	Ping An Bank Co., Ltd.	SZDBCNBSXXX	SZDBCNBSXXX
11	Industrial Bank Co., Ltd.	FJIBCNBAXXX	FJIBCNBAXXX
12	HSBC Bank (China) Company Limited	HSBCCNSHXXX	HSBCCNSHXXX
13	Citibank (China) Co., Ltd.	CITICNSXXXX	CITICNSXXXX
14	Standard Chartered Bank (China) Limited	SCBLCNSXXXX	SCBLCNSXXXX
15	DBS Bank (China) Limited	DBSSCNSHXXX	DBSSCNSHXXX
16	Deutsche Bank (China) Co., Ltd.	DEUTCNBJXXX	DEUTCNBJXXX

(*Continued*)

Table 10.9 (*Continued*)

S/N	English Name	CIPS Code	SWIFT BIC
17	BNP Paribas (China) Limited	BNPACNSHXXX	BNPACNSHXXX
18	ANZ China Shanghai Branch	ANZBCNSHXXX	ANZBCNSHXXX
19	The Bank of East Asia (China) Limited	BEASCNSHXXX	BEASCNSHXXX
20	China Citic Bank	CIBKCNBJXXX	CIBKCNBJXXX
21	China Guangfa Bank Co., Ltd.	GDBKCN22XXX	GDBKCN22XXX
22	Bank of Shanghai	BOSHCNSHXXX	BOSHCNSHXXX
23	Bank of Jiangsu	BOJSCNBNXXX	BOJSCNBNXXX
24	Bank of Tokyo-Mitsubishi UFJ (China), Ltd.	BOTKCNSHXXX	BOTKCNSHXXX
25	Hang Seng Bank (China) Limited	HASECNSHXXX	HASECNSHXXX
26	Mizuho Bank (China), Ltd.	MHCBCNSHXXX	MHCNCNSHXXX
27	Bank of China (Hong Kong) Limited (Hong Kong Renminbi Clearing Bank)	BKCHHKHH838	BKCHHKHH838
28	China Everbright Bank	EVERCNBJXXX	EVERCNBJXXX
29	JPMorgan Chase Bank (China) Company Limited	CHASCNBJXXX	CHASCNBJXXX
30	China Central Depository and Clearing Co., Ltd.	NDCCCNBJXXX	NDCCCNBJXXX
31	Shanghai Clearing House	CHFMCNSHXXX	CHFMCNSHXXX

Source: Arranged as per internet information.

clearing and settlement institutions operating in France. Financial institutions around the world participate in CIPS by using SWIFT network. CIPS is also directly connected with two domestic clearing institutions: China Central Depository & Clearing Co., Ltd. (CCDC) and Shanghai Clearing House (SCHC) in order to support "bond connect" transaction and settlement.

So far, the daily average volume of cross-border RMB businesses processed by CIPS is maintaining a high growth rate of 10% per month. CIPS is gradually becoming the main channel of RMB cross-border businesses. According to transaction data, London, Frankfurt,

Singapore, Hong Kong, Taiwan and Seoul are the districts with the highest degree of RMB transaction activity in the world.

10.4.3 *The RMB Settlement and Clearing System of Several Offshore Financial Centers of the EU (Including the UK)*

The CIPS system of Paris, Luxembourg, Frankfurt, and London are listed in Tables 10.10 to 10.13, respectively.

Table 10.10   The CIPS System of Paris

S/N	CIPS Code	SWIFT Code	English Name
1	BKCHFRPPXXX	BKCHFRPPXXX	Bank of China, Paris Branch
2	PCBCFRPPXXX	PCBCFRPPXXX	China Construction Bank, Paris Branch
3	BNPAHKHHXXX	BNPAHKHHXXX	BNP Paribas, Hong Kong Branch

Source: Arranged as per internet information.

Table 10.11   The CIPS System of Luxembourg

S/N	CIPS Code	SWIFT Code	English Name
1	ABOCLULBXXX	ABOCLULBXXX	Agricultural Bank of China, Luxembourg Branch
2	ABOCLULLXXX	ABOCLULLXXX	Agricultural Bank of China (Luxembourg) Co., Ltd.
3	ICBKLULCXXX	ICBKLULCXXX	Industrial and Commercial Bank of China, Luxembourg Branch
4	COMMLULLXXX	COMMLULLXXX	Bank of Communications (Luxembourg) Co., Ltd.
5	BKCHLULLXXX	BKCHLULLXXX	Bank of China, Luxembourg Branch
6	PCBCLULXXXX	PCBCLULXXXX	China Construction Bank, Luxembourg Branch
7	CMBCLULLXXX	CMBCLULLXXX	China Merchants Bank, Luxembourg Branch

Source: Arranged as per internet information.

Table 10.12 The CIPS System of Frankfurt

S/N	CIPS Code	SWIFT Code	English Name
1	ABOCDEFFXXX	ABOCDEFFXXX	Agricultural Bank of China, Frankfurt Branch
2	ICBKDEFFXXX	ICBKDEFFXXX	Industrial and Commercial Bank of China, Frankfurt Branch
3	COMMDEFFXXX	COMMDEFFXXX	Bank of Communications, Frankfurt Branch
4	BKCHDEFFXXX	BKCHDEFFXXX	Bank of China, Frankfurt Branch
5	PCBCDEFFXXX	PCBCDEFFXXX	China Construction Bank, Frankfurt Branch

Source: Arranged as per internet information.

Table 10.13 The CIPS System of London

S/N	CIPS Code	SWIFT Code	English Name
1	ICBKGB2LXXX	ICBKGB2LXXX	Industrial and Commercial Bank of China (London) Co, Ltd.
2	PCBCGB2BCLR	PCBCGB2BCLR	China Construction Bank, London Branch
3	PCBCGB2LCLR	PCBCGB2LCLR	China Construction Bank (London) Co., Ltd.
4	BKCHGB2LXXX	BKCHGB2LXXX	Bank of China, London Branch
5	CMBCGB2LXXX	CMBCGB2LXXX	China Merchants Bank, London Branch
6	BEASGB2LXXX	BEASGB2LXXX	Bank of East Asia, London Branch
7	COMMGB3LXXX	COMMGB3LXXX	Bank of Communications, London Branch

Source: Arranged as per internet information.

10.5 Macro-Economic Conditions and Decision-Making Systems of the EU

10.5.1 *Economic Conditions of France*

(1) *Economic Strength of France*

In 2016, France's total GDP was about a quarter of China's. France is the sixth economy, fifth trading country, fourth country of foreign aid and the first tourist destination in the world (Table 10.14).

(2) *The Industrial Structure of France*

The major industrial departments of France include mining industry, metallurgy, steel, automobile manufacturing, shipbuilding, machinery manufacturing, textile industry, chemistry, electrical appliances, power industry, daily goods, food processing and construction industry. France's nuclear power equipment, oil and oil processing technologies are ranked the second in the world, only second to the USA. And the country's aviation and aerospace industry ranks as third in the world, second to the USA and Russia. The leading departments in France's industry are traditional industrial departments, among which steel, automobile and construction are the three pillars. France is the largest country of agricultural production in the EU, and a major export country of agricultural and sideline products. France's grain production is one-third of the grain production of the entire Europe, and its export of agricultural products is the second in the world, only second to the USA.

(3) *Major Industries of France*

A. Aviation and aerospace

France's technologies in the aviation industry are quite systematic and comprehensive, and mainly include large civil airplanes, transport airplanes, military aircraft, military helicopters and key components such as aircraft engines. In the civil aviation field, the Airbus company and

Table 10.14   The GDP of EU Countries in Comparison with the USA in Recent 6 Years

Unit: 100 Million Euros, EUR/USD Rate: 1.26

S/N	Country	2016	2015	2014	2013	2012	2011
1	EU	148,197.9	147,200.2	140,078.7	135,541.2	134,457.6	131,923.7
2	USA	147,373.8	143,148.0	138,040.5	132,472.4	128,216.3	123,158.1
3	Germany	31,440.5	30,436.5	29,324.7	28,262.4	27,582.6	27,031.2
4	UK	23,669.1	25,800.6	22,608.0	20,483.3	20,657.4	18,761.5
5	France	22,288.6	21,942.4	21,476.1	21,152.6	20,869.3	20,592.8
6	Italy	16,724.4	16.454.4	16,218.3	16,046.0	16,132.7	16,374.6
7	Spain	11,138.5	10,756.4	10,370.3	10,256.3	10,397.6	10,704.1
8	Netherlands	7,026.4	6,834.6	6,630.1	6,527.5	6,451.6	6,429.3
9	Sweden	4,620.6	4,470.1	4,326.9	4,357.5	4,233.4	4,049.5
10	Poland	4,242.7	4,300.4	4,109.9	3,947.2	3,893.7	3,802.4
11	Belgium	4,216.1	4,102.5	4,008.0	3,917.3	3,875.0	3,791.1
12	Austria	3,493.4	3,399.0	3,304.2	3,225.4	3,171.2	3,086.3
13	Denmark	2,773.4	2,717.9	2,652.3	2,587.4	2,545.8	2,478.8
14	Ireland	2,755.7	2,620.4	1,945.4	1,803.0	1,755.6	1,719.4
15	Finland	2,156.2	2,095.8	2,054.7	2,033.4	1,997.9	1,968.7
16	Portugal	1,849.3	1,795.0	1,730.8	1,702.7	1,684.0	1,761.7
17	Czech	1,765.6	1,684.7	1,566.6	1,577.4	1,614.3	1,640.4
18	Greece	1,758.9	1,757.0	1,779.4	1,806.5	1,912.0	2,070.3
19	Romania	1,695.8	1,599.6	1,503.6	1,442.5	1,335.1	1,333.1
20	Hungary	1,124.0	1,096.7	1,049.5	1,014.8	990.9	1,008.2
21	Slovakia	809.6	786.9	759.5	741.7	727.0	706.3
22	Luxembourg	541.9	523.4	499.7	465.5	441.1	431.6
23	Bulgaria	473.6	452.9	427.6	420.1	419.5	412.9
24	Croatia	458.2	440.7	429.8	434.9	439.3	447.1
25	Slovenia	397.7	385.7	373.3	359.2	360.0	369.0
26	Lithuania	386.4	373.3	365.9	350.0	333.5	312.8
27	Latvia	250.2	243.7	236.3	228.3	220.6	202.0
28	Estonia	209.2	202.5	197.6	188.9	179.3	166.7
29	Cyprus	179.0	176.4	175.7	181.2	194.7	197.3
30	Malta	99.0	92.7	84.4	76.3	71.6	68.3

Source: Arranged as per internet information.

the USA's Boeing company are the top two manufacturers of passenger airplanes. The Eurocopter company founded in 1992 is a manufacturer of heavy-load helicopters, and is currently ranked the first in the world, with its share of 50% of the world market.

B. Nuclear energy and energy industry

France is the second largest nuclear power production country in the world, with an installed capacity of nuclear power second to the USA. Currently, France has 59 nuclear reactors in operation and 1 under construction. In 2007, France's nuclear power accounted for 79% of its total generated power, with an energy self-sufficiency rate of 50%. France is in a world-leading position in the civil nuclear power field. It not only possesses the technologies of the entire process covering uranium mining and extraction, overall design and construction of nuclear power plants and nuclear waste disposal, but also has strong capacity of industrialization.

C. High-speed railway

France's wheel track high-speed railway is in a leading position in the industry. The TGV company started research and development since the beginning of the 1960s. After 20 years of hard work, it commercially launched the first high-speed train in 1981. The fourth-generation high-speed train independently developed by the French company Alstom will achieve a commercial speed of 350-360 km/h, which is comparable with the commercial speed of maglev trains (400 km/h).

D. High-end manufacturing

France's manufacturing industry accounts for about 20% in national economy, and the proportion is higher than the USA, Japan, Germany and Canada, which are similar in competitive force. France's manufacturing industry has a balanced production capacity and a stable scale. The country possesses complete core technologies in advantageous fields of the manufacturing industry, and most of them are results of independent innovation.

E. Automobile manufacturing

France is the fourth largest automobile export country in the world. Major companies in this field include PSA Peugeot Citroen and Renault S.A., which are the eighth and tenth largest automobile manufacturers in the world.

F. Pharmaceutical industry

France's pharmaceutical industry has an important position in the world. France is the first largest drug producing country in Europe and the third largest drug export country in the world. A representative company is the Sanofi-Aventis group formed by a merger in 2004. The company is the third largest pharmaceutical company in the world, and ranked the first in Europe.

G. Agriculture

France is the largest country of agricultural production in the EU, and a major export country of agricultural and sideline products in the world. France comprehensively develops agriculture and animal husbandry, and mainly produces wheat, barley, maize, beet, potatoes, tobacco, grapes, apples, vegetables and flowers and plants. It is a major export country of agricultural products and agri-food. France has become the largest export country of agricultural products in the EU and the largest export country of processed food in the world. The country's agricultural product export is only second to the USA, and it is really a powerful country in agriculture.

10.5.2 *Economic Conditions of Other Major Countries of the EU (Including the UK)*

(1) *The UK*

The service industry is the UK's pillar industry in national economy. Agriculture only takes up a small proportion, and traditional manufacturing industries such as steel, coal and textile are gradually shrinking in the UK's industrial structure transformation. The UK's industries are mainly classified into 5 departments: (1) agriculture, fishery and forestry; (2) manufacturing; (3) construction; (4) energy and natural resources; (5) service industry. The proportions of added value of various industries in the British economy are as follows: The service industry including finance, wholesale, retail and real estate takes up 72%; manufacturing and construction industries take up 23%; energy and natural resources take up 4%, and agriculture, fishery and forestry take up 1%.

The financial service industry is one of the pillar industries of London and even the UK. Since the financial "big bang" in 1986 and the independence of Bank of England in 1997, financial industry has been developing rapidly in the UK. According to statistics of International Financial Services London in May 2009 (IFSL, the same below), financial service industry took up 5.5% in UK economy in 2001, but the percentage rose to 7.6% in 2007. The UK's trade surplus in the financial industry in 2008 was 35.6 billion pounds, which was higher than the value 19.3 billion pounds in 2005. At the end of 2008, the employment figure of the financial service industry was 1 million. London's financial and business service departments took up 40% of total output, and the Greater London's GDP took up one-fifth of the UK's.

(2) *Germany*

After the global financial crisis, Germany actively adjusted industrial policies and increased investment in manufacturing and construction. For example, Germany increased production of high-end products including automobiles and precise instruments. The country's automobile production index rose from 79.8 in 2009 to 100.03 in 2010. The proportion of industry in GDP rose from 27.67% in 2009 to 30% in 2010. And the proportion of manufacturing in industry rose from 66% in 2009 to 79.46% in 2010. The country's exports were also gradually increasing; therefore, its economic growth was guaranteed. Since the European debt crisis, Germany outshone others in economy and became the first country in Europe which achieved positive economic growth. The proportions of three main industries of Germany were 0.86%, 30.71% and 68.43%, respectively. The proportion of industry, especially high-end manufacturing is rising, while the proportion of service industry has fallen.

(3) *Netherlands*

Major traditional industries of Netherlands include: shipbuilding, sugar refinery, chemical industry, automobile assembly and machinery manufacturing. Netherlands is one of the major commercial centers for business investments in Europe, and many transnational corporations have set up their European headquarters in this country. A characteristic of Dutch economy is that the export-oriented economy is playing a leading role. 80% of raw materials of this country are imported, and 60% of products are exported to different parts of the world. Netherlands' total volume of foreign trade is ranked the eighth in the world, and 80% of its foreign trade is conduced in the EU. The total export value of commodities and services of this country accounts for about 60% of its GNP, and the proportion is higher than Germany, the USA and Japan. In summary, Netherlands is a power country in trade, agriculture, transportation, industry, financial and insurance services, technology, and water conservancy.

(4) *Italy*

The Italian economy has one common characteristic of western industrially developed countries: the primary industry is taking up a small proportion in the national economy; while the secondary industry and tertiary industry are taking up high proportions, which are still increasing. According to the added values of three main industries in 2012 published by the statistics bureau of Italian central bank, the proportion of added values of agriculture, forestry and fishery of Italy rose slightly from 2011; the proportion of construction industry fell significantly; and the service industry rose slightly.

(5) *Spain*

Currently, proportion of agriculture in national economy of Spain is gradually decreasing; meanwhile, due to rapid development of the service industry, the proportion of industry has also significantly decreased. Spain's service industry accounts for 65% to 70% of GDP, while the proportion of agriculture is less than 3%. Main industries of Spain include automobile, shipbuilding, chemical industry and steel, which have great scale and competitive force compared with other members of the EU.

(6) *Switzerland*

In Switzerland, about 74% of GDP is contributed by the service industry. Industry takes up a proportion of 25% in GDP and is an important pillar of economy. Key industries of Switzerland include chemical industry, capital goods and banking. In addition, agriculture takes up about 0.9% in GDP. Switzerland has multiple highly developed industrial clusters in chemical medicine, financial services, mechatronics, watch industry and IT industry, which are occupying an important position in the world.

10.5.3 *The Decision-Making Structure of EU Countries*

(1) *European Council*

The European Council is the highest authority of the EU, and consists of heads or government leaders of EU countries and the president of the European Commission. The main task of the European Council is to determine the EU's overall political orientation and matters of priority. Since the European Council is not a legislative institution of the EU, it does not hold discussions on EU law. Instead, it stipulates the EU's policy agendas. Traditionally, the European Council reaches conclusions in meetings to determine the subject matter in concern and the actions to be taken.

(2) *Council of European Union*

In the Council of European Union, government ministers from EU countries participate in meetings, hold discussions, modify and pass laws and coordinate policies. The ministers have the right to request their governments to take part in actions determined in the meeting.

Together, the Council of European Union and the European Parliament constitute the EU's major decision-making body.

(3) *European Parliament*

The European Parliament is the EU's directly elected parliament. It fulfills the EU's legislative function together with Council of European Union and European Commission. The parliament is comprised of 751 members. Although European Parliament has the legislative power, which the European Commission does not have, as with most parliaments of EU's member countries, it does not have the formal power of initiative in legislation. The EU's executive body European Commission is in the charge of European Parliament; especially, the parliament can elect the commission's president, and approve (or decline) the appointments of the entire commission.

(4) *European Commission*

The European Commission is the EU's executive body, and is responsible for proposing legislation, implementing decisions, maintaining the EU's treaties and managing the EU's daily businesses. Members of the European Commission take the oath of office in the European Court of Justice in Luxembourg. They promise to respect treaties and fulfill their duties independently during execution of tasks. The commission operates as a cabinet government and has 28 members. Every member country of the EU has a member in the commission, but the member's office oath represents the overall interest of the entire EU instead of the interests of his/her own country. The commission's current president is Jean-Claude Juncker.

(5) *Others*

In addition, the EU's bodies also include the European Court of Justice and European Court of Auditors located in Luxembourg.

10.5.4 *The Marshall Plan's Influence on Euro-Dollar*

The wide use of USD in Europe is attributed to the profound influence of Marshall Plan on the development of European countries and the world's political and economic pattern. Marshall Plan is the USA's plan to provide economic assistance for Western European countries' reconstruction after World War II. It formally started in July 1947 and lasted for 4 years (Table 10.15). During the period, Western European countries received assistance from the USA in the form of finance, technologies and equipment totaling to 13 billion USD, which was equivalent to 130 billion USD in 2006.

Table 10.15 Assistance Received by Western European Countries in the Marshall Plan

Unit: 100 Million USD

Country	1948/1949	1949/1950	1950/1951	Total Amount
Austria	2.32	1.66	0.7	4.88
Belgium and Luxembourg	1.95	2.22	3.6	7.77
Denmark	1.03	0.87	1.95	3.85
France	10.85	6.91	5.2	22.96
Germany	5.1	4.38	5	14.48
Greece	1.75	1.56	0.45	3.66
Iceland	0.06	0.22	0.15	0.43
Ireland	0.88	0.45	—	1.33
Italy	5.94	4.05	2.05	12.04
Netherlands	4.71	3.02	3.55	11.28
Norway	0.82	0.9	2	3.72
Portugal	—	—	0.7	0.7
Sweden	0.39	0.48	2.6	3.47
Switzerland	—	—	2.5	2.5
Turkey	0.28	0.59	0.5	1.37
UK	13.16	9.21	10.6	32.97

Source: Internet information such as Wikipedia.

The Marshall Plan has long been considered as an important factor which facilitated integration between Europe and the USA. It eliminated or weakened the tariff and trade barriers which had long existed between Western European countries and the USA, and closely united the Western European countries and the USA in economy. Under the driving force of the Marshall Plan, the USA obtained large amount of export shares of commodities, currency and labor, and the USD became the major settlement currency for international trade of Western Europe. A new international system and order which facilitates economic integration between the USA and Western Europe was gradually established and improved.

10.5.5 *Investment and Trade Cooperation Between China and France*

According to statistics of Ministry of Commerce, China's investment in France made a substantial progress in recent years. The forms of investment are diversified and include mergers and acquisitions, factory establishment, and founding of district headquarters, R&D centers and cooperation zones. In 2015, France attracted Chinese direct investments totaling 328 million USD, and China's direct investment stock in France reached 5.724 billion USD. In terms of bilateral investment, France is China's fourth investment source country in Europe, and investments are focused on fields including energy, automobiles, chemical industry, light industry and food. Most of the investments are made by manufacturing companies. By January 2016, France has 5,010 investment projects in China, with a total investment of 14.953 billion USD. In 2015, 208 new French companies were set up in China, with an actual investment of 1.224 billion USD and a year-on-year decrease of 71.9%. France's investments in China cover a variety of fields including electricity, automobiles, aviation, communication, chemical industry, water utilities and pharmaceutical industry.

10.6 Relevant Laws on EU Investments

10.6.1 *Laws on Investments Between EU Countries*

(1) *In Principle: Free Flow of Capital*

According to Article 63 of *Treaty on the Functioning of the European Union*, all stipulations which restrict capital flow among EU member countries and between an EU member country and a third country should be banned.

(2) *In Practice: Restrictions by Law*

The member countries still regulate investments as per their own Bilateral Investment Treaties (BITs). France has 96 BITs with different countries around the world, and 12 BITs with EU countries. Currently, the EU countries are dedicated to formulating a uniform investment policy for use within the EU (including France). Additionally, the EU, as a whole, has started reaching investment agreements with third countries, such as Canada, South Korea and Vietnam.

Although the EU hopes the European Commission could reach uniform investment and trade agreements with countries around the world on behalf of the EU countries, the member countries are holding different opinions. In 2015, Austria, Finland, France and Germany jointly petitioned the European Commission to express their objection to uniform investment agreements. They stated such agreements would hinder the countries' effort to attract and protect investors. So far, EU countries have signed more than 1,200 investment agreements with other countries around the world, most of which are investment protection agreements and do not involve promises on market admittance. The protection terms generally contain "non-discriminatory principle", "fair and just treatment", "timely, sufficiently and effectively collection of compensations" and "investor-country dispute resolution mechanism".

The investment agreements between the EU countries and other countries differ from one another, and some of them are even in conflict with the EU law. The conflicts created inconvenience for investors heading for the EU. More importantly, the simple investment protection agreements cannot meet the EU's requirements to expand investment market and attract international investors into the EU market.

The *Treaty of Lisbon*, which took effect in December 2009 assigned powers on investment (common business policies) to the EU. Additionally, the treaty also modified the decision-making bodies and procedures related to investment. The EU became the major management institution of the member countries on investment, and the European Commission could conduct negotiations on investment agreement with a third country on behalf of the member countries, but it is also regulated by the European Parliament and the Council of European Union.

10.6.2 *Regulations on Investments Between the EU and a Third Country*

(1) *Europe-Canada Economic and Trade Agreement*

The *Europe-Canada Economic and Trade Agreement* signed between the EU and Canada set out a series of prohibitions against foreign capital restriction: (1) Prohibit restrictions on company supplies, investment amount or turnover in the form of quantity, monopoly or exclusivity. And prohibit restrictions on shares and number of recruits of the foreign company. (2) Prohibit restrictions which only allow the foreign capital to participate in the market in specific forms, such as joint venture and whole ownership. (3) Prohibit restrictions on the foreign capital's export proportion and domestic product composition. And prohibit formulation of terms regarding preferential domestic purchase. (4) Prohibit restrictions on the nationality of senior managers of the foreign company. Certainly, there are exceptions in the above protection of foreign capital, such as matters related to environmental protection and special professions.

The negative list of *Europe-Canada Economic and Trade Agreement* includes direct shipping services, audio-visual products, cultural industry, oil and natural gas industry, uranium mining, agriculture, accounting, auditing and customs clearance. Although the financial industry is not in the negative list, Canada put forward reserved opinions as long as 94 pages on the opening-up of the financial industry. Additionally, the EU made reservations in R&D, health care and transportation industries. In terms of merger review, Canada promised to lift the threshold from 354 million CAD to 1.5 billion, and the promise applies to all EU investors which are not state-owned companies.

(2) *Negotiation on China-Europe Investment Treaty*

In April 2012, leaders of China and European countries reached a consensus on starting the BIT negotiation in the China-Europe summit, and set up a negotiation work team in the same year. By the end of June 2015, China and Europe have held 14 rounds of negotiation on BIT.

One focus of the negotiation is the market admittance policy. Since the parties lack mature management experience and industry knowledge on the negative list model, they held multiple rounds of negotiation. Other difficulties include the terms related to IPR protection, competitive neutrality of state-owned companies, environmental protection and labor protection. Besides Canada, the EU also reached a BIT with South Korea. In the negotiations, the EU often presses our country on the grounds of the bilateral civil and criminal stipulations between Europe and South Korea, and requests our country to enlarge the scope of IPR protection. In addition, the EU is discontent with the subsidies and loan policies for our country's state-owned companies in certain industries, and wishes to build a fairer market competition order. In terms of environmental protection and labor protection, the environmental protection terms on which the EU insisted had more constraining and executive forces than our country's existing laws. The EU requested our country to implement terms of the agreement by adjusting domestic laws, and introduced many international treaties and standards. However, the EU's requests were difficult for our country to accept.

China and the EU have common appeals in certain fields. For example, in the aspect of investment protection, our country wishes to keep a balance between investment protection and government control, and we can learn from the EU's advanced management experience. Our country also hopes to receive non-discriminatory treatment in the EU and establish a dispute resolution mechanism acceptable to both parties. Therefore, the conclusion of the treaty will greatly help our country invest in Europe.

10.7 Advantages and Disadvantages of Setting up RMB Overseas Funds in France

10.7.1 *Advantages*

(1) *The French Government Strongly Supports Our Country's Work and Has a Strong Will of Cooperation*

After the UK exited from the EU, the French government declared multiple times its support for setting up an RMB offshore financial center in Paris, and hoped Paris could replace London as the EU's financial center. It created favorable conditions for our country to set up RMB overseas funds in France under the condition of sovereign cooperation. In addition, France has been an active advocate of uniform EU investment policies, therefore it has been playing a leading role in the negotiation on *China-Europe Investment Treaty*. More friendly investment policies will help attract RMB investment funds to France.

(2) *China and France Have a Large Scale of Trade Cooperation*

In 2015, the bilateral volume of trade between China and France reached 51.37 billion USD, which was about one-tenth of the bilateral volume of trade between China and the EU, and was far ahead among the EU countries, only second to Germany and Netherlands. China has a small surplus in China-France trade, and China-France trade cooperation has a huge potential for development (Table 10.16). Currently, the proportion of RMB use in China-France trade settlement is higher than that in the settlement between China and many other countries.

Table 10.16 Comparison of Bilateral Volume of Trade Between China and the USA and EU Countries in Recent 4 years

Unit: 100 Million USD

S/N	Country	2015			2014		2013		2012	
		China Imports	China Exports	Total	China Imports	China Exports	China Imports	China Exports	China Imports	China Exports
1	EU	2,930.65	4,032.41	6,963	3,361.31	4,388.25	3,241.72	4,057.44	2,866.9	3,963.99
2	USA	1,478.1	4,092.1	5,570	1,590.6	3,960.6	1,523.4	3,684.1	1,329	3,517.8
3	Germany	876.23	691.55	1,568	1,050.13	727.03	941.56	673.43	919.21	692.1
4	UK	189.34	595.67	785	237.27	571.41	190.79	509.42	168.05	462.97
5	Netherlands	87.78	594.53	682.3	93.4	649.29	98.25	603.15	87.03	588.97
6	France	246.22	267.48	513.7	270.63	287.02	231.1	267.14	241.18	268.99
7	Italy	168.2	278.34	446.5	192.82	287.56	175.74	257.53	160.68	256.53
8	Switzerland	410.96	31.67	442.6	404.41	30.88	560.76	35.11	228.17	34.92
9	Spain	55.87	218.52	274.4	62.04	214.97	59.72	189.29	63.34	182.37
10	Belgium	70.06	162.08	232.1	100.59	172.16	98.48	155.6	99.64	163.77
11	Poland	27.42	143.45	170.9	29.35	142.57	22.32	125.75	19.97	123.86
12	Sweden	64.17	70.99	135.2	67.92	71.68	69.87	67.99	69.22	64.15
13	Czech	27.8	82.26	110.1	29.87	79.93	26.15	68.38	24.07	63.23
14	Denmark	40.95	61.51	102.5	40.57	65.48	33.76	57.11	29.05	65.4

(*Continued*)

Table 10.16   (*Continued*)

S/N	Country	2015 China Imports	2015 China Exports	Total	2014 China Imports	2014 China Exports	2013 China Imports	2013 China Exports	2012 China Imports	2012 China Exports
15	Hungary	28.76	51.97	80.73	32.6	57.64	27.15	56.92	23.23	57.38
16	Austria	49.68	24.98	74.66	58.52	23.96	50.3	20.38	47.24	20.4
17	Ireland	42.86	28.23	71.09	37.34	28.02	41.93	24.77	37.97	20.98
18	Finland	34.85	35.41	70.26	40.51	50.99	39.06	58.32	38.32	74.41
19	Norway	41.46	28.57	70.03	44.68	27.31	34.68	27.37	30.68	30.2
20	Slovakia	22.37	27.94	50.31	33.76	28.29	34.58	30.84	36.55	24.23
21	Romania	12.95	31.62	44.57	15.21	32.23	12.08	28.23	9.8	27.97
22	Portugal	14.62	28.95	43.57	16.63	31.37	13.99	25.07	15.15	25.01
23	Greece	2.86	36.65	39.51	3.46	41.86	4.33	32.19	4.27	35.93
24	Malta	4.41	23.8	28.21	5.91	31.93	7.25	25.15	8.85	22.45
25	Luxembourg	3.09	23.23	26.32	3.04	19.49	2.57	18.08	2.63	19.56
26	Slovenia	2.9	20.92	23.82	3.31	19.92	3.03	18.33	2.56	15.67
27	Bulgaria	7.48	10.43	17.91	9.85	11.78	9.57	11.17	8.39	10.55
28	Croatia	1.12	9.86	10.98	1.01	10.27	1.04	13.9	0.75	13

Source: Arranged as per internet information.

Therefore, it is feasible and necessary to facilitate RMB internationalization in France and the EU by setting up RMB overseas funds.

(3) *China and France have a Great Potential for Capacity Cooperation*

France has a scientific and reasonable industrial structure, and has prominent advantages in aviation and aerospace, nuclear power and energy industry, high-speed railway, high-end manufacturing, automobile manufacturing, pharmaceutical industry and agriculture. China and France have a great potential for capacity cooperation. They can conduct capacity cooperation in developing countries and emerging economies in Africa and along BRI in order to provide project opportunities for the use of RMB overseas funds.

(4) *China and France have a Great Potential for Financial Cooperation*

Paris has a highly developed capital market and is the largest corporate bond market in Europe, accounting for a market share of 35%. The Societe Generale and Credit Agricole in Paris are ranked high in the banking industry of the Eurozone. Paris' asset management scale is only second to London in the entire Europe, and the headquarter of the Europe's first cross-border exchange (the first stock exchange in Europe and the second derivative exchange in the world) is located in Paris. The advantages of the capital market of Paris could provide rich market experience and an investor base for RMB offshore investment and financing business.

(5) *The China-France Bilateral Investment Treaty Provided Legal Assurance for Setting Up RMB Overseas Funds in France*

China and France reached a bilateral investment treaty, which stipulates that one Party should provide treatment for investment and investment-related activities of the investor of the other Party in its land and sea territory not lower than the treatment for its domestic investors — national treatment and most-favored-nation treatment. If the investor of one Party has invested in the other Party's land and sea territory, the other Party should guarantee relevant natural person or company could freely transfer interests, bonuses, profits and other income under the current account. These bilateral investment stipulations provided legal assurance for setting up RMB overseas funds in France.

(6) *France's RMB Business Has "African" Characteristics*

14 countries in Africa used to be in the French franc area. The French banks have been developing in these countries over many years and are the major providers of local financial services. Currently, the RMB deposit in Paris is ranked the second in Europe, and a large part of it came from China-Africa transactions. Therefore, Paris could become an RMB financial platform for China-Africa cross-border trade and investment.

(7) *France Has a Developed RMB Settlement and Clearing System*

Currently, the Paris Branch of Bank of China, Paris Branch of China Construction Bank, and Hong Kong Branch of BNP Paribas have been connected to the CIPS system. Among them, the Paris Branch of Bank of China is the RMB clearing bank appointed by People's Bank of China. In terms of settlement and clearing, RMB investment and trading activities have smooth transmission routes in France and the EU district, and normal operation of RMB overseas funds can be guaranteed.

10.7.2 *Disadvantages*

(1) *The Current Scale of China-France Investment Cooperation Is Limited*

Currently, China's total investment in France is small. In 2015, China's direct investment in France was only 328 million USD. By the end of 2015, China's direct investment stock in France was 5.724 billion USD. In terms of bilateral investment, France had an accumulated investment of 14.953 billion USD in China by

January 2016. In 2015, France's actual investment in China was 1.224 billion USD. In the perspective of investment, the current scale of investment between China and France cannot support operation of RMB overseas funds in France, which must therefore irradiate to other countries.

(2) *Investments Among the EU Countries Are Restricted by Bilateral Investment Agreements*

So far, the EU still does not have a set of uniform investment standards and policies in the real sense. China and Europe have completed the 16th round of negotiation on *China-Europe Investment Treaty*, and market admittance is the most crucial item in negotiation. Difficulties of the negotiation include terms on IPR protection, competitive neutrality of state-owned companies, environmental protection and labor protection. These restrictions created unfavorable conditions and obstacles for RMB overseas funds in France to invest in other countries of the EU.

(3) *China and France Lack the Experience of Cooperative Investment in a Third Country*

China has been advocating capacity cooperation with developed countries in developing countries by making use of their comparative advantages. However, according to public information, there is not a successful cooperation case in this regard. Therefore, although theoretically China and France could cooperate to push forward the use of RMB overseas funds in African countries and countries along the BRI route, we still need to explore, accumulate experience and draw conclusions in practice.

(4) *It is Difficult for Paris to Overtake London as a Financial Center*

France expects to overtake the UK after the UK exits from the EU. However, according to statistics, RMB clearing business in London steadily increased since the UK held the "Brexit" vote. Additionally, UK's exit from the EU will facilitate development of economic, trade and investment relations between London and countries outside of the EU, among which the China-UK relationship, especially the RMB business cooperation is playing an important role. It will facilitate construction of the RMB financial center in London and widen the gap between London and Paris.

10.8 Suggestions on Setting up RMB Overseas Funds in France

10.8.1 *Make Use of the Government's Advantages in Cooperation, and Guarantee the Funds' Position in Sovereign Cooperation*

The key to success of setting up RMB overseas funds in France is to make use of the government's advantages in cooperation and guarantee the funds' sovereign cooperative position. Therefore, our country should take advantage of the high-level visits of both countries to establish the sovereign fund position of RMB overseas funds in France in order to guarantee policy and legal convenience during operation.

10.8.2 *Make Use of Industry Advantages of France and EU Countries*

To set up RMB overseas funds in France, we need to make full use of the comparative advantages of EU countries, and support industries which have globally leading technologies. France's nuclear power equipment and oil processing technologies are on a world-leading level; its aviation and aerospace industries are also among the tops, second to the USA and Russia. The country's agricultural product export is ranked the second in the world, only second to the USA. The UK's service industry is its pillar industry of national economy. Germany's high-end products such as automobiles and precise instruments are on a world-leading level. Shipbuilding, sugar refinery, chemical industry and automobile assembly of Netherlands and Spain have prominent advantages. The Switzerland's chemical medicine, watch industry and IT industry are on an important position in the world.

10.8.3 *The Investment Region Irradiates to Africa and Countries Along "Belt and Road"*

The developed countries have basically fixed economic structures, and therefore have strong inertia in currency use. Due to a strong will for development, the developing countries and emerging economies are more probable to produce a currency substitution effect under the driving force of capital. At present, RMB has been widely used in surrounding countries and has become a major currency in cross-border trade settlement. With the progress of the BRI, infrastructure of our country and countries along the BRI route will be further connected, political and economic connections will be strengthened, and building an optimal currency area in Africa and districts along the BRI route is the working objective of RMB internationalization.

10.8.4 *Lead the Practice with Green Finance and Inclusive Finance Concepts*

In recent years, financial institutions of various countries have been actively developing green finance. The most influential principles in this regard are the Equator Principles — a set of voluntary industrial rules implemented by about 100 banks around the world. The Equator Principles have become the reference standard, industrial convention and development direction of international project financing. These principles require analyzing and evaluating influence on nature, environment and districts in project financing activities, and taking measures to prevent damage to the ecological system and community environment. Inclusive finance is a financial system which widely provides reasonable, convenient and secure financial services for the general class of people. While constructing the green finance and inclusive finance system, China could make full use of its late-mover advantages, learn from the world's advanced rules, optimize various financial systems and mechanisms and play a leading role in financial innovation.

10.8.5 *Construct and Improve RMB Financial Infrastructure*

The founding of European Payments Union in 1950 provided payment infrastructure assurance for the success of currency integration of the EU. Our country should learn from the experience of international currencies such as EUR and USD, push forward construction of RMB cross-border settlement infrastructure, accelerate construction of the RMB cross-border payment system (CIPS), and increase security and efficiency of cross-border RMB clearing, in order to provide necessary financial infrastructure for RMB internationalization.

10.8.6 *Improve Investment Agreements Between China and the EU*

Providing assurance for overseas investment and trade through bilateral or multilateral agreements is a precondition for currency internationalization. One important result of the Marshall Plan is that the USA and Western European countries made a series of institutional arrangements, and the USA obtained large export shares for exporting commodities, currency and labor to Western European countries. Consequently, the USD became the major settlement currency for international trade in Western Europe, and a new international system and order which facilitates economic integration between the USA and Western Europe was gradually established. China should strengthen policy communication with EU countries, facilitate trade and investment, solidify work results in the form of legal documents, and enter into agreements which facilitate free trade and investment cooperation, in order to lay a solid foundation of policy and legal assurance for RMB internationalization, and strengthen RMB's functions of valuation, settlement, transaction and reserves.

10.8.7 *Prevent Investment Risks*

Most of the investment risks in France and other developed countries of the EU are market risks and company operation risks, which affect the rate of return on investment. In developing countries, political, policy and legal risks are more prominent. There are uncertainties related to the host country's sovereignty, such as political instability, regime change, armed conflicts, social instability and policy instability. Operation of RMB overseas funds in France involves multiple developed countries and developing countries, therefore we must take care to prevent risks. In developed countries, we should fully consider issues such as environmental protection, residents' rights protection, labor cost and commercial and cultural differences. Whereas in developing countries, we should fully consider the political risks, development risks, construction risks, project operation risks and commercial risks to ensure sustainable development of RMB overseas funds.

RMB Internationalization in Arab League Countries

Arab league countries are mostly located in the intersection of Asia, Africa and Europe and have frequent trade contacts with China. Those countries also have extremely important positions in geo-politics and geo-economy. In the global credit currency system, pushing forward RMB internationalization in Arab league countries will lead to a win-win result. It not only reflects China's political and economic strength, but also brings benefits for the countries in cooperation.

11.1 Introduction

On January 21, 2016, Chinese president Xi Jinping visited the head-quarter of Arab league and pointed out in his speech: China and Arab league countries should make use of their large scale of foreign trade and the tools of currency swap and bilateral investment agreement, and by focusing on high-tech cooperation in nuclear energy, new energy and aerospace, they should deepen Belt and Road Initiative

(BRI) investment and financing cooperation and enlarge RMB's scope of settlement.

Arab league countries have extremely important strategic positions for China. Since the launch of the BRI, core countries of the Arab league, including Saudi Arabia, UAE and Egypt have been allocated to the "Middle East plate" among six plates. They had become the intersection of the "Belt" on the land and the "Road" on the sea, and an important hub of the BRI leading to Europe and Africa. China's economic ties with Arab league countries have been deepening. Currently, our country is ranked the second in total volume of trade with Arab league countries; and for the 9 countries in the Arab league, our country is their largest trade partner. For our country, Arab league countries are ranked the seventh in total trade volume, and they are the largest energy supply partner and an important project contracting market (Zhang Shuangshuang, 2015). Therefore, pushing forward RMB internationalization in Arab league countries has become a crucial topic.

11.2 Current Situation of RMB Internationalization in Arab League Countries

11.2.1 *Trade Settlement*

Currently, Industrial and Commercial Bank of China and Bank of China have set up RMB clearing centers in Qatar and the UAE, respectively. Industrial and Commercial Bank of China has established offices in the UAE, Qatar, Kuwait and Saudi Arabia. The four state-owned commercial banks — Bank of China, Agricultural Bank of China, Industrial and Commercial Bank of China and China Construction Bank have set up branches in Dubai, the capital of the UAE. In 2015, 74% of transaction amount between China and the UAE was settled in RMB, and the proportion of RMB payment in Qatar was 60%. The above data signifies RMB's popularity in this region. On September 17, 2017, China Development Bank signed the *Contract for 260 Million RMB's Overseas Loan Project* with SAI-Bank for RMB settlement in China-Egypt capacity cooperation, and signed the *Memorandum of Understanding for "Belt and Road" RMB Special Loan Cooperation Between China and Egypt* with Banque Misr. The former was our country's first overseas RMB loan project in Egypt, and the first overseas project of RMB granting for financial institutions in Arab league countries and Africa. The successful implementation of the project aroused great reactions in Egyptian financial field. Additionally, National Bank of Egypt proposed to sign a China-Arab inter-bank consortium cooperation agreement with China Development Bank to carry out cooperation on joint financing, bank consortium loans and sub-loans under RMB account.

11.2.2 *Financial Transaction*

Bank of China issued an RMB bond of 2 billion yuan, with a period of 2 years in Dubai in July 2015. About 25–30% of investors of the bond came from Middle East. In May 2015, Bank of China and Dubai International Financial Exchange signed a cooperative agreement on deepening financial transaction cooperation. In December 2015, People's Bank of China provided a QFII quota of 50 billion yuan for the UAE, and the UAE became the first country in the Middle East region which acquired QFII qualification (Kuwait and Qatar acquired the qualification in 2011 and 2012, respectively).

11.2.3 *Reserve Currency*

By the end of July 2017, there were 36 countries in the world which had signed currency swap agreements with People's Bank of China. Among Arab league countries, the UAE signed 5 billion RMB/20 billion AED, Egypt signed 18 billion RMB/47 billion EGP, Qatar signed 35 billion RMB/20.8 billion QAR, and Morocco signed 10 billion RMB/15 billion MAD. Recently, China Development Bank is cooperating with Egyptian central bank and helping Egyptian government increase RMB exchange reserves through large amount of RMB loans. Therefore, RMB internationalization has made the first breakthrough in Egypt.

11.3   Political and Economic Situations of Arab League Countries

Arab league has 22 member countries at present (including Qatar, which was expelled in June 2017) and a total area of 14.2 million square kilometers, in which West Asian and North African countries take up 28% and 72%, respectively. The total GDP of Arab league in 2015 reached 2.94 trillion USD. Arab league countries have a rich reserve of oil resources, with 650 billion barrels of proved reserves, accounting for 57.5% of the world total (Zhang Shuangshuang, 2015).

In terms of economic aggregate, Saudi Arabia, the UAE and Egypt are the top three in Arab league, which take up 22.24%, 12.17% and 11.32%, respectively. The three countries account for 45.73% of the total GDP of Arab league. Typically, Saudi Arabia and the UAE represent gulf oil producing countries and Egypt represents North African countries in the Arab league, and the three countries are playing a leading role in affairs of Arab countries. Additionally, according to statistics, China's exports to Arab countries in recent 15 years has been focused on Saudi Arabia, the UAE, Egypt, Algeria, Iraq and Morocco, which accounts for 75% of China's total exports to Arab league countries (Zhang Shuangshuang, 2015). Therefore, in the aspects of economic aggregate, political strength and our country's economic and trade relations, it is reasonable to analyze strategies of RMB internationalization in Arab countries by using Saudi Arabia, the UAE and Egypt as examples.

(1) *Saudi Arabia*

In terms of macro-economy, Saudi Arabia is the most important oil-producing and export country in the world, and its export volume of crude oil and refinery products account for about one-eighth of the world total export volume. Export of oil and refinery products is the major income source of Saudi Arabia and accounts for 50% of the country's GDP. Since 80% of the fiscal revenue of Saudi Arabia is dependent on oil, the country's economic conditions are closely related to oil price trend. International oil price has been staying low in recent years, and Saudi Arabia's GDP growth had stagnated and even fell, but Saudi Arabia's GDP per capita is still ranked high among wealthy countries in the world. Since January 2017, the average inflation rate of Saudi Arabia has been varying between –0.7- –0.1%, and the country's economy has been in a small degree of deflation.

In terms of exchange rate policies, Saudi riyal has been following the USD since 1986 at a rate of 1:3.5 in values. However, in recent years, with the significant fall of oil price, Saudi currency is under increasing devaluation pressure, and devalued to 1:3.7615 after the decease of the king. Despite so, Saudi Arabia still maintains the follow-up exchange rate policy, because crude oil income valuated in USD accounts for 90% of the country's total income, and the follow-up policy could reduce income fluctuations.

In terms of balance of payments, Saudi Arabia's exports are focused on oil and oil products, which account for 85% of the total export, and there are also some exports of building materials and transit goods. Imported products of the country include mechanical and electrical products, equipment, tools and foods. Export of oil and oil products is the source of Saudi Arabia's long-term large trade surplus, and the country's surplus of current account is closely associated with international oil price.

In terms of foreign exchange reserves, Saudi government accumulated a large amount of overseas capital due to long-term large trade surplus. By the end of 2015, Saudi government had a foreign exchange reserve of 602.667 billion USD. Saudi Arabia's principles of overseas asset operation include low risks, portfolio diversification and liquidity maintenance.

(2) *The United Arab Emirates (UAE)*

In terms of macro-economy, the UAE's oil reserves rank the seventh, and natural gas reserves rank the third in the world, but over 80% of the country's GDP is created by non-oil-gas industries (Han Lu, 2017). In 2016, the UAE's GDP was about 349 billion USD in current price, and 379 billion USD in constant price, with a year-on-year growth of 3%. The GDP of non-oil industries accounted for 83.3% of total GDP in current price, while oil-and-gas GDP accounted for

16.7%. In recent years, the significant fall of international oil price caused fluctuations of the UAE's GDP. To reduce dependency on oil exports, the UAE has been increasing proportion of non-oil industries in national economy, such as tourism, building materials, petrochemical industry, finance and trade logistics. The UAE's inflation rate has been fluctuating in a normal range around 2% in recent years.

In terms of exchange rate policies, the UAE has been adopting a managed floating exchange rate policy. Since the use of Dirham in 1973, the UAE currency's exchange rate to the USD has been maintained around 3.67.

In terms of balance of payments, the UAE has set up multiple domestic free trade zones (about 40 in number, mostly in Dubai) to encourage trade development (esp. non-oil trade). And the most well-known is the Jebel Ali free trade zone, which was the earliest in the Middle East and North African districts.

In terms of foreign exchange reserves, the UAE's foreign exchange reserve was 89.9 billion USD by July 2017. On March 23, 2012, the UAE government announced that it has included RMB into its official foreign exchange reserve.

(3) *Egypt*

In terms of macro-economy, Egypt's GDP has been growing steadily in recent years; especially, the growth rate reached 4.2% and 4.3% in the fiscal years of 2014/2015 and 2015/2016, which signified a relatively fast speed. According to the World Bank's global economic prediction report in June 2017, Egypt's GDP growth rate in 2016/2017 fiscal year was expected to be 3.9%, which was consistent with the Egyptian government's predictions. According to the World Bank's predictions, with the economic reforms of Egypt and the improvement of investment environment, Egypt's economic growth rate will stay above 4% in the next two fiscal years, and is expected to reach 5.3% in 2018/2019. The inflation rate of Egypt in recent years has been basically around 10%. In 2015/2016, Egypt's annual overall CPI gradually increased. Since Egypt adopted freely floating exchange rate policy in November 2016, the country's inflation rate has been rising sharply, and the annual inflation rate has reached 30%.

In terms of exchange rate policies, Egypt started implementing a managed floating exchange rate policy since 2003. In 2005, the Egyptian government accepted terms of the IMF on freely convertible current account, and boosted people's confidence in Egyptian pound, but it did not implement free convertibility of the capital account. Before January 2003, Egypt was adopting a fixed exchange rate system and following the USD. The government supported Egyptian pound with a high interest rate and large foreign exchange reserves, and curbed economic growth. After the exchange rate reform, EGP/USD exchange rate passed a reasonable devaluation process, and Egyptian economic growth was accelerated. In December 2012, Egyptian central bank declared to reform the dollar auction system in order to prevent Egyptian pound devaluation and the further decrease of Egyptian foreign exchange reserves. It also set a maximum amount for dollars transacted in auctions by the commercial banks. On November 3, 2016, Egyptian central bank declared to allow free floating of exchange rate of Egyptian pound, in order to get rid of domestic economic difficulty and better fulfill its loan commitments with the IMF.

In terms of balance of payments, in order to improve the long-term trade deficit, the Egyptian government is dedicated to improving product quality, expanding export, and increasing Egyptian products' competitive force in the international market. Meanwhile, it set up economic free trade zones in different districts to increase import and export trade volumes. And it also started the process of opening up trade and reducing tariff, and reduced restrictions on goods import and export. In the 2015/2016 fiscal year, Egypt's external deficit was 2.81 billion USD (with a surplus of 3.73 billion USD in the last year). Egypt's external deficit in 2015/2016 was mainly reflected in two aspects: 1. The deficit of current account rose sharply from 12.14 billion USD of the last fiscal year to 19.83 billion USD. 2. Net in-flow of capital and financial account rose from 17.93 billion USD of the last fiscal year to 21.18 billion USD.

In terms of foreign exchange reserves, Egypt's foreign exchange reserves decreased sharply from 33.7 billion USD in June 2010 to 15.5 billion USD in June 2012 under the influence of the turmoil since the 2011/2012 fiscal year. The decrease of foreign exchange reserve was mainly due to the decrease of foreign exchange investment in Egyptian security exchange market, rapid decrease of tourism income and reduction of foreign direct investment. In March 2013, Egypt's foreign exchange reserves reduced to as low as 13.4 billion USD. Since then, Egypt received assistance from Saudi Arabia, the UAE and Kuwait, and its foreign exchange reserves maintained at 15–19 billion USD. Since November 2016, Egypt started implementing the freely floating exchange rate system. As Egyptian foreign exchange fund flowed into the banking system, Egypt increased borrows of foreign debt, and IMF issued a 12 billion USD loan. Egypt's foreign exchange reserves increased. By the end of July 2017, Egypt's foreign exchange reserves reached 36 billion USD, which exceeded the historically highest level before the "1.25" revolution in 2011.

11.4 Pushing Forward RMB Internationalization in Arab League Countries

11.4.1 *Cooperation Basis*

(1) *BRI Construction Provided Mechanism Assurance for China-Arab Capacity Cooperation Supported by RMB*

The BRI created a good channel for RMB internationalization, i.e. encouraging Chinese companies to "step out" for international capacity cooperation by taking advantage of the complementary nature of industrial structures and economic elements of China and countries along the BRI route. By considering the national development strategies of the host country, we should output China's advantageous capacity, and support the entire process of capacity cooperation with RMB.

Countries along the BRI route are important targets for our country's international capacity cooperation. Due to rich oil reserves and important graphical locations, the Arab league countries such as

Saudi Arabia, the UAE and Egypt are extremely important cooperation partners of our country. In recent years, due to the decrease of oil reserves and the fall of international oil price, Arab league countries have formulated economic structure adjustment plans to increase proportion of non-oil economy in their entire national economy. They intend to make a "gear shift" in economic development impetus in order to achieve long-term development.

The UAE emphasized the development of tourism, building materials, petrochemical industry and trade logistics, and put forward the "2021 strategic plan" in order to create a "non-oil economy". To facilitate tourism development, the UAE invested a large amount of capital in constructing public infrastructure, including airports, hotels and roads. Such constructions increased demands in the building material industry, especially energy-saving building materials, and the UAE has become the largest-scale building market in Middle East (Han Lu, 2017). In terms of petrochemical industry, the UAE intends to develop downstream industries by making use of its advantages in raw materials in order to increase additional value of oil and natural gas industry. Egypt is also implementing economic transition strategies. It used to rely on industries such as oil, natural gas and textile, but now it has decided to boost the economy through investments in infrastructure and industry. In June 2015, our country's National Development and Reform Commission and Ministry of Commerce and Egypt's Ministry of Industry and Trade and Investment Department signed an inter-governmental framework agreement for China-Egypt capacity cooperation and the minutes of meeting, and clarified the project list and cooperation model. The agreement signified a phased result of China-Egypt capacity cooperation. Our country has first-mover advantages in fields such as infrastructure construction, building material production and industrial equipment manufacturing, and has more rights of speech in negotiation on the settlement currency. Therefore, we could try to provide RMB-valuated financial services from Arab league countries. For example, Chinese financial institutions could provide overseas RMB loans, and the companies of Arab league countries could make payments for construction projects or equipment with RMB.

(2) *Renewable Energy Development in Arab League Countries Created "Green Opportunities" for RMB Internationalization*

Arab league countries are well-known for their rich oil reserves, but their oil consumption is also remarkable. Saudi Arabia is the sixth largest country of oil consumption and the seventh of natural gas consumption. The UAE and Egypt are the 12th and 15th natural gas consumption countries, respectively. The UAE's natural gas consumption even exceeded India, which has a 1.2 billion population (Wu Lei, 2014). The rich oil reserves increased energy subsidies of Arab league countries. In Saudi Arabia, automotive oil costs less than 0.2 USD/liter, and energy subsidies take up 5% of GDP (while food subsidies only take up 0.7%). Domestic oil consumption takes up 25% of the country's export volume (Zhang Qi, 2013). Due to low energy price and increased demands of economic construction, the finance and environment of oil producing countries are largely consumed by domestic crude oil consumption. Al-Amad, the director of Regional Center for Renewable Energy and Energy Efficiency indicated that according to calculations, if domestic energy consumption is growing at the current speed, Arab league countries will have no oil for export by 2030 (Wang Erde, 2013). For this reason, Arab league countries reached a consensus on the "Renewable Energy Application and Development Strategy for Pan-Arab Districts in 2010–2030" in the third Arab Economic and Social Development Summit in 2013. They intended to increase installed renewable energy generating capacity to 75 kMW before 2030, accounting for 9.4% of total generating capacity of Arab districts.

Meng Gang (2017) pointed out that China should share green industry development experience with developing countries and lead green financial innovations during the BRI construction. In the renewable energy field, our country is the largest market of solar energy and wind energy, and we have a group of leading enterprises as well as cost and technical advantages. Secondly, our country should make use of the leading energy-saving technologies and experience in industries including steel, electricity, machinery, non-ferrous metals, petrochemical, textile and information, and push forward export of energy-saving technologies (Jin Ruiting, 2016). In addition, our country's nuclear power technology is gradually gaining competitive force in the international market. In 2013, Pakistan invested 13 billion USD to purchase three large nuclear power projects from China, and it was the first time for China's third generation nuclear power technology with proprietary IPR to "step out" of border (Li Xin, 2016). The Arab league countries, which are seeking traditional energy substitution are also inviting China for the bidding of several nuclear power projects. While Chinese companies are "stepping out", financial institutions could follow up and provide RMB loans for Arab league countries. At present, China Development Bank has signed 260 million RMB loans with SAI-Bank in Egypt to support China-Egypt capacity cooperation projects. Egyptian companies could apply for loans from SAI-Bank, and make payments to Chinese suppliers with RMB.

(3) *The Serious Rich-Poor Polarization of Arab League Countries Created Opportunities of "Domestic Currency Cooperation" in Inclusive Finance*

The political turmoil that started in Tunisia in 2009 caused economic stagnation and even regime change of several Arab league countries. The main cause of "Arab Spring" is the serious rich-poor polarization of Arab league countries and the reduction of employment rate; while Islam, which the common people have faith in greatly emphasizes on social equity. As a result, the common people and the ruling elites were in serious conflict. According to statistics, the Arab world is the only district with continuous increasing of impoverished population in 2010. In the Arab district, 40% of people are living below an income of 2.75 USD/day, and over 4% are living below the poverty line 1.25 USD/day (Ridhaaboudi, 2017). The high population growth rate of Arab league countries is also a major cause of rich-poor polarization. Young people over working age (15–30 y/o) account for one-third to a quarter of the total population, but 20–40% of the people in the

15–24 y/o age group are unemployed. In Middle East and North African districts, the employment rate of young people is less than 30%, and did not even have a better performance in the past 20 years (the number of East Asia is 53%). In the year 2007 before "Arab Spring", the unemployment rate of Egyptian young people was 63% (Bai Ruomeng, 2017).

The development of medium-small enterprises is in an important position in the national economy of Arab league countries, and it can solve the employment issue of large numbers of people. Data indicated that medium-small companies account for 90% of total number of companies in Arab league countries, and they create a value exceeding 50% of GDP. In Egypt, the medium-small companies account for 80% of total number of companies, and they create a value over 56% of national GDP (Jiang Chuanying, 2012). Therefore, leaders of Arab league countries are paying great attention to the development of medium-small companies in recent years. In 2017, the leaders of Arab league countries reached an important consensus on facilitating medium-small enterprise development in the annual meeting of Association for Financial Inclusion in Sharm el Sheikh, Egypt.

According to Meng Gang (2017), our country should promote enlending platform construction experience such as medium-small enterprise loans in Central Africa in countries along "Belt and Road", encourage cross-border e-commerce and mobile payment industry to "step out", and push forward development of inclusive finance. Currently, China Development Bank has successfully conducted multiple sub-loan businesses in Egypt. The major model is to issue loans to local large financial institutions, and the financial institutions will in turn sub-loan to medium and small enterprises which require capital. While China-Arab trade is growing at full speed, and Arab league countries are vigorously developing inclusive finance to improve social equity, our country should push forward RMB inclusive financial services, such as providing RMB loans to Arab small and medium enterprises (for payment in China-Arab trades), and helping Arab league countries construct telecommunication infrastructure for mobile payment. We could also encourage Chinese cross-border e-commerce companies to settle businesses in Arab league countries in RMB, and in this way, push forward RMB internationalization through inclusive finance.

(4) *In Recent Years, Decreased Dependency of Europe and America on Middle East Oil Paved the Way for RMB Business Expansion*

Oil exports of Saudi Arabia in the 1960s–1970s were mostly focused on Europe and America, but after the 1990s, oil exports of the country started concentrating on the Asia Pacific region. After 2000, Saudi Arabia's oil exports to the Asia Pacific region have been taking up a high percentage (Zou Zhiqiang, 2016). Currently, due to the USA's shale gas revolution and the substantial increase of Canada's oil exports to the USA, Saudi Arabia's oil exports to the USA have fallen to less than 1 million barrels/day, and even less than the bottom level after financial crisis in 2009. Oil imports from Saudi Arabia only account for 13% of the USA's total oil imports.

Currently, China is the largest oil import country in the world, and the Middle East region's oil exports to China will reach twice of the current quantity before 2035. As an important buyer in the world oil market, China is developing forward oil contracts which are valuated in RMB and convertible with gold, and will formally launch them into the market in this year. The forward oil contracts are the first bulk commodity futures contracts open to foreign institutional investors. In the first half of 2017, China's oil import increased by 13.8%, while Saudi Arabia's oil supply only increased by 1%. China's increase in oil import was mostly supplied by Russia. In 2015, Saudi Arabia was still China's largest oil export country, but now Russia has taken its position. By August 2017, Russia's export to China was 1.2 million barrels/day, and Saudi Arabia was 942,000 barrels/day, accounting for 12% of China's total imports. In addition, RMB settlement has been achieved in China-Russia oil trade. While volume of trade with Europe and America has decreased, oil producing countries such as Saudi Arabia are not willing to lose China as their large customer. Conducting oil trade settlement with RMB will increase demands of China to import from Arab league countries. Besides, our country's economic cycle highly matches the cycle of emerging markets, while the international currency system led by USD and the global governance system led by the USA are only being reformed at a slow rate. Therefore, in the special period when Europe and America are reducing dependency on Middle East oil, our country should set up a diversified oil settlement system, and steadfastly push forward oil settlement in RMB.

(5) *Long-term Low Price of Oil and USD Assets Weakened the Position of "Petro-dollar"*

By reviewing the history, we can find that "petro-dollar" has been existing on the basis of high oil price and economic prosperity of the USA. In 1974, the USA and Saudi Arabia reached an agreement that the oil trade between both countries would be settled in USD, and the USA would provide arms and ammunition for Saudi Arabia to protect the country from possible invasions of Israel. In December of the same year, the USA opened the US public debt market for Saudi Arabia, and ensured Saudi Arabia's priority in purchasing US public debts. Thus, the "petro-dollar" chain was closed, i.e. Saudi Arabia obtains USD income by exporting oil, and the USD flows back to the USA to contribute to American economic development, and Saudi Arabia also benefits from the increase of asset price. When oil price was on a high level, oil producing countries accumulated large amount of dollar exchange surplus, which finally flowed back to developed countries. But since oil price stays low at present, oil producing countries in the Arab world are enabling foreign exchanges in stock to flow back to their own countries in order to implement economic adjustments (Zhang Shuai, 2016). Besides, the USA implemented quantitative easing to rescue domestic economy after the financial crisis in 2008. As a result, the USD had a substantial devaluation, price of USD-valuated assets reduced, and oil producing countries in the Arab district suffered huge loss. The basis of "petro-dollar" was weakened. Multiple Arab league countries had the intention to abandon USD as the oil valuation currency. For example, Saudi Arabia is trying to use the Argus Sour Crude Index (ASCI) which valuates oil with a basket of currencies, in place of the West Texas Intermediate (WTI), which valuates oil with USD (Zhang Shuai, 2016). In addition, the Arab countries in the Middle East accumulated large amount of foreign exchange reserves by exporting oil, and many sovereign wealth funds created based on these reserves need to spread risks. Currently, RMB has been formally included into the SDR currency basket, and multiple countries have included RMB-valuated assets into their foreign exchange reserves. Therefore, we should push forward RMB internationalization by taking advantage of the opportunity of the "petro-dollar" weakening.

(6) *China-Arab Trade Development Needs RMB Capital Support*

China is ranked the second in volume of trade with Arab league countries. In 2005–2015, volume of trade between China and Arab league countries increased 6 times. Oil trade has become and will remain as the pillar industry of China-Arab trade. Arab league countries account for 40% of China's oil imports, and the proportion may grow higher in future. China-Arab trade has a complementary nature. For example, China and Saudi Arabia have cooperated in renewable energy, aerospace and nuclear energy projects in recent years, and Saudi Arabia not only exports oil to China, but also exports industrial products such as petrochemicals, which China needs. The UAE's emphasis on non-oil economy has been reflected in its trade and economic connections with China. While the total volume of trade is decreasing, non-oil trade between China and the UAE reached 47.5 billion USD, accounting for 86% of total trade in 2015. In future, the UAE will vigorously develop building materials, petrochemical industry and trade logistics. These industries are highly complementary for China and the UAE, and will take the volume of trade between two countries to a new level. While the volumes of trade and investment between China and Arab league countries are increasing, comprehensively developing RMB businesses in Arab league countries will help lead more Chinese enterprises into the Arab league countries, facilitate trade and investment cooperation between Chinese and Arab league companies, increase efficiency of using resources, increase the degree of openness and mutual cooperation, and increase the comprehensive strength of both China and Arab league countries.

(7) *The Huge Potential of Arab League Countries will Attract Direct Investment from China*

Although China has a large amount of foreign exchange reserves and strong investment abilities, China's direct investment in Saudi Arabia is still small. According to statistics of Ministry of Commerce, China's non-financial direct investment in Saudi Arabia in 2013 was 479 million USD, only accounting for 0.5% of China's total investment abroad of 90.1 billion USD. The small-scale investment was mainly because Saudi Arabia had accumulated large amount of foreign exchange reserves by oil export and did not lack capital for development. However, with the fall of crude oil price in recent years, Saudi Arabia is gradually opening up to foreign capital in certain fields; especially, Saudi Arabia has loose policies on foreign direct investment in downstream industries of oil and natural gas and industrial manufacturing.

Egypt is not only an Arab league country, but the third largest economy of Africa. Currently, China and Egypt have a large volume of trade, and Egypt is China's third largest trade partner in Africa. But due to small stock of investment and the small quantity of contracted works, Egypt is not among China's top ten investment destination countries in Africa. By the end of 2015, China's direct investment stock in Egypt was only 663 million USD. According to statistics, Egypt is the fifth largest country of foreign direct investment in-flow, only second to India, China, Indonesia and America. And China's overseas investment rose sharply by 44% in 2016 and reached 183 billion USD. China became the second largest country of overseas investment. In 2015, China's direct investment in Africa was 2.98 billion USD, while its direct investment in Egypt was only 60.5 million USD, accounting for only 2%. China's investment in Egypt still has a large space for development. As more Chinese companies come to Egypt to make investment and build factories, China-Egypt economic and trade cooperation will be strengthened, and favorable conditions will be created for RMB internationalization in Egypt.

(8) *Arab League Countries Keep Issuing Preferential Policies on Foreign Direct Investment*

In May 2017, the Egyptian parliament passed a new *Investment Law*, which stipulated that the approval period for investment projects should not exceed 97 days, and defined the concept of investment zone, technical zone and free zone in terms of economic and industrial development degrees (Table 11.1). The parliament also issued a

Table 11.1   Policies of Egypt's New *Investment Law*

S/N	Stipulation of New *Investment Law*	Detailed Regulations
1	Investment zone	Set out by the prime minister's order, and covering logistics, agriculture and industry (not limited by the free trade zone). The new zone's independent board of directors has the sole right of management, which includes project admittance (approval of other government departments is not required)
2	Technical zone	Set out by the prime minister's order, and covering IT, telecommunications, designing and manufacturing of electronic devices, data center, programming and technical education. The new zone's independent board of directors has the sole right of management, which includes project admittance (approval of other government departments is not required). The equipment and instruments used in projects in the new technical zone are only subject to taxes stipulated in the new *Investment Law*.
3	Free zone	Set out by the prime minister's order, mainly serving exports, and covering all industries other than oil, chemical fertilizer, steel production, transportation and natural as production. The new zone's independent board of directors has the sole right of management, which includes project admittance (approval of other government departments is not required). The equipment and instruments used in projects in the new technical zone are only subject to taxes stipulated in the new *Investment Law*.

Source: Egypt's *Investment Law*.

series of tax reduction and financial return policies to attract foreign investment. In terms of taxation, the new *Investment Law* stipulated that a maximum of 50% tax reduction can be applied to investment projects located in "districts mostly in need of development", and a 30% reduction can be applied to investment projects which "widely use manpower, are carried out by medium-small enterprises, produce or use renewable energy, or conducted under national or strategic tourism plans". If the project is put into operation within 2 years, the investor will obtain a 50% return of land-transferring fees from the department of finance.

The Saudi government is also trying to create a favorable investment environment. Firstly, it simplified the foreign investment approval procedures, and set up a swift visa channel for convenience of foreign workers in Saudi Arabia to visit their relatives. The visa application process will take 5 working days in maximum. Secondly, foreign investments in Saudi Arabia are treated based on their ratings. Leading enterprises in an industry and medium-small enterprises with proprietary IPR are given a higher rating. Thirdly, the government will screen investment projects, and specifically encourage projects which can increase Saudi Arabia's economic competitive force, facilitate IPR's localization in Saudi Arabia and increase the competitive force of exported commodities. At last, the government raised the share proportion limit for foreign capitals. Foreign capital is allowed to take up 100% in the shares of wholesale and retail projects (the proportion used to be 75%) (Chen Mo, 2016).

Due to the favorable investment environment, huge investment growth potential and important geographical location, the Arab countries have become important countries attracting China's overseas direct investment. RMB valuation development will increase the number of Chinese companies making investment in Arab countries and provide more support for Arab countries to accomplish economic transitions.

(9) *The Currency Swap Agreements will Lay the Foundation for RMB Business Development in Arab League Countries*

Currently, People's Bank of China has signed currency swap agreements with the central banks of several Arab league countries to provide liquidity support for these countries. The currency swap agreements signified the trust of Chinese and Arab central banks for each other's currencies, and our country also requests the central banks of relevant countries to formulate commercial bank operating rules for the use of RMB in order to gradually achieve domestic settlement with RMB. Although the amount of currency swaps between China and Arab league countries is not as large as the currency swaps between China and ASEAN countries, it was still a good start for Arab banking industry to use RMB in settlements. After the currency swaps, the Arab banking industry will be motivated to conduct RMB settlements for Chinese companies or Arab companies with trade contacts with Chinese companies in order to reduce USD cashing pressure, and Chinese companies could also reduce financial costs. Once the domestic currency cooperation has achieved a win-win situation, it will create a virtuous cycle, in which more Egyptian banks will seek to conduct settlements with RMB, and produce demands such as overseas RMB loans.

11.4.2 *Major Problems*

(1) *Our Country's Crude Oil Futures Market is Still Not Complete*

In the 1990s, our country became the first to set up a crude oil futures market in Asia, but due to problems in operation and supervision, the market had to be closed at last. The present Shanghai futures market only trades fuel oil futures contract. Although it launched medium sour crude futures (the major trade category in the world is light sour crude futures), it is still far behind the world's leading crude oil futures market. Xu Dong (2017) conducted research on several globally well-known crude oil futures exchanges and discovered that a successful crude oil futures market needs a complete financial transaction system, such as a complex and organic ecological system formed by linkage between the derivative market, currency market and foreign exchange market (Table 11.2). Besides, active crude oil transactions mean the absence of a market monopolist, while our country is not prepared to fully open the oil field, especially when it concerns national security. "Petro-dollar" was built on control of the oil transaction and settlement process, which

Table 11.2 Comparison of Major Crude Oil Futures Exchanges in the World

Country/Exchange	Trade Category	Valuation and Settlement Currency	Delivery Method	Reason of Launch	Result of Launch	Reason of Success (or Failure)
USA/NYMEX	WTI	USD	Physical delivery	Hedging	Success	The selected underlying asset is a mainstream category in the country. Most spot crude oil in the world is marked with USD price, and the traders avoided exchange risks. Good liquidity and price transparency. Support of a developed financial system. Development of the OTC market (over-the-counter market)
UK/ICE	BRENT	USD	Cash delivery. The developed forward market provided authoritative settlement prices for futures delivery	Hedging	Success	The exchange occupied its position through geo-politics in the 1990s. Good liquidity and price transparency. Support of a developed financial system. Arbitrage mechanism of London and New York markets. Development of the OTC market

UAE/DME	OMAN	USD	Physical delivery	Intending to acquire rights of speech in export prices of Middle East crude oil	Ordinary	The Middle East oil is mainly used for exports. Flow direction is singular. Transaction amount is small. The exchange turned into a spot market
India/MCX	WTI	Rupee	Physical delivery and cash delivery co-exist	Intending to seize crude oil pricing power as a large country of oil import	Ordinary	It has time zone advantages and can conduct cross-timing transactions with New York market. The domestic financial system is not complete (valuation currency is an uncommon currency, and there is foreign exchange control)
Japan/TOCOM	MECO	JPY	Cash settlement at Oman/Dubai. Average price evaluated by S&P	Intending to seize crude oil pricing power as a large country of oil import	Failure	Slow growth of economy and an inactive futures market. Japanese crude oil completely depends on imports. Flow direction is singular. Cash settlement, with no function of price discovery

Source: Xu Dong (2017).

means the presence of mature oil infrastructure — crude oil futures exchanges. Therefore, there are still many obstacles on the way to achieve "petroleum RMB".

(2) *RMB has a High Market Interest Rate and Long-term Interest Rate*

According to research, a currency's market interest rate and long-term interest rate will affect and are inversely proportional to its internationalization degree. Since the bank will add points on the basis of SHIBOR or LIBOR in loan pricing, and the points reflect the borrower's credit risks, the points added while using SHIBOR and LIBOR are essentially the same, and reflect the same credit risks. At a lower interest rate, domestic currency loans will be more popular abroad. But when the interest rate of a currency is high, people will be less inclined to accept loans in this currency, and the currency's internationalization process will be affected. Relevant policies of the People's Bank of China have included the overseas RMB loan scale into the overall regulation and control of credit scale. At present, the banks' income from overseas RMB loans is relatively lower than domestic RMB businesses. When the loan scale is limited, the overseas RMB business will directly affect the bank's overall profit and loss, and therefore reduce the bank's preference to conduct overseas RMB business.

(3) *Fluctuation Range of RMB Exchange Rate is Gradually Increasing*

According to research, the (expected) fluctuation range of a currency will have great influence on the currency's internationalization. Since March 17, 2014, the floating range of RMB/USD trading price in the inter-bank spot exchange market increased from 1% to 2%. Especially, when the US economy is recovering, the expectation of one-way appreciation of RMB does not exist. Based on trend of RMB/USD exchange rate in recent years, RMB sharply appreciated after a continuous downfall. Consequently, the governments and companies will consider the RMB's fluctuation risks as hard to manage. With an unclear trend of RMB exchange rate and an increased fluctuation range, foreign governments will prefer more stable currencies for settlement and reserves, and foreign companies will be more inclined to obtain USD financing to reduce exchange risks. The situation increased the difficulty of promoting RMB as a settlement and reserve currency.

(4) *The RMB Offshore Market is Not Sufficiently Developed*

Although the offshore RMB markets in Hong Kong, Singapore and Europe are growing rapidly in scale, they still have the problem of low liquidity and lack sufficient financial products, and cannot satisfy the traders' demands for risk avoidance, value preservation and value increase. These problems limited RMB's functions of financial transaction and reserves. Additionally, although RMB repayments and the exchange risks associated with repayments can be transferred to the companies actually using the funds through the bank credit granting model, the overseas borrowers often lack RMB income compared with domestic companies, and they do not have sufficient demands for RMB use. The situation greatly affected the development of overseas RMB loan business. At present, the main risk avoidance method which our banks provide for overseas RMB loan business is forward exchange settlement with the borrower. But since the RMB forward market is not mature, and transactions over 1-year period are inactive, the customer's risk avoidance demand cannot be fully satisfied. The above situation also negatively affected the promotion of overseas RMB loans.

11.4.3 *Suggestions*

(1) *Push Forward RMB Valuation and Settlement for Bulk Commodities of Arab League Countries*

Bulk commodities are the leading commodities in international trade and mainly include petroleum, steel, non-ferrous metals, ores and bulk agricultural products, among which oil trade is the most important, frequent, and typical. One of the causes of the failure of JPY internationalization is that JPY's functions of valuation and settlement in international trade were not fully developed. The USA is a large country of oil consumption. It reached an "unshakable" agreement with Saudi Arabia in the 1970s which established USD as the only pricing currency of oil. Since then, the USA has been tightly controlling the valuation and settlement of international oil trade, oil finance and many oil producing countries via USD. Although the USA is not an OPEC member, it has great influence on international oil price. Bulk commodity trade is the key to currency substitution in the international trading field and has strong currency inertia. Iraq and Iran once tried to valuate and settle oil trades with currencies other than USD, but failed due to political turmoil arising for various causes. In 2015, China and Russia successfully tried RMB settlement for oil trades. In 2016, China surpassed the USA as the largest oil import country. Taking this as a good starting point, China should make use of its comprehensive advantages in investment and financing, vigorously push forward RMB valuation and settlement for bulk commodities such as oil in countries along the BRI route, such as Saudi Arabia and Egypt, gradually increase the use of RMB in international trade, and achieve internationalization of RMB functions.

(2) *Set Up a Crude Oil Futures Market and Improve RMB Valuation System for Crude Oil*

To implement RMB settlement for oil, our country should not only have strong oil demands, but have plenty of rights of speech in the oil pricing system, which depend on a complete crude oil futures transaction system. Although our country still has some problems in oil pricing in relevant markets, which could not quite objectively reflect the supply and demand relationship, and our country does not have the corresponding foreign exchange, currency and derivative transaction markets, our country should increase market efficiency as early as possible, enabling the buyer to obtain a reasonable price and the seller to increase supply efficiency, achieve effective international price comparison, and finally connect with the international crude oil transaction system and achieve the goal of RMB settlement for oil.

(3) *Further Improve the RMB Settlement System in Arab League Countries and Set Up More RMB Clearing Banks*

Currently, our country has set up RMB clearing banks in Qatar and proposed to set up a clearing center in the UAE. RMB payment has made great progress in Arab countries in the Middle East, but it still has huge potential in the North Africa. Egypt imports large quantity of commodities from China each year. China's volume of exports to Egypt in 2016 was 10.78 billion USD. Egypt is China's third largest trading partner in Africa, and by setting up RMB clearing banks in Egypt, we could more effectively push forward RMB internationalization in Arab countries in North Africa. Additionally, China mainly exports mechanical and electrical products and automobiles to Egypt. Since China has certain technical advantages, it should have more rights of speech in selection of payment currencies. While Egypt is short of foreign exchanges, setting up RMB clearing banks or encouraging more Egyptian banks to connect to the RMB settlement system could help facilitate RMB payment in China-Egypt trade, and therefore reduce the foreign exchange reserve pressure of Egypt.

(4) *Set Up Bank Cooperation Organizations in Arab League Countries*

The internationalization processes of GBP, USD, JPY and EUR were all inseparable from the close cooperation of banks of various countries centering on the domestic banks. Therefore, the key to pushing forward RMB internationalization through BRI is to create an RMB-centered regional currency cooperation system with extensive participation of countries along the BRI route. Arab league countries have a solid foundation for political and economic cooperation with China, and have high expectations for Chinese investment, trade and capital. China should seize the good opportunity at present and set up bank cooperation organizations in Arab league countries in order to create an RMB-centered regional currency cooperation system with extensive participation of banks of Arab league countries, facilitate investment, financing and trade cooperation along the BRI route, and accelerate the process of RMB internationalization.

(5) *Solidify Policy Communication Results with Free Trade and Investment Cooperation Agreements*

A currency's leading position in overseas investment and trade is the precondition for its internationalization. China should strengthen policy communication with Arab league countries, facilitate trade and investment, solidify work results in the form of legal documents, and enter into agreements which facilitate free trade and investment cooperation in order to lay a solid policy and legal foundation for RMB internationalization and better implement RMB's functions of valuation, settlement, trade and reserves. In recent years, Chinese government has signed economic and trade cooperation agreements with governments of 30 countries, and China's Ministry of Commerce, relevant departments of 60 countries and international organizations co-issued the cooperation initiative for facilitating BRI trade during the "Belt and Road" summit. On this basis, China should continue to push forward economic and trade cooperation with Arab league countries, enter into bilateral or multilateral free trade and investment cooperation agreements, and encourage RMB's use in investment and trading activities.

(6) *Actively Study Requirements of Different Parties and Push Forward Overseas RMB Loans*

Wen Yuan (2017) classified prospective borrowers of overseas RMB loans into four categories: currency authorities, fiscal authorities, financial institutions and companies, and classified the foreign countries into four categories: surrounding countries, aid receiving countries, resource countries and developed countries. In the above classification, Arab leagues countries are between the resource type and developed type, and due to the special geographical location of the Middle East, they also have the characteristics of surrounding countries. Therefore, we should pay special attention to the currency authorities, financial institutions and local companies while pushing forward overseas RMB loans in Arab leagues countries. The first RMB loan in Egypt, i.e. the 260 million RMB loan cooperation between China Development Bank and SAI-Bank, and the memorandum of understanding for RMB loan cooperation between Banque Misr and China Development Bank indicated the demands of financial institutions and currency authorities in this respect. According to survey results, Chinese companies in Arab league countries and Chinese companies which have trade contacts with Egypt have strong demands for RMB settlement. And these Chinese companies often have technical advantages over Arab countries, therefore the Arab countries are willing to pay with RMB in relevant industries and fields. Our country could promote buyer's credit business at appropriate times, and grant RMB credit to Arab companies which import products from China, and satisfy the requirements of both Chinese and Arab companies.

(7) Cultivate RMB's Investment and Foreign Exchange Reserve Functions with Currency Swaps

In history, the British central bank effectively solved GBP's credit crisis through currency swaps. And Japan constructed a regional currency cooperation framework in the East Asia district through currency swaps. So far, People's Bank of China has signed bilateral domestic currency swap agreements with central banks of more than 21 countries and districts along "Belt and Road", with a total scale of 3 trillion yuan. The currency swap agreements signed between China and Arab league countries will not only provide liquidity support for both China and Arab league countries, but promote RMB as the bilateral trade settlement currency, promote direct investment and financial asset investment valuated in RMB, and encourage the Arab league countries to increase RMB exchange reserves. Reserve currency refers to assets and deposits valuated in a foreign currency and is mainly held by the government or official institutions as foreign exchange reserves. In September 2010, the central bank of Malaysia purchased RMB bonds with a value of 10 billion USD in Hong Kong as its foreign exchange reserve, and it was the first time for RMB to become a reserve currency of the central bank of another country. By December 2016, RMB assets accounted for 1.07% in IMF's database of official foreign exchange reserve currencies, and at least 40 countries and districts included RMB as a reserve currency with different methods. In recent years, Arab countries such as Egypt has been seriously lacking in USD liquidity, therefore they have a strong demand for our country's liquidity support. Motivating Arab league countries to increase RMB exchange reserves through currency swaps is an effective marketized operation method.

11.5 Conclusion

Arab league countries are important strategic supports for our country. They not only have important positions in geo-politics and geo-economy, but have frequent trade contacts with China. This chapter analyzed the feasibility of pushing forward RMB internationalization in Arab league countries, and put forward 9 cooperation bases, 4 major problems and 3 suggestions.

Nine cooperation basses:

1. BRI construction provided mechanism assurance for China-Arab capacity cooperation supported by RMB. Countries along the BRI route are important partners for our country's international capacity cooperation. Our country should seize the opportunity created by Arab league countries' transition to non-oil economy, output our advantageous industries, such as infrastructure construction, and provide financial services with domestic currency.

2. Renewable energy development in Arab league countries provided a "green opportunity" for RMB internationalization. The rich oil reserves and low price of energy increased energy consumption of Arab league countries, and these countries have started developing

renewable energies as a solution. Our country should encourage companies in the fields of solar energy, wind energy, biomass energy and nuclear energy to "step out" and provide RMB loans for Arab league countries to support projects involving Chinese capital.

3. The serious rich-poor polarization of Arab league countries created opportunities of domestic currency cooperation in inclusive finance. The root cause of the political turmoil triggered by "Arab Spring" is the serious rich-poor polarization of Arab society, and an important method to solve social equity problem is to encourage the development of medium-small companies. Our country's financial institutions should reproduce the enlending platform construction model in Egyptian banking industry, widely promote the model in Arab league countries, and encourage cross-border e-commerce and mobile payment industries to "step out" and provide inclusive financial services based on RMB valuation.

4. Reduced dependency of Europe and America on Middle East oil provided opportunities for RMB business development. While Canada has increased oil exports to the USA, and the USA increased shale gas production, the Arab league countries with rich oil resources, such as Saudi Arabia and the UAE have shifted their focus of export to Asian countries such as China. Since China's influence on the oil price of Arab league countries in the Middle East is gradually increasing, China should make use of this opportunity to push forward RMB settlement for oil.

5. Long-term slump of the oil price and USD assets weakened the "petro-dollar" position. Since the oil price and USD assets have stayed low over the long term, Arab league countries in the Middle East are seeking other currency assets to spread risks. At this moment, our country should open up the financial market to attract oil capital.

6. China-Arab bilateral trade development needs RMB capital support. China is an important trade partner of Arab league countries, and implementing RMB's trade settlement function will help Arab league countries reduce financial cost and the consumption of foreign exchange reserves.

7. The huge investment potential of Arab league countries will attract more Chinese direct investment. At present, the volume of trade between China and Arab league countries does not match the amount of direct investment, and RMB capital still has a large space for investment.

8. Arab league countries have been issuing preferential policies on foreign direct investment. While the crude oil price is staying low, the Arab oil producing countries are striving to attract foreign capital and issuing stipulations to simplify investment procedures. Our country should actively study their policies and make use of various favorable conditions.

9. The currency swap agreements laid the foundation for RMB business development. China and Arab league countries have signed a series of currency swap agreements, and created conditions for wide use of RMB in Arab league countries.

Four potential problems:

1. Our country's crude oil futures market is still not complete. RMB valuation and settlement for oil requires a complete crude oil futures market, while our country's crude oil pricing system still has mechanism obstacles and could not objectively reflect market supply and demand. Nor is the system effectively connected with the international market.

2. RMB's market interest and long-term interest are staying high, therefore RMB loans are at a disadvantageous position compared with USD and JPY, and overseas customers are not motivated to use RMB loans.

3. The fluctuation range of RMB exchange rate is gradually increasing. With the deepening of our country's exchange rate reform, the fluctuation range of RMB will further increase, therefore other countries' risk preference for RMB assets will decrease.

4. RMB offshore market is not sufficiently developed. As a result, countries holding RMB could not conduct adequate hedging transactions, and value preservation and increase of assets could not be realized.

Seven items of suggestion:

1. Push forward RMB valuation and settlement for bulk commodities of Arab league countries.
2. Set up a crude oil futures market and improve the RMB pricing system for crude oil.
3. Further improve the RMB settlement system in Arab league countries and set up more RMB clearing banks.
4. Set up bank cooperation organizations in Arab league countries.
5. Solidify policy communication results with free trade and investment cooperation agreements.
6. Actively study requirements of different parties and promote overseas RMB loans.
7. Strengthen RMB's investment and foreign exchange reserve functions through currency swaps.

RMB Internationalization in Russia

The rapid development of the bilateral relationship between China and Russia in recent years is attributed to both the emphasis of the leaders and the changes in international situation. The Europe and America imposed sanctions against Russia due to the Ukraine crisis. Consequently, the financing channels of Russian financial industry in the European and American markets were closed; and as a countermeasure, Russia reduced oil exports to Europe. However, Russian economy is still energy-oriented, and Russia's GDP is heavily dependent on the income of oil exports. Due to blocks in market financing channels of European and American currencies and reduction of oil exports to Europe, Russia is seeking RMB capital and expanding energy exports to China, and has agreed to use RMB as the valuation currency for oil exports to China.

12.1 Introduction

Chinese President Xi Jinping pointed out that China-Russia relation is one of the most important bilateral relations of China. At present, China and Russia highly trust each other in the political field, and their relationship is moving forward in all aspects. Therefore, both countries should make use of the good relationship and achieve tangible cooperation results. According to Putin, the president of Russia, China and Russia are having the best relationship in history. Both countries should make advancement hand-in-hand and face development challenges together.

Pushing forward RMB internationalization in Russia has great significance. Firstly, China and Russia have frequent economic and trade contacts carried out in large volumes. In 2001, China-Russia trade volume reached 10.67 billion USD, which was the first time to exceed 10 billion USD. Since then, the bilateral trade volume between China and Russia has been increasing rapidly. Before Russia joined WTO, China-Russia trade volume has always been increasing, except a little drop in 2009 due to the financial crisis. In recent two years, the trade volume between both countries dropped again, due to the fall of international oil price. In the first 7 months of 2017, China-Russia import and export reached a total amount of 46.822 billion yuan, and the amount of the entire year was expected to exceed 80 billion USD. The bilateral economic and trade relationship between China and Russia provided a carrier for RMB internationalization, and is helpful for implementing RMB settlement in cross-border trade. Secondly, Russia is a large country of energy export. RMB valuation in China-Russia oil trade will serve as a great example. Currently, the oil exports of Russia's third largest oil export company to China are completely settled in RMB, and Russia has replaced Saudi Arabia as China's largest oil export country. Since the demand of the USA and Europe for crude oil in Middle East is reduced, the oil export countries in Middle East, such as Saudi Arabia started worrying. RMB valuation and settlement for crude oil in Russia will help promote the same system in the Middle East. Thirdly, Russia is an important neighboring country of China. RMB internationalization will lead more capital of our country to expand the market. In recent years, Russia has been transforming its economic development model from consumer-driven to investment-driven economy, and has listed the far east as an important district for investment promotion. Our country has technical advantages in fields such as transport and industry, and Russia is in great need for investment capital under the sanctions of Europe and America. Therefore, we should push forward

RMB-valuated direct investment in Russia by taking advantage of the current international situation.

12.2 Current Situation of RMB Internationalization in Russia

12.2.1 *Trade Settlement*

Domestic currency settlement for China-Russia trade started in 2002. The central banks of both countries agreed that border trade could be settled with freely convertible currencies, RMB or rouble in Chinese banks registered in Heihe city, Heilongjiang province, China or Russian banks registered in Blagoveshchensk, Amurskaya Oblast, Russia. In 2011, the scope of domestic currency settlement of both countries was expanded from border trade to general trade. All trades between economic entities of both countries could be settled with the domestic currency. On March 22, 2017, Industrial and Commercial Bank of China became Russia's RMB clearing bank.

In 2002–2011, most China-Russia trades with domestic currency settlement were settled in rouble, especially after Russia fully opened the capital account in 2006. According to statistics, about 14% of China-Russia trades were settled in rouble, and only 0.1% were settled in RMB in 2009 (Sun Shaoyan, 2015). In 2011, our country issued the *Management Methods for Trials of RMB Settlement in Overseas Direct Investment*, and improved the situation of rouble dominance in domestic currency settlement for China-Russia trades.

12.2.2 *Financial Transactions*

RMB transactions are active in Russian financial market. In January to September 2016, China-Russia cross-border receipt and payment exceeded 20 billion RMB, with a year-on-year growth of 50%. Currently, 50 billion RMB is in circulation in the Russian market. In 2015, Russian government declared to include issuance of RMB-valuated bonds into its plan, but delayed the action over and over. No reliable news could be heard in this respect so far. In March 2017, Russian Aluminium issued RMB bonds with a total scale of 10 billion yuan and a first phase of 1 billion yuan in our country's onshore market.

12.2.3 *Reserve Currency*

The central banks of China and Russia signed a currency swap agreement in October 2014, with a scale of 150 billion RMB/815 billion rouble. After RMB was included into SDR in 2016, the central bank of Russia declared to start purchasing RMB-valuated assets, and formally include RMB into its foreign exchange reserve basket.

12.3 Russia's Political and Economic Situation

Russia is a large country in terms of politics, economy and military, and is playing an important role on the world stage. After the collapse of the Soviet Union, Russia achieved economic liberalization quickly, but many problems which ensued have been troubling the Russian leaders. The rich reserves of oil and natural gas enabled Russia to obtain large amount of income via energy export in 2002–2007, when energy price stayed high. As a result, Russia achieved rapid growth of economy. However, since the global economic crisis in 2008, Russian economy has been frustrated with little hope of recovery (Table 12.1). Even when the energy price recovered in 2012 and 2013, Russia still did not achieve the expected economic growth. Some scholars think it was due to the low degree of rule of law in Russia, because Norway was even more dependent on energy resources than Russia, but Norway was not quite affected by energy price fluctuation (Kuboniwa Masaaki, 2012). Some scholars attribute Russian economic decline to an imbalanced economic structure, including an overly large proportion of energy and raw material industry in the industrial structure, an overly large proportion of labor-intensive industry in the service industry structure, and an overly large proportion of primary commodities in the export structure (Guo Xiaoqiong, 2017). The oil price fall starting from October 2014, and the Ukraine crisis in the same year caused more negative influence on Russian economy. Accordingly, Russia formulated a series of economic reform measures to reduce impact of western sanctions on its economy, and seek a sustainable economic development path in the medium and long terms. Russian economy was stabilized in 2016, with a GDP growth rate of –0.2% (compared to –3.7% in 2015). IMF predicted that Russian economic growth rate in 2017 would reach 1.4%.

Table 12.1   Russian Economy in Recent Years

Key indicators	Values				
	2012	2013	2014	2015	2016
1. Real GDP (100 million rouble)	428,696	434,444	437,227	421,050	420,208
2. Real GDP (100 million USD)	13,798	13,653	11,515	6,866	6,288
3. GDP growth rate (%)	3.40	1.30	0.6	−3.7	−0.2
4. Nominal GDP (100 million USD)	20,161	20,790	18,806	13,114	12,850
5. Nominal GDP per capita (USD/person)	14,099	14,508	13,087	8,964	8,762
6. GDP composition (industry proportions)	100	100	100	100	100
(1) Industry	31.40	31.23	31.74	37.5	33.1
(2) Agriculture	3.35	3.40	3.57	3.9	4.7
(3) Service	65.26	65.37	64.69	58.6	62.2
7. Total fixed-asset investment (100 million USD)	4,045	4,155	3,563	2,374	341.35
8. Inflation rate (%)	6.6	6.5	11.4	12.9	5.4
9. Annual average exchange rate (USD/ domestic currency)	31.07	31.82	37.97	61.32	66.83

Source: Federal Statistics Service.

12.4 Push Forward RMB Internationalization in Russia

12.4.1 *Basis of Cooperation*

(1) *The Sanctions Imposed by Europe and America Accelerated the "De-dollarization" Process of Russia*

In November 2013, the then Ukrainian president Yanukovych suspended the process of signing political and economic treaties with the European Union and froze Ukraine's progress of joining the European Union. His actions caused discontent of the domestic public, and he was dismissed from office by the parliament. A serious conflict between pro-Europe and pro-Russia forces broke out in Ukraine. As Crimea conducted a referendum for joining Russia, the Ukraine crisis continued. Since April 2014, the USA and EU countries imposed sanctions against Russia on the ground that Russia violated international law and infringed on Ukraine's sovereignty and territorial integrity (Table 12.2). In terms of timing, the Europe and America imposed six rounds of sanctions against Russia. The first three rounds were focused on the 17 state-owned large companies of Russia, which were the "close friend circle" of Russian president Putin. Since the fourth round, the sanctions stepped into the essential phase. Major state-owned banks of Russia were prohibited from obtaining financing in the European and American markets. The fifth round of sanctions was extended to large military industrial enterprises and energy enterprises and aimed to frustrate Russia's middle and long term economic development. And the sixth round was an extension of the fifth.

In the financial field, 5 largest state-owned commercial banks of Russia were forbidden from obtaining financing in bond markets exceeding 90 days in the European Union. American companies and individuals are forbidden from purchasing debts exceeding 30 days issued by the above Russian banks. According to statistics, Russian state-owned banks conducted 47% of financing via the European Union market in 2013. It can be seen that the freezing of this financing channel had a huge influence on Russian banks.

In the military industry field, the largest Russian military industrial enterprise Russian Technologies, whose high-tech and industrial product export accounts for 23% of total Russian export was sanctioned. The company's assets in the USA were frozen, and American individuals and companies were forbidden from transacting bonds issued by the company.

In the energy field, the main objective of sanctions by Europe and America was to damage Russia's capacity of middle-term and long-term development. European and American companies were forbidden from providing product and technical support for projects which develop Russia's long-term energy supply capacity, such as

Table 12.2 Economic and Financial Sanctions Imposed by Europe and America Against Russia

Sanction Initiator	Date	Content
USA, EU	2014-4-28	The USA declared to freeze the assets of 7 Russian citizens and 17 Russian companies in the US territory to punish Russian companies and individuals for supporting protectors in the east of Ukraine. Accordingly, the EU expanded the name list for sanctions.
USA, EU	2014-7-17	Expand sanctions in the financial, energy and national defense fields. The USA declared to sanction three Russian banks and Russian shipbuilding enterprises which had cooperation with Russian military and restrict trade exports to Russia. The EU declared to forbid Russian state-owned companies from taking part in European financial market transactions, restrict export of relevant commodities and technologies to Russia, suspend capital support for Russia, and expand the sanction name list by adding 4 individuals and 4 companies.
USA	2014-9-12	Forbid American companies and individuals from purchasing debts exceeding 30 days issued by relevant Russian banks. Forbid American companies and individuals from purchasing debts exceeding 90 days newly issued by relevant Russian oil companies. Freeze the assets of 5 Russian state-owned national defense companies in the USA. Forbid exporting relevant commodities, services and technologies to 5 relevant Russian energy companies.
USA	2014-12-18	The US president Obama signed a new act on sanctions against Russia. The act was not in force yet, but it stipulated the economic measures of the USA to sanction Russia and support Ukraine. Restrict capital and technical support for the energy and technological fields of Russia. Provide 350 million USD's military equipment support for Ukraine. Sanction Russian arms export companies.
EU	2015-6-22	The EU will extend economic sanctions against Russia for half a year, till January 31, 2016.

Source: Federal Statistics Service.

deep water oil development, north pole energy exploration and shale gas extraction.

The sanctions of Europe and America caused huge influence on Russian economy, which can be analyzed in three aspects: aggravation of capital outflow, blockage of financial channels, and rising of inflation rate.

The first is the aggravation of capital outflow. In the first season in 2014, when Ukraine crisis broke out, Russia's capital net outflow was 70 billion USD, exceeding that of the entire year of 2013. Russia's foreign direct investment reduced by 70% in 2014, and 92% in 2015. But the overseas direct investment in global market in the same period was in a rising trend. Capital was transferred away from Russia to avoid risks. After a series of stabilizing measures taken by the Russian government, the capital outflow crisis was gradually put under control, but Russia was still desperately in need of capital.

The second is the blockage of financial channels. The European Union closed doors of financing against the five largest banks of Russia, and forbade major Russian energy companies, such as Rosneft Oil from obtaining capital in European Union market. The USA forbade its citizens and organizations from investing in bonds of major Russian companies. The above sanctions caused serious influence on Russian companies, which were accustomed to low-cost investment and loans of Europe and America. On one hand, the major Russian banks were in short of capital; on the other hand, energy companies with ongoing large projects were in need of money. But the situation also provided opportunities for the development of RMB financing in Russia.

The major rating agencies of the USA downgraded the credit ratings of Russian sovereignty and relevant companies (also as a means of sanctions). Standard & Poor's downgraded Russia's sovereign credit rating from BBB– to BB+ (garbage rating). Fitch rated Russia's sovereign credit as BBB– (lowest in speculative ratings). Since financial institutions use the ratings as important references, the downgrade of credit ratings will increase Russia's financing cost and cause more negative influence on Russian economy.

Additionally, the USA temporarily closed the payment business of three Russian financial institutions including Rossiya Bank, while 90%

of Russia's foreign trades process payment via the dollar payment system, SWIFT. Although the USA recovered the Russian payment business later, the act of sanctions enabled Russia to realize that it must develop its own payment infrastructure to cast off dependency on the USD system.

The third is the rising of inflation rate. As a countermeasure against European and American sanctions, Russia restricted imports of agricultural products from European Union, and turned to Turkey and Brazil for the above imports. However, agricultural products of those countries have higher prices and pushed up the inflation rate of Russia. In 2015, Russia's inflation rate was about 13%, only second to the financial crisis period in 2008. Food price rose up by 14% and affected the livelihood of the common people. Therefore, it may shake the ruling foundation of Russian government. To reduce inflation rate, Russia adopted a deflation currency policy and successfully reduced the inflation rate to 5.4% in 2016.

At present, the five largest banks of Russia have signed RMB loan agreements with China Development Bank. In May, September and December 2015, China Development Bank signed loan agreements of 6 billion yuan, 12 billion yuan and 10 billion yuan with Sberbank, JSC VTB Bank and Vnesheconombank, respectively, to support China-Russia bilateral economic and trade cooperation. Currently, the project of JSC VTB Bank is progressing smoothly, with an actual withdrawal of 9.6 billion yuan. During the meeting of prime ministers of both countries in November 2016, JSC VTB Bank signed the loan agreement for credit grant of the second sum of 12 billion yuan. In July 2017, in the witness of the heads of both countries, China Development Bank signed the *Financing Cooperation Agreement* with Gazprombank and Rosselkhozbank, with an amount of 10 billion yuan and 1 billion yuan, respectively. Meanwhile, China Development Bank is actively seeking cooperation with Russian banks which are not sanctioned and have certain strength, such as Alpha Bank. China Development Bank promised to provide a loan of 200 million USD for Alpha Bank to support Huawei's government and corporate network project in Russia.

In the background of European and American sanctions, new demands for cooperation between Russian financial institutions and corporate customers emerged in order to explore ways to get around USD. The cooperation mainly involves five fields: (1) Multi-currency loan business except USD. Loans are issued in RMB (including CNH and CNY), HKD and EUR. (2) Capital and bond business. The banks and customers will issue domestic currency bonds to each other and establish a domestic currency swap market. (3) Payment and settlement business. The banks and customers will establish an agent bank relationship and conduct payment and settlement in the domestic currencies. And they will open offshore multi-currency accounts. (4) Investment and fund business. Russia will attract Chinese capital investment via fund establishment, equity investment, direct investment and project company formation. (5) Derivative businesses of loan projects, such as rentals and insurance. Our country should take advantage of the historical opportunity of European and American sanctions and facilitate business development in different fields.

(2) *The Fall of International Oil Price Urged Russia to Strengthen Trade and Economic Connections with the Asia Pacific Region*

On June 26, 2014, the international crude oil price of West Texas crude oil market was 106.71 dollars/barrel, but the price fell to 53.77 dollars/barrel only half a year later (Figure 12.1). The oil price fall was attributed to multiple factors: 1. Slow growth of global economy caused lack of demands; 2. The dollar is in an interest-rate rise cycle, which caused the price fall of crude oil valuated in USD. 3. Extraction of shale oil and gas increased total supply of energy in the world; 4. Speculators of crude oil futures manipulate market price with techniques and expectations (Mi Jun et al, 2016). Since the fall of international oil price took place in the same period of the European and American sanctions against Russia, some people think the fall of oil price was purposely created by the Europe and America in order to punish Russia for annexing Crimea.

Since Russia is highly dependent on energy export income, a sluggish oil price will have serious impacts on Russian economy, which can be analyzed in the following aspects:

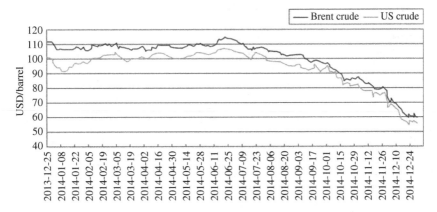

Figure 12.1 Fluctuation of International Crude Oil Price in 2014

Source: The website of China's Ministry of Commerce.

Firstly, low oil price has an impact on Russian currency market. According to research, correlation between rouble's exchange rate and international oil price has reached 92% (Zhang Hongxia, 2016). Since Russia has achieved free convertibility of capital account, the oil price fall caused negative expectation of the market for Russian economy. As a result, capital flowed out, rouble devalued, and inflation rate rose up in Russia. To reduce inflation rate, the central bank of Russia implemented currency deflation policies, and the currency's market interest rate went higher. For example, the central banks' one-week benchmark interest rate was 8.25% (up to 17% during the crisis in 2014), and the 3-month inter-bank offer rate reached 8.79%.

Secondly, low oil price affected Russia's real economy (Figure 12.2). In the 21st century, export of energy and raw materials contributes to 40–70% of Russia's economic growth. Decrease of oil export income caused slow-down of Russian economy. Since investments in industrial fields such as oil and natural gas are dependent on the oil export income, the influence of low oil price extended to the building and trade industries and reduced their total demands. Additionally, due to low oil price, capital's expectation for Russian economic development will turn negative. Since capital can flow freely, Russia will be more severely in short of capital, and even needs to sell off assets to obtain liquidity.

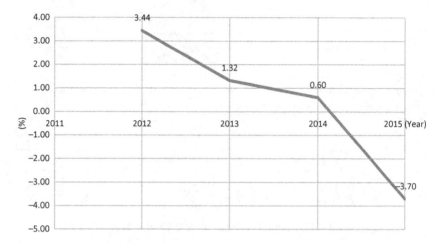

Figure 12.2   Russia's Economic Growth Rate in Recent Years

Source: The website of China's Ministry of Commerce.

Thirdly, low oil price forced Russia to transform its economic development model. This aspect of impact is more or less positive. At present, Russia is overly dependent on energy export. Due to the singular economic structure, the country is easily influenced by international market fluctuation. In addition, Russian companies lack innovation capacity, and their exported products lack technological content and competitive force, with the exception of only some military products. Although the sluggish international oil price caused tremendous economic difficulty for Russia, it also helped the country realize the unsustainable nature of its economic model and carry out reforms accordingly.

The fall of international oil price reduced the total domestic demand of Russia. Due to a serious lack of economic growth impetus, Russia accelerated implementation of its "look east strategy" and strengthened economic and trade connections with Asia Pacific countries. For example, Russia is enthusiastically participating in international organizations such as Asia-Pacific Economic Cooperation, ASEAN Regional Forum and Asian Infrastructure Investment Bank. So far, Russia has made initial achievements in its Asia Pacific strategy. Russia's volume of trade with member countries of Asia-Pacific Economic Cooperation accounts for 20% of the country's total trade volume. The oil and natural gas pipelines built by Russia in the far east region (such as the pipeline from Sakhalin to Vladivostok via Khabarovsk) will provide important energy support for economic and trade development of Russia and Asia Pacific countries. It can be anticipated that Asia Pacific countries will replace the European Union as Russia's largest trade partners.

Since Russia has shifted the focus of economy and trade to the Asia Pacific region and strengthened trade contacts with China, more Russian companies will earn RMB income and the liquidity of Russian offshore RMB market will be increased. Consequently, overseas demands for RMB loans will be increased, and RMB's functions of valuation, settlement and financial transactions will be developed in Russia.

(3) *Russia has Implemented Import Substitution Policies to Increase Demands for Chinese Commodities*

To tackle the economic crisis in 2014, the Russian government issued the *Preferential Measures for Maintaining Sustainable Development of Economy and Social Stability* on January 27, 2015. The document included 60 items on the measures to stimulate economic growth, support economic development through economic departments, maintain social stability and monitor economic and social situation, and aimed to protect important departments related to national security from risks, stabilize the severely fluctuating domestic economy, and implement structural reforms to increase Russia's middle-term and long-term economic strength (Table 12.3). Item 1–15 were financial stabilizing measures, and were the most important among the anti-crisis policies in 2015. Item 6–20 included import substitution strategies and were mainly focused on national security-related fields, such as food and medicine. Item 21–23 concerned "cost decreasing and benefit increasing" and support for medium-small enterprises. Other measures included policies to support important industries of national economy.

After the economy gradually stabilized, the Russian government issued the *Development Plan of Russian Federal Government to Guarantee Stability of Society and Economy in 2016*. The plan was considered as the 2.0 version of Russia's anti-crisis plan, but it emphasized on the import substitution strategy, which could strengthen middle-term and long-term competitive force of Russian economy (Table 12.4).

Table 12.3 Preferential Directions of Anti-crisis Plan in 2015

Aspect	Preferential Measures (60 items in total)
I. Measures to stimulate economic growth	1. Stabilizing measures (Item 1–15, focused on the financial and industrial departments, involving financial stability, capital support for banks and state-owned companies, non-performing asset clearance of banks, credit loan expansion, especially financing support for industrial departments and import substitution departments)
	2. Import substitution and support for non-raw material export (Item 16–20, involving equipment and services in the government's import plan, government purchase plans, plans for supporting state-owned holding companies, guarantees and simplified procedures for export stimulation, capital injection for state-owned policy banks)
	3. Reduce company cost (Item 21–22, involving weakening and delays of compulsory insurance and inspection measures in the fields of production and transport security)
	4. Support small and medium enterprises (Item 23–33, expanding participation of small and medium companies in public infrastructure projects, making innovation in capital support, simplifying tax procedures, reducing tax burden, simplifying procedures for entrepreneurship and patent application, and lowering thresholds of industries)
II. Supportive measures of economic departments	Item 34: Provide capital guarantee for implementing preferential directions of the national plan. Item 35: Unconditionally guarantee the completion of preferential tasks in national investment policies
	1. Agriculture (Item 36–38, reducing operation cost of agricultural companies and providing credit support)
	2. Housing construction and public housing (Item 39–40)
	3. Industry, fuels and energy (Item 41–48)
	4. Transport (Item 49–51)
III. Measures to ensure social stability	1. Facilitate adjustment of employment structure (Item 52–55)
	2. Social support for the public (Item 54–56)
	3. Guarantee for health care, drugs and medical products (Item 57–59)
IV. Monitor economic and social situations	Organize predictions for economic and social situations, and formulate measures to implement this plan (Item 60)

Source: Yin Hong (2017).

Table 12.4   Preferential Directions of Anti-crisis Plan in 2016

Aspect	Preferential Measures (120 Items in Total)
I. Urgent measures to stabilize society and economy	1. Government support in social protection and employment (Item 1–11, rescuing unemployment and issuing unemployment compensation, raising old-age pension and issuing mother fund, and maintaining stability of drug price and other prices related to people's livelihood)
	2. Support by certain economic departments (Item 12–35, plans for supporting automobile industry, including environmental protection automobiles, plans for supporting light industry, transport equipment manufacturing, agricultural machinery manufacturing, agricultural import substitution, housing construction, communication facilities and tourism, capital injection plans for large state-owned companies)
	3. Support for non-raw material export (Item 36–41, including support for high technology exports)
	4. Remove restrictions of advanced technology development (Item 42–44, necessary support for import substitution of food industry production equipment, road construction technologies and mining equipment, and for increasing international competitive force)
	5. Develop small and medium enterprises (Item 45–48, including support for not less than 70,000 small and medium enterprise projects, establishing not less than 20,000 employment positions, setting up not less than 220 small-enterprise innovation projects, and specific measures for small and medium enterprise financing and accelerated depreciation)
II. Structural measures to ensure steady development of economy and society	1. Create favorable conditions for investment (Item 49–56, improving investment environment, boosting investment enthusiasm, reducing bankruptcies, and reducing unnecessary administrative interference)
	2. Reduce economic costs (Item 57–72, reducing company cost in terms of financing, taxation and administrative charges, strengthening supervision of investment efficiency of monopolies, reducing debt burdens of federal and local finances, improving laws regarding industrial, agricultural and tourism parks)
	3. Small and medium enterprises (Item 73–92, expanding the scope of small and medium enterprises, reducing financing costs and simplifying tax procedures)
	4. Social support and social system development (Item 93–104)
	5. Regional balanced development (Item 105–109)
	6. Support for economic departments (Item 110–120)

Source: Yin Hong (2017).

The import substitution strategy was once used by Latin American countries in the 1960s–1970s. It means encouraging domestic enterprises in certain industries to conduct industrial production, and in this way, gradually casting off over-dependency on imports. Regretfully, the import substitution strategy of Latin American countries did not make a success. It is worth noting that Russia's import substitution strategy is different from that of Latin American countries. Russia does not overly emphasize trade protection policies such as quota and tariff; instead, it supports certain industries with policies in a market competition environment. The supported industries include food, national defense and medicine. The Russian government provides low-cost capital for qualified projects in the above industries. For example, the "Russian industrial development fund" had an annual interest rate of 5% and a period of 5–8 years. The fund's total scale in 2015 was 200 billion rouble, and more than 2,500 projects actually used 600 billion rouble's financial subsidies in that year (Xu Poling, 2017). Based on Russia's economic situation and industry importance, the food industry will first implement the import substitution strategy; second to the food industry is household appliances and automobile. And the last are Russia's traditional fields of advantages, such as aerospace, national defense and military industry (Most heavy machinery in these fields needs to be imported to Russia).

By taking advantage of the low exchange rate of rouble and the gradual growth of labor productivity in manufacturing industry, Russia achieved initial effects in import substitution strategy. In 2015, Russian industrial enterprises above designated size had an increase in profit, and the proportion of unprofitable companies reduced by 30% compared to the same period in 2014. However, import substitution strategy is not a new concept in Russia. In 1998 and 2008, when Russia was under the influence of international oil price fluctuation, the Russian leaders discussed this topic many times, but as the energy price recovered to the high level, economic prosperity ensued, and Russia lost the impetus to consider this long-term strategy. As a result, Russia is still troubled by the raw material economy at present. Only by implementing the import substitution strategy in the long term will Russia be able to adjust its economic structures.

According to the import substitution theory of Prebisch and Singer, if an industry of a country which does not even have production capacity intends to develop a competitive force surpassing its international peers, the country needs to increase import tariff of the final product in the beginning stage, and even forbid import of certain products (e.g. stipulation on forbidding imports of foreign products in national defense and national security fields formulated by Russia on December 24, 2013), and apply preferential import policies such as tax reduction and exemption on capital items and intermediate items used in the import substitution strategy. It can be noticed that import substitution is a long process. Russia will increase imports of capital and intermediate items in some key fields during implementation of the strategy, and our country could provide support for Russia in large machinery, parts and components. For Russia, importing these intermediate items from our country is not accompanied with political risks. Therefore, while Russia is implementing the import substitution strategy, our country should analyze vacancies in Russian market of capital and intermediate items, increase exports to Russia in relevant fields, seize the opportunity to occupy market shares, and push forward RMB valuation and settlement in trades of certain industries.

(4) *Chinese Technologies have Won the Favor of Russia Due to Investment Transfer of Developed Countries*

As the largest country in size, Russia has huge demands in transport infrastructure construction. So far, Russia has a railway length of 87,600 kilometers, ranked the second in the world. But most of the Russian railway network was built in the Soviet Union era, and concentrated in the part bordering Europe (this part accounts for 80% of the entire area of Russian railway network). Such a network is very unbalanced for a large country of railways.

Currently, Russia has three high-speed railway lines. The "Sapsan" line connects Moscow and St. Petersburg, with a total length of 650 kilometers and a max speed of 250 km/h. The line was put to operation since December 2009. The "Allegro" line connects St. Petersburg and Finnish capital Helsinki, with a total length of 443 kilometers and a maximum speed of 220 km/h. Another high-speed railway line used for Sochi Winter Olympics was completed in 2013, with a total length of 163 kilometers and a maximum speed of 180 km/h (Jiang Fachen, 2016). In terms of quantity and operation quality, Russian high-speed railway is still far behind the world advanced level.

The Russian government is paying great attention to high-speed railway development. It planned to construct 4,200 kilometers' high-speed railway lines before 2030, with a maximum designed speed of 400 km/h. Additionally, it planned to construct a railway trunk line of 7,000 kilometers, with a speed of 140–200 km/h (Cai Yuchen, 2015).

Siemens of Germany, Alstom of France, Kawasaki Heavy Industries of Japan and Bombardier of Canada are all world class enterprises in the high-speed railway field, and they have great interest in Russian high-speed railway market. For example, the Moscow-Kazan high-speed railway project had an expected investment of 1 trillion rouble. Siemens and Alstom participated in the bidding process, and Germany and France proposed to provide financing support of 1–2 billion euros. However, due to the economic sanctions caused by Ukraine crisis in 2014, the European and American companies had to withdraw from the Russian market.

As far as high-speed railway is concerned, China has obvious advantages in high-cold train technologies, stable running of trains and comprehensive prices. The Harbin-Dalian high-speed railway put to operation in 2012 was the first high-speed railway line operated in high-cold regions in the world. With the increase of operation mileage and duration, China's high-cold train technologies were gradually improved. Due to low cost of labor force, our country's high-speed railway has obvious advantages in price/performance ratio, with a whole train price 30% lower than the international peers. Because of advantages in technology and price, Chinese high-speed railway has strong competitive force in Russian high-speed railway market. Since high-speed railway projects often require huge amount of investment, our country could make full use of advantages in technology and capital, and push forward simultaneous "internationalization" of RMB and high-speed railway technologies via project loans. Currently, our country's CRRC Corporation has signed a cooperation agreement with the Russian railway company on the Moscow-Kazan high-speed railway project. And China Development Bank will provide a supportive loan of 500 billion rouble as the only Chinese financial institution involved in the project.

(5) *Russia's Far East Development Strategy will Further Deepen China-Russia Economic Cooperation*

Russia's far east region has a rich reserve of energy and borders major geo-political countries such as China and Japan; therefore, it is in an important geographical location. As a measure of economic stimulation, Russia included far east development as a national strategy in recent years. For example, in the state of the union message of 2014, president Putin requested to implement the far east development plan and proposed to develop the Pacific coast economic belt and open up a north pole ship route.

In the far east development plan, the Russian government proposed to establish 14 "leading development zones", which will provide preferential treatment for investment enterprises and individuals in terms of taxation and land. For example, the Russian government encourages the people to make investments in the far east region through the *Russian Act for Free Allocation of Land in the Far East Region*. It canceled the minimum requirement of 10% of project total investment for private investments in the far east region, in order to attract more private capital. The Russian government also promised to provide preferential loans for state-owned companies which make investments in factory establishment in the far east region. These preferential measures will help the far east region attract investments of about 270 billion rouble in 2016–2017. Rosneft Oil has declared to invest 1.3 trillion rouble to build a petrochemical enterprise in the far east region. And Russian Railway will invest 500 billion rouble for modernization improvement of Baikal-Amur railway and trans-Siberian railway (Zhang Hongxia, 2016).

The placement of far east development strategy on a fast track by Russia has provided more opportunities for deepening China-Russia economic and trade relations. In May 2014, PetroChina and Gazprom signed the *Purchase and Sales Contract of China and Russia on the East-Line Natural Gas Supply*. According to the contract, the Russian company will transmit 38 billion cubic meters' natural gas to China each year. Energy is the blood of modern industries, and construction of oil and gas pipelines in the far east region is crucial for our country's industrial development. For Russia, it opens up a new natural gas market apart from Europe. In August 2017, the Russian president Putin attended the commencement ceremony of Amurskaya natural gas processing plant, which was completely contracted to Chinese companies for construction. After completion, the natural gas processing plant will not only become the largest in the world, but signify that China-Russia energy cooperation has gone deeper than oil and gas trade into the downstream processing stage.

With the gradual progress of Russia's far east development, China and Russia are also actively cooperating in transport infrastructure. For example, both countries are co-constructing Tongjiang Railway Boundary River Bridge and the Large Harbor of Zarubino, in order to increase cross-border trade transport capacity. Our country should take advantage of the economic and trade opportunities brought about by Russia's far east development strategy, and push forward overseas RMB loans for large projects and RMB valuation and settlement for trade, services and investment in the background of increased trade and economic contacts between both countries.

(6) *The Complementary Nature of China-Russia Economy and Trade Provided Opportunities for Cross-border RMB Settlement*

China and Russia are important trade partners for each other. China is the largest source country for Russian imports. Although Russia's export to China has fluctuated in recent years, it has remained in top 5. Russia mainly exports raw material products such as minerals, and 80% of its imports are finished industrial products, such as

Table 12.5 China's Rank and Proportion in Russia's Foreign Trade with its Trading Partners

Year	Import Rank	Import Proportion (%)	Export Rank	Export Proportion (%)
2002	5	5.2	4	6.4
2003	4	5.8	4	6.2
2004	4	6.3	6	5.6
2005	3	7.4	4	5.4
2006	2	9.4	4	5.2
2007	2	12.4	7	4.3
2008	1	13.0	7	4.5
2009	1	13.4	6	5.5
2010	1	17.0	4	5.0
2011	1	15.7	3	6.7
2012	1	16.4	3	6.8
2013	1	16.9	3	6.8

Source: Zhu Zijing (2016).

machinery. China mainly imports raw material products such as minerals. Machinery and transport tools account for 45% of China's exports and the proportion is gradually rising with each year.

China and Russia strongly complement each other in trade (Table 12.5). Zhu Zijing (2016) studied the complementary nature of China-Russia trade and pointed out that more than 95% of China's exports to Russia are finished industrial products, while primary commodities only account for a very small percentage. Although miscellaneous products still account for a large proportion in the finished industrial products exported from China to Russia, the proportion is gradually decreasing with each year. With the advancement of technologies, the proportion of machinery and transport equipment in our country's exports to Russia has been increasing. Another characteristic of China-Russia bilateral trade is that most trades are conducted in goods. By the third season of 2014, goods trade took up 68% in the total trade volume, while service industry and other industries only took up 32% (Song Yina, 2016). According to research, the service industry has the strongest complementary nature in China-Russia trade, therefore our country has great potential to achieve RMB settlement in cross-border trade of the service industry.

Strengthened cooperation in technology, agriculture and energy will push forward financial cooperation of China and Russia, and financial cooperation will become a new field for strategic integration and mutual benefit of both countries. According to Yin Jianfeng's research (2011), a currency's internationalization degree is closely related to the corresponding country's pricing power in the international trading system. The simple model of "trade settlement + offshore market" cannot bring about long-term advantageous position of the currency. Instead, we should make use of the complementary advantages of trade products, build the currency internationalization model of "capital output + transnational enterprises", and create a series of transnational industrial chains, in order to increase international trade pricing power. As far as China-Russia trade is concerned, our country should take advantage of the highly complementary nature of the bilateral trade, encourage Chinese companies to develop a transnational industrial chain by using Russia's comparative advantages, and increase additional values of brands and technologies, in order to seize pricing power in China-Russia cross-border trade and push forward RMB internationalization in Russia.

(7) *Russia will Attract More Chinese Capital while Developing Investment-type Economy*

After the collapse of Soviet Union, Russia applied a "shock therapy", which reduced the position of investment in its economic development model. High consumption became the new engine of economy. In 1992, investment contributed to 35.7% of Russian GDP, but the number in 1995 was only 25.4%, while the contribution rate of consumption rose from 49.9% to 71.2% (Yin Hong, 2016). It should be pointed out that Russia's consumption-driven economy was built on "de-industrialization" due to severe economic recession. In addition, due to the "bull market" of energy price in the beginning of the 21st century, Russia became overly dependent on consumption and neglected the effect of investment. Russia's fixed-asset investment level in 1999 was only 22% of the level in 1990 when Soviet Union collapsed. Due to over-dependency on consumption-driven economy, Russia stays weak in industrial basis, and its industrial products only have a weak competitive force. Russia has always been troubled by the "Dutch disease".

Currently, Russian society has reached a consensus on the important role of investment in economic growth. The Russian prime minister Medvedev pointed out that Russian needs to increase investment in order to get out of the difficult situation. Contribution of investment in GDP growth should be raised from 20% to 24%. Currently, because of the control measures of the Russian central bank, Russia's inflation rate has reduced from 14% during the 2014 crisis to about 5%, and a low inflation rate is favorable for investment expansion.

Although China and Russia have frequent trade contacts, they have achieved little in investment relations. And the investments between both countries are overly concentrated. For example, most of Russian investments in China are focused on nuclear power plants, auto processing, chemical industry and building materials. And our country's large-project investments in Russia are in the fields of oil, natural gas and transport infrastructure. Due to unfavorable investment environments, most Chinese companies only invest in small projects in Russia in the fields of tailoring, catering, wood processing and household appliance assembly. The products in those fields only have low additional values and technological content.

In the background of European and American sanctions and low energy cost, Russian companies are unable to obtain financing in the western capital market, and the economic decline caused large outflow of capital (In 2012–2015, capitals of 53.9 billion USD, 60.3 billion USD, 152.1 billion USD and 57.5 billion USD flowed out of Russia, respectively). Russia is gradually improving its investment environment, e.g. improving economic legal system and cracking down on gray clearance in order to attract foreign capital. In 2015, Russia's rank in the international business environment rose from the 120th in 2012 to the 40th, among 183 countries. When China and Russia are deepening their economic and trade relationships, Chinese companies and technologies are growing more and more attractive for Russia. In this background, our country should push forward RMB valuation and settlement for Chinese direct investments, and also provide domestic currency loans to facilitate RMB investments in Russia.

(8) *The Rouble Internationalization Strategy could be Helpful for Development of Offshore RMB financial Centers in Russia*

As a traditional power and emerging market country, Russia has adopted the rouble internationalization strategy, which has created both competition and cooperation with RMB internationalization. Therefore, we also need to understand the rouble internationalization strategy, in order to push forward RMB internationalization in Russia.

Rouble internationalization is a long-term national strategy of Russia. In 1996, Russia achieved complete convertibility of rouble under current account. In 2003, president Putin indicated that Russia should achieve free convertibility of rouble as early as possible. In 2006, the Russian central bank removed a series of restrictions of the capital account and achieved complete convertibility of rouble under the capital account.

Another aspect of rouble internationalization is to enable rouble to become an international settlement currency. Due to geographical locations and history, the CIS countries are important carriers in rouble internationalization process. Belarus, Kazakhstan, Kyrghyzstan and Tajikistan have the highest rate of rouble use, among which Belarus uses rouble most frequently (Table 12.6). 51.9% of trades between Belarus and Russia in 2009 were settled in rouble. Completely free convertibility of rouble is quite helpful for its internationalization, and many CIS countries use rouble as the settlement currency first, because rouble could be easily converted into other currencies. In 2015, the Eurasian Economic Union initiated by Russia was formally founded, with Russia, Kyrghyzstan, Kazakhstan, Belarus and Armenia as its

Table 12.6 Currencies of Payment Between Russia and
EEC Member Countries in 2009

Unit: %

EEC Member Countries	Russian Rouble	USD	EUR
Belarus	51.9	33.6	14.0
Kazakhstan	48.5	48.1	2.1
Kyrghyzstan	25.2	62.9	11.9
Tajikistan	45.8	51.3	2.6

Source: Li Zhonghai (2011).

member countries. Since then, economic and trade connections between CIS countries has been strengthened, and their volume of trade with Russia has increased. Therefore, CIS countries could further use the rouble they obtained in trades with Russia and other CIS countries.

To accomplish rouble internationalization, Russia made a great deal of effort in pushing forward rouble valuation of energies. Firstly, Russia set up its own oil exchange in St. Petersburg and launched rouble-valuated crude oil futures contracts to challenge the petro-dollar system. But it should be noted that the current international oil transaction system is quite complex, and the European and American markets have diversified petro-financial derivatives, which Russia could not surpass in a short time. Secondly, although Russia requests countries with which it has energy trade connections to use rouble in settlement, few countries consented.

Additionally, Russia intends to transform Moscow into a world financial center to pave the way for rouble internationalization. The Russian government put forth a plan of two stages for this purpose. The first stage is to implement the regional financial center function of Moscow in 2008–2010. In this stage, works are focused on improving domestic capital market, such as securities and bonds, establishing and improving investment policies, enriching categories of financial products, protecting investors' rights and interests, and enabling Moscow to produce an irradiation effect on CIS countries. The second stage is to transform Moscow into a financial center with global influence. To serve this purpose, Russia planned to attract more foreign capitals, reduce transaction costs and improve foreign exchange laws and regulations.

It should be noted that although rouble can have a crowding-out effect on RMB, the financial infrastructure developed under rouble internationalization strategy will facilitate offshore RMB transactions in Russia and help improve RMB's financial transaction functions. Therefore, the internationalization of rouble and RMB is not a zero-sum game, and our country should encourage Moscow to become an offshore RMB transaction center in Russia.

12.4.2 *Major Problems*

(1) *China-Russia Trade Structure Needs Improvement*

China is a large country of manufacturing industry, while Russia is mostly an export country of raw materials such as energies and steel. In 1995–2011, the proportion of manufactured products in China's exports to Russia rose from 80% to 94%, while the proportion of primary commodities, resources and services reduced from 9.86% to 1.67%. However, China's manufactured products exported to Russia were mostly labor-intensive products, such as textiles, shoes, hats and foods. Among manufactured products exported from China to Russia in 1995, 41.89% were labor-intensive, 31.62% were capital-intensive, while knowledge-intensive products only accounted for 6.48%. With the improvement of our country's manufacturing industry structure, the proportion of knowledge-intensive products in exports to Russia has been rising with each year, and reached 33.83% by 2011. But capital-intensive products in the same year dropped to 6.02% and labor-intensive products still accounted for 54%. The above data means our country's exports to Russia are still focused on low-end products. On the contrary, the proportion of knowledge-intensive products in Russia's exports to China has been falling, from 61.55% in 1995 to 6.97% in 2011 (Qi Shaozhou, 2017). According to research, Russia's trade competitive force is only rising in the energy industry, but falling in other manufacturing industries. One reason is that Russia is overly dependent on energy exports, and neglects investment increase in certain key fields and future industries. On the other hand, the high barrier of Russia in its trade with China is also a cause of the above situation. In 2015, Russia charged a tariff of 15–20% over Chinese goods, which was twice of the tariff for other countries (Zhang Hongxia, 2017). Additionally, Russia's labor force is always scarce, therefore our country has comparative advantages over Russia in labor-intensive products such as textiles. It is also a major cause of the current situation of China-Russia trade.

With the increase of labor cost of our country and the development of manufacturing industry of Southeast Asian countries, the labor-intensive industry has been relocated, and our country cannot dominate Russia's low-end product market over the long term with labor cost advantages. In terms of RMB internationalization, China and Russia should optimize the trade structure and transform patterns of economic and trade cooperation. Since our country's bargaining capacity is weak in goods with low additional value, we lack the ability to persuade Russia to settle those trades in RMB.

(2) *The Banks' Cross-border RMB Settlement Business Lacks Diversity*

Currently, the major demands of Chinese and Russian companies in domestic currency settlement are focused on spot transaction products of RMB-rouble. Our country's banking industry still has a large space for exploration in interest rate swap, forward exchange rate, L/C and pledge financing, and RMB settlement has great advantages in these aspects. For example, a foreign currency L/C over 90 days needs to be included into the financial institution's short-term foreign debt limit, but RMB L/Cs are not subject to the limitation. It provides greater financing convenience for the banks and companies. According to survey, Russian companies have strong demands for rouble and RMB swaps over 3 years, but the currency swap agreements between central banks of both countries still lack the scale and duration, and the exchange rate and interest rate swap market of RMB/rouble is still far from maturing. The above situation restricted development of RMB business in Russia.

Due to the singular RMB settlement business, rouble is taking up an overly large proportion in domestic currency settlement in China-Russia trade. In 2008, rouble settlement accounted for 99.6% of domestic currency settlement (about 20 billion USD), while RMB only accounted for 0.6%. In 2016, China-Russia cross-border RMB receipt and payment reached 30.46 billion RMB, which was still lower than the proportion of rouble settlement.

(3) *Russian Businesses Only have a Low Degree of Recognition of RMB*

Since the Russian government is pushing forward rouble internationalization, RMB and rouble are in competition regarding valuation and settlement for a single trade. In addition, Russia has been suffering from severe economic conditions with the rising of trade protectionism in recent years, and Russia has the seller's rights of speech in national security-related strategic materials such as energy. Besides, the Chinese commodities exported to Russia still only have low technical content. Therefore, most Russian companies and individuals prefer rouble as the settlement currency. Although rouble devalued significantly since 2014, and the currency value fluctuation caused thoughts of currency substitution in many companies, the USD is still the primary currency for settlement between Russia and foreign countries. Russian businesses' recognition of RMB still needs improvement.

12.4.3 *Suggestions*

(1) *Our Country should Seize the Strategic Opportunities for RMB Business During American and European Sanctions Against Russia*

As Russia was accused of interfering with the USA's general election in 2016, the US Congress passed an act on a new round of sanctions against Russia on October 25, 2017. American organizations and individuals are forbidden from conducting major transactions with Russian national defense and intelligence departments, investing in

Russia's major oil pipeline projects (especially deep sea oil and natural gas in the north pole and shale oil development projects, which are major growth points of Russia's energy exports and are expected to reach 20–30% of Russia's energy exports in 2050), and investing over 10 million USD in Russia's privatization of state-owned assets. The NordStream-2 project was seriously affected by this. The project is aimed to construct a natural gas pipeline from Russia to Germany, which will provide natural gas of 55 billion cubic meters for the European Union each year. At this time, the USA did not consult with the European Union before imposing the sanctions, as it did in the Ukraine crisis in 2014; therefore, the European Union was discontent with the sanctions' influence on its benefits, and accused the USA of trying to increase international competitive force of its own shale gas through the sanctions.

The sanctions of Europe and America blocked financial channels of Russia in the international financing market. Russia lacks capital for key projects, and its demands for overseas RMB loans and products like dim sum bonds and panda bonds increased. And Russia is willing to open up its energy and infrastructure fields for our country's investment. However, we should understand that the Europe and America are not always on the same footing in terms of sanctions against Russia, just like the unilateral sanction imposed by America this time. With an increase of dependence on Russian energies, the European Union may ease the sanctions in future. Therefore, our country should seize the valuable strategic opportunity for RMB business created by the European and American sanctions, increase the width and depth of RMB business in Russia, and increase Russian companies and individuals' degree of recognition of RMB.

(2) *Precisely Meet the RMB Demands Generated in Russian Economic Reforms*

Over the long term, Russian economy has benefited from the international oil price, which has maintained at a high level; however, the international crude oil market has fluctuated in recent years, seriously affecting Russia's singular economic model. The European and

American economic sanctions starting from 2014 also had negative impacts on the Russian economy. As a result, Russia started and accelerated its economic reform process. It is paying more attention to the Asia Pacific region, upgrading economy from consumer-driven to investment-driven, and encouraging development of innovative economy. Our country is a major country in the Asia Pacific region and is in an important position in Russia's reforms. Therefore, we should seize the good opportunity by actively participating in Russia's far east development, strengthening and expanding our energy pipeline network, increasing RMB direct investment in Russia in the infrastructure field, such as roads, ports and bridges, and expanding our advantageous industries to Russia. In this process, Chinese banks should actively meet the financing requirements of relevant Russian industries, departments and companies, and by providing RMB loans, push forward RMB valuation and settlement in China-Russia direct investment and trade, and also seek more opportunities of overseas RMB loan business.

(3) *Actively Set Up and Make Full Use of China-Russia Financial Cooperation Platforms*

Russia is an original member of the BRICS New Development Bank and co-founded the China-Russia sovereign wealth fund together with China. BRICS New Development Bank is an attempt of emerging economies to set up a diversified international financial order; it aims to gather idle fund of emerging economies and seek investment opportunities in infrastructure and sustainable development projects among members. Meanwhile, the Bank could strengthen financial connection between the BRICS countries, simplify procedures of investment and loans, and also function as an IMF to provide assistance for member countries in financial difficulty (Wang Jipei, 2014).

In 2012, China and Russia co-founded the Russia-China Investment Fund (RCIF), with an initial raising of 2–4 billion USD. 70% of the fund was used in projects in Russia and CIS countries, and 30% was used in projects in China. RCIF mainly focuses on infrastructure, logistics and natural resource development projects in the far

Table 12.7   RCIF Investment Projects

Project	Date of Signature	Industry	Location
Holding the shares of Russian Forest Product Co., Ltd.	2013-10	Forestry	Russia
Investing in the construction of China-Russia cross-border railway bridge	2014-5	Transportation	China, Russia
Investing in GLP's Chinese logistics business	2014-5	Logistics	China
Investing in tourism and aging community projects	2014-5	Tourism, aging	China, Russia
Investing in construction of China-Russia High-Tech Park	2014-10	Technology	China
Investing in agricultural projects in border regions	2015-5	Agriculture	China, Russia
Setting up financing platforms	2015-5	Finance	Russia
Investing in SSJ100 passenger plane rental project	2015-5	Service	China
Holding the shares of JSC Detsky Mir	2016-1	Retail	Russia

Source: Jin Xin (2016).

east region (Table 12.7). Additionally, it also provides investment in Russia's financial field.

Our country should make use of financial platforms directly related to Russia, and direct Chinese capital into high-quality projects in different fields. Meanwhile, we should push forward RMB valuation in direct investment in Russia and facilitate RMB direct investment and capital output to Russia.

(4) *Expand RMB's Usage Scope in Russia Under China-Russia Currency Swap Account*

Currently, the capital under China-Russia currency swap agreement is used for three purposes: 1. Paying for commodities and labor imported from our country. 2. Investing in our country's inter-bank bond market. People's Bank of China issued the *Notice on Relevant Matters in Trials of Three Types of Institutions Including Overseas RMB Clearing Bank Using RMB to Invest in Inter-Bank Bond Market* in 2012. The notice allowed overseas participating banks of cross-border trade RMB settlement to invest in our country's inter-bank bond market with RMB. Our country should strengthen propaganda work, and direct Russian banks holding RMB cash to actively invest in our country's inter-bank bond market and expand channels of cross-border RMB back-flow. 3. Investing in relevant assets of other RMB offshore centers. During the first 9 months of 2014, RMB was used in 28% of all security settlements confirmed by China mainland and Hong Kong, and RMB has been steadily advancing toward the goal of becoming an investment currency. Therefore, Russia could actively participate in RMB security investment.

(5) *Improve China-Russia Cross-border Payment and Settlement Services*

To expand RMB's scope of use in Russia, we need to extend the banks' RMB-related services. Although our country has set up multiple banking branches in Russia, the Russian market entities still mainly conduct RMB current businesses, and seldom conduct transactions of RMB-related derivatives such as forward foreign exchange sales and purchase and interest rate swaps. The situation is unfavorable for promoting RMB-related products in Russia. Therefore, we should strengthen propaganda among Russian companies and citizens, and introduce how to make use the banks' RMB services to reduce exchange risks and even benefit from RMB investment. Meanwhile, we could increase Russia's QFII quota, approve founding of multiple RMB investment funds in Russia, and encourage Russian financial institutions or entities with RMB businesses to invest in our country's onshore or offshore bond and security market, in order to preserve and increase the value of RMB capital in Russia.

(6) *Explore New Highlights in RMB Settlement in Cross-border E-commerce*

Cross-border e-commerce is a new highlight in China-Russia trade relations. Our country's e-commerce platforms are developing rapidly in Russia and have gained a large number of followers. During the "double 11" shopping festival in 2014, Russia was the country with the second largest trade volume in the world, while China was the first. The AliExpress website under Alibaba was rated as the most popular online shop in Russia in 2015, with a monthly PV of 23.80 million persons-time. Today, Russia has become the largest import country for China's cross-border e-commerce, and our country's online shopping platform Taobao ships goods with a value of 4 million USD to Russia each day (Jiang Zhenjun, 2017).

To meet the large demands in Russia, our country's payment platform for cross-border e-commerce has been established, such as the Webmoney software of AliExpress. In consideration of the huge growth potential of China's cross-border e-commerce in Russian market, we could try to add the RMB payment option in payment software and allow Russian companies and individuals with RMB holdings to make payments with RMB. In this way, we could open up a new channel of RMB use for pushing forward RMB internationalization in Russia.

12.5 Conclusion

This chapter has put forward eight cooperation bases, three major problems and six suggestions in terms of pushing forward RMB internationalization in Russia.

Eight cooperation bases:

1. The financial sanctions imposed by Europe and America accelerated Russia's "de-dollarization" process. Since European and American countries forbid Russia's major financial institutions from obtaining financing in their markets, Russia is turning to RMB capital market for support.

2. The fall of international oil price urged Russia to strengthen trade and economic connection with the Asia Pacific region. Russian economy was seriously affected by the fall of international oil price, therefore Russia hopes to develop a diversified economy, and strengthen trade and economic connection with the Asia Pacific region in order to reduce impacts of oil price fluctuation on domestic economy.

3. Russia's import substitution policy increased its demands for our country's products. As a countermeasure against the European and American sanctions, Russia reduced imports from Europe and America, and turned to China for commodity imports. China-Russia bilateral trade volume increased as a result. And our country's commodities mostly possess necessary properties and technical advantages, which has laid a foundation for RMB valuation and settlement.

4. Due to investment transfer of developed countries, Chinese technologies are gaining the favor of Russia. Since Russia is in an economic turmoil, the investments of many developed countries are flowing out from Russia. Therefore, Russia turned to China in expectation for investments in relevant industries such as high-speed railway.

5. Russia's far east development strategy deepens China-Russia economic cooperation. Our country has first-mover advantages in transportation and industry, and could provide RMB-valuated services for the far east region of Russia.

6. The complementary nature of China-Russia economy and trade could provide an opportunity for cross-border RMB settlement. Strengthened cooperation between China and Russia in technology, agriculture and energy will facilitate cooperation in finance, and financial cooperation will become a new field for strategic integration and mutual benefit of both countries.

7. Russia will attract more Chinese capital in its development of investment-oriented economy. While Chinese capital is gaining popularity in Russia, we should push forward RMB valuation and

settlement for Chinese direct investment, and by providing domestic currency loans, promote RMB investments in Russia.

8. The rouble internationalization strategy also helps with the development of offshore RMB financial centers in Russia. The financial infrastructure developed under rouble internationalization strategy will facilitate RMB offshore transaction in Russia and help improve RMB's financial transaction functions.

Three major problems:

1. China-Russia trade structure still needs improvement. Since our country's exports to Russia are mostly concentrated on commodities with low additional values, we have low bargaining capacity and cannot easily persuade Russian businesses to settle in RMB.

2. The banks' cross-border RMB settlement business lacks diversity. Currently, the major demands of Chinese and Russian enterprises in domestic currency settlement are focused on spot transaction products of RMB/rouble. Our banking industry still has a large space for exploration in interest rate swap, forward exchange rate, L/C and pledge financing, and RMB settlement has great advantages in those fields.

3. Russian businesses only have a low degree of recognition of RMB. Since the Russian government is continuously pushing forward rouble internationalization, RMB and rouble are in competition in valuation and settlement for single trades.

Six suggestions:

1. Seize the strategic opportunities for RMB business created by American and European sanctions against Russia. The sanctions caused financing gaps and market vacancy in Russia. Consequently, the Russian government is seeking cooperation with China with more openness and enthusiasm in fields such as overseas RMB loans, RMB bond issuance, RMB-valuated overseas direct investment and Russian businesses' direct investment in China.

2. Precisely meet the RMB demands generated in Russia's economic reform. During Russia's economic reform process, our country should actively meet the financing requirements of relevant Russian industries, departments and companies, and by providing RMB loans, push forward China-Russia direct investment and RMB valuation and settlement in China-Russia trades, and also seek more opportunities of overseas RMB loan business.

3. Actively set up and make full use of China-Russia financial cooperation platforms. Our country should seize the good opportunity created by the sanctions, direct China-Russia investment funds to raise RMB capital and facilitate RMB direct investment and capital output to Russia.

4. Expand RMB's scope of use in Russia under the currency swap account. Our country should strengthen propaganda work, and direct Russian banks holding RMB cash to actively invest in our country's inter-bank bond market in order to expand RMB back-flow channels.

5. Improve China-Russia cross-border payment and settlement services. We should conduct promotions on how to use the banks' RMB services to reduce exchange risks and even obtain benefits from RMB investments. Meanwhile, we could increase Russia's QFII quota to expand RMB back-flow channels in Russia.

6. Explore new highlights in RMB settlement in cross-border e-commerce. In consideration of the huge growth potential of our country's cross-border e-commerce in the Russian market, we could try to add RMB payment options in payment software, and allow Russian companies and citizens with RMB holdings to make payment with RMB. In this way, we could open up a new channel of RMB use for pushing forward RMB internationalization in Russia.

Chapter 13

RMB Internationalization by Banks

Take China Development Bank for example. In November 2016, the State Council approved the *Articles of Association of China Development Bank*, and China Development Bank successfully implemented the "three steps" strategy. It clarified its mission and strengthened its advantages. By taking advantage of the opportunity of supporting Belt and Road Initiative (BRI) infrastructure, capacity and financial cooperation with the special loan of 250 billion yuan, China Development Bank could create a coordination and promotion mechanism of RMB internationalization together with People's Bank of China, facilitate regional and global economic integration, take part in offshore financial market construction, improve comprehensive marketing and risk control capabilities, strengthen high-end think tank research, connect payment systems, push forward RMB valuation and settlement for bulk commodities, and build a global value chain originating in China.

13.1 Chinese Financial Institutions' Participation in BRI Financial Cooperation

13.1.1 *Before the Belt and Road Initiative Came Forth in 2013*

Since most countries along the BRI route are developing countries with political turmoil, economic downturn and high risks of investment and financing, China's financial institutions only had a small number of establishments in those countries, and only participated in a small number of projects before the BRI came forth in 2013. China's development and policy-related financial institutions, such as China Development Bank, Exim Bank of China and China Export & Credit Insurance Corporation supported most major projects related to economic diplomacy, energy and resources and "stepping out" of Chinese companies.

13.1.2 *After the BRI Came Forth in 2013*

In recent four years, China's banking industry has fully engaged in BRI construction. Firstly, by the end of 2016, 9 Chinese banks have set up 62 primary institutions in 26 countries along the BRI route. Secondly, many Chinese banks have formulated BRI credit policies or measures, and supported major projects in fields including highway, railway, port, electricity and communication by means of bank consortium loans, industrial funds, loans for contracted foreign projects and preferential loans. Thirdly, Chinese banks have actively made innovations in business, system and management to facilitate BRI construction and provide diversified financial services for Chinese and foreign companies. Fourthly, China Development Bank and XXX Bank have provided BRI special loans of 250 billion yuan and 130 billion yuan, respectively to support infrastructure, capacity and financial cooperation. 100 billion yuan was added to the Silk Road Fund, and financial institutions will conduct overseas fund business with a scale of about 300 billion yuan. Fifthly, major breakthroughs have been made in RMB's valuation, settlement, investment and reserve functions on the way of RMB internationalization.

13.2 China Development Bank and RMB Internationalization

13.2.1 *China Development Bank's Institutional Positioning*

(1) *The History of China Development Bank as a Developmental Financial Institution*

In April 1994, China Development Bank was founded as China's earliest and largest policy-related financial institution. In 1998, China Development Bank put forward the concept of developmental finance and carried out major reforms of the credit and liability businesses, including adjusting credit structure, pushing forward credit construction, paying attention to the recycling of principal and interest, ensuring asset quality and strengthening risk control. The bank combined government credit, medium-term and long-term financing and marketized operation, actively pushed forward construction of "bottleneck" fields in economy and society, supported major domestic and international projects, and gradually developed into a major bank for medium-term and long-term investment and financing and the largest bank for overseas investment and financing cooperation in China. At the end of 2008, China Development Bank started commercialized reform as a policy-related financial institution, and carried out explorations in the economic downturn period. On one hand, it should steadily push forward commercialized transformation and prevent risks in the process. On the other hand, it should actively handle the international financial crisis and make use of the function of developmental finance to stabilize periodic fluctuation of economy. After commercialized transformation, difficulties started to emerge for China Development Bank. Since the bond credit policy extends with each year, the difficulty level and cost of bond issuance also increased. The external supervision and assessment are conducted as per the standard of commercial banks, which goes against the requirements to serve national strategy and obtain only a small profit. The operation model of China Development Bank — medium-term and long-term, wholesale, large amount and bond bank — became unsustainable.

(2) *The "Three Steps" Strategy was Successful*

In July 2013, China Development Bank formally put forward the "three steps" road map for deepening reforms. The "three steps" strategy has been successfully implemented. Step one was to solve the long-term bond credit problem. In the beginning of 2015, the State Council approved the China Development Bank's plan for deepening reforms, clarified the bank's positioning as a developmental financial institution as well as relevant policies and mechanisms, ensured long-term stability of bond credit policy, and completely solved the bank's problems in bond issuance and financing. Step two was to set up the bank's shareholding group architecture. To implement the decisions of the Party Central Committee and the State Council, China Development Bank set up a group architecture which meets the needs to serve national development strategies. Step three was to push forward legislation of China Development Bank. In November 2016, the State Council approved the *Articles of Association of China Development Bank*. The new articles of association clearly positioned China Development Bank as a developmental financial institution and emphasized characteristics of developmental finance. The successful implementation of "three steps" strategy is an important milestone in the reform and development history of China Development Bank. It completely solved the bank's problems in institution positioning, operation model, supportive policy and company governance, which had existed over many years. The "three steps" strategy has set up a group architecture of China Development Bank which serves national strategies and laid a solid foundation for pushing forward RMB internationalization in BRI construction.

13.2.2 *China Development Bank and RMB Internationalization*

In May 2017, president Xi Jinping announced in the Belt and Road Summit for International Cooperation: China Development Bank will provide special loans equivalent to 250 billion RMB to support infrastructure construction, capacity cooperation and financial cooperation of the BRI. As the largest developmental financial institution in the world, and the largest bank for overseas investment and financing, long-term and medium-term credit and bond issuance in China, China Development Bank has accumulated rich experience in supporting major infrastructure construction and pushing forward international cooperation with developmental financial methods, and is playing a unique role in serving BRI construction and RMB internationalization. Firstly, it has established close connections with relevant ministries and commissions and the government departments of the cooperative country. Therefore, it helps achieve policy connections. Secondly, it always makes plans at first. China Development Bank has rich experience in planning and cooperation, and could provide financing support for the cooperative country's economic and social development. Thirdly, it relies upon state credit, therefore it could raise long-term stable financial capital to meet the medium-term and long-term capital needs of major projects. Fourthly, it operates on the small-profit principle and does not pursue profit maximization, therefore it could more easily provide low-cost capital for major strategic projects. Fifthly, it has specialized subsidiaries such as CDB Capital, CDB Securities and CDB Leasing, which could provide diversified financial services for the cooperation project. Sixthly, marketized operation is the bank's basic operation model. During project operations, the bank keeps on improving the market mechanism and credit environment in order to prevent financing risks.

13.3 Advantages of China Development Bank to Push Forward RMB Internationalization

13.3.1 *Wholesale Bank*

Based on different customer resources, the banking business can be classified into retail banking and wholesale banking. Major customers of wholesale banking business include domestic and overseas large enterprises, financial institutions and government departments, and wholesale banking business generally involves large amount of capital. According to international currency history, a currency's internationalization process can be divided into the stages of starting, rapid progress and steady maintenance. In terms of the relationship between currency internationalization and banking business, the starting stage is characterized by retail banking. When retail banking has developed to a certain level, wholesale banking will start its development, and currency internationalization will enter the rapid progress stage. After a virtuous cycle is formed, currency internationalization will enter the steady maintenance stage, in which the banks rely mainly on retail business, and conduct wholesale business as a supplement. China Development Bank relies upon state credit, and raises long-term capital through bond issuance. Compared with the medium-term and short-term capital sources of commercial banks, it does not have the contradiction of "short-term deposit, long-term loans", and therefore it has obvious advantages in supporting major wholesale businesses such as infrastructure and capacity cooperation. Currently, China Development Bank is responsible for implementing the BRI special loan equivalent to 250 billion RMB. It could make use of the advantages of wholesale banking business in scale, influence, irradiation and driving force, and more actively push forward RMB internationalization into the rapid progress stage.

13.3.2 *Bank-government Cooperation*

Based on the successful experience of major international currencies, the governments of various countries have played an important role. The British government seized the historical opportunity and became the leader of the first industrial revolution. It strongly advocated manchesterism, exported advantageous products overseas, invested in many countries in the form of capital, and established GBP as an international currency. The US government strongly pushed forward USD internationalization, and by making use of international rules such as "Bretton Woods System" and GATT, it vigorously developed the financial market and strengthened USD's core position in international trade and financial fields. The key to making a success in developmental finance in China is to build a bridge between the government and the market. China Development Bank took into consideration China's national condition, learned from globally advanced principles, transformed government advantages into market driving force, and played a unique role in improving our country's financial ecology and facilitating reforms of investment and financing mechanism. While pushing forward RMB internationalization in BRI construction, China Development Bank could make use of the advantages of bank-government cooperation, closely cooperate with relevant government departments, conduct policy communication and coordination with countries along the BRI route, and create a sound cooperation environment with smooth Currency swap on the government relation level.

13.3.3 *Overseas Deployments*

Since the 1990s, China's commercial banks has started implementing the "step out" strategy. Most of their overseas branches were set up in developed countries or relatively developed countries and districts. In recent years, they have started setting up branches in countries along the BRI route, but since different countries have different approval policies, the speed of deployments cannot meet the needs of Chinese companies of "stepping out" in the short term. China Development Bank started comprehensive overseas deployments since 2005. Its overseas branch network mostly takes the form of work teams, and covers 197 countries and districts, which basically include all countries and districts along the BRI route. The bank's overseas business has mostly adopted the model of medium-term and long-term wholesale bank, which has flexible work methods, high level of connection and smooth capital transmission route. China Development Bank has also created good interactive relationships with the host country's government, central bank, major commercial banks and other financial institutions, and established cooperation mechanisms with financial institutions including major Chinese banks and China Export & Credit Insurance Corporation. The bank could make use of the advantages of overseas bank-government-company cooperation platform in major projects. It has strong capacity to direct social capital, and could effectively push forward RMB internationalization in BRI construction.

13.3.4 *The Driving Force of Market*

In the perspective of currency circulation scope and extent of use, a currency's circulation and use in the home country is controlled by the country's sovereign force, and currency internationalization is essentially the result of competition between various countries in comprehensive strength. Currency internationalization is driven by market demands and reflects the political and economic position of the issuing country's sovereign credit in the world. Therefore, we must observe economic rules while pushing forward RMB internationalization. The government's direction is necessary, but marketized operation should be the fundamental driving force of RMB internationalization. Developmental finance is a form of finance which operates on marketization. China Development Bank's transformation from a policy-related bank to a developmental financial institution is the result of successful marketized operation. It could both obtain a small profit and serve the nation's strategic objectives. China Development Bank has a rich experience in marketized operation. It encourages the companies to play a principal role in BRI construction, and by following the principle of market driving, commercialized operation, discussion, co-development, sharing, equality and mutual benefit, it conducts economic and financial cooperation with relevant countries and effectively pushes forward RMB internationalization.

13.3.5 *Plan First*

"Plans developed within the tent, decide victories a thousand miles away." China Development Bank's "plan first" has become its unique brand in developmental finance. Plans are different from projects. Projects are localized, specific and implemented in the short term; while in comparison, plans focus on comprehensive development, and on solving macroscopic, strategic and long-term issues. By scientifically formulating development plans, the decision-making entity and executive entity could actively grasp objective rules, develop advanced and systematic objectives and pathways, and guide practice with issues. During BRI construction, China Development Bank adheres to the "plant at first" principle, increases the initiative, foresight and innovation in works, cooperates with Chinese and foreign government departments in major cooperative planning, mobilizes the initiative of companies, allocates various elements and resources, systematically constructs key large projects, and encourages various parties to create a joint force. While pushing forward RMB internationalization, China Development Bank could take advantage of the "plan first" principle, strengthen cooperation with Chinese and foreign governments, banks, companies and think tanks, make an overall plan and blueprint for implementing various functions of RMB in its internationalization, and make major breakthroughs in a targeted manner.

13.3.6 *Equity Investment*

With the development of capital market, the advantages of equity investment are becoming prominent. Equity investment could become a major source of company financing, and could function as a financial lever to lever up credit's right financing such as bank credit and increase the rate of return of the company's capital. In the beginning stage of BRI construction, the capital markets of many countries along the BRI route are still underdeveloped and need the support of policy capital to create a virtuous cycle of equity investment and creditors' investment. President Xi Jinping announced in the Belt and Road Summit for International Cooperation that China will strengthen support for BRI construction with equity capital, and add 100 billion RMB to the Silk Road Fund. China will also encourage financial institutions to conduct RMB overseas fund business, with a scale of about 300 billion RMB. China Development Bank has accumulated rich experience of equity investment through the platforms such as CDB Capital and China-Africa Fund. Therefore, it could flexibly provide diversified investment-based or portfolio-based financial products according to the characteristics and needs of the company and project, including quasi-equity investment methods such as ordinary equity investment, preferred stock, convertible bond and mixed capital tool as well as mezzanine investment methods. It could also set up a "mother fund" to invest in other funds, and facilitate RMB financing in countries along the BRI route, in a variety of aspects.

13.3.7 *Bond Bank*

Currently, a major obstacle of RMB internationalization is the small percentage of RMB valuation and settlement in international trade, but this is only a superficial phenomenon. Apart from trade structure and currency inertia, the in-depth causes of this phenomenon mainly include the fact that available overseas RMB financial products are too few in quantity, and cannot meet the needs of asset value preservation and liquidity. RMB internationalization has fallen into a dilemma. If the overseas RMB capital pool is too small, RMB internationalization cannot be achieved. If the overseas RMB capital pool is too large, there will not be enough investment products for the large amount of capital, and an "asset shortage" will occur. Therefore, in order to push forward RMB internationalization, we must set up an RMB offshore market, and steadily increase high-quality RMB-valuated financial assets in the international financial market, especially the fixed-income financial products, such as bonds, which have smaller risks and strong credit guarantee capacity. China Development Bank has a state credit rating and is a pioneer of marketized bond issuance. In 2007, the bank issued RMB bonds of 5 billion yuan in Hong Kong as the first domestic financial institution. Through bond issuance, China Development Bank could transform short-term scattered funds in the market into large amount of capital, and effectively implement RMB's international currency functions while supporting major projects in BRI construction.

13.3.8 *Comprehensive Marketing*

In overseas investment and trade activities, RMB internationalization has two direct driving forces: low cost and convenient service. Most countries in the BRI region are developing countries. Their financial system and services are relatively weak, and the banking industries have a large space for cooperation. Diversity of financial products for real economic cooperation between China and foreign countries needs to be increased. To meet the urgent requirements of our country's market economy system reforms, China Development Bank focused on medium-term and long-term credit as its core business in the beginning of its foundation, and subsequently made innovation in business, system and management. The bank's capabilities were strengthened and formed a complete comprehensive marketing system under the group architecture. Therefore, it could provide diversified financial services for Chinese and foreign companies, including investment, loans, bonds, rentals and securities. In recent years, China Development Bank has taken the lead to encourage Chinese companies to participate in the BRI construction, established coordination mechanisms with various financial institutions engaged in pushing forward RMB internationalization, widely participated in or supported RMB overseas direct investment, RMB offshore financial market construction, trade settlement and currency swap, and provided convenience for Chinese and foreign parties to use RMB funds. Therefore, comprehensive marketing has prominent advantages in pushing forward RMB internationalization during the BRI construction.

13.3.9 *Risk Control*

The capability of risk management and control is China Development Bank's core competitive strength. China Development Bank has established the objective of stabilizing asset quality, and is dedicated to protecting national financial and economic security. Its dynamic risk management and control system with developmental finance characteristics has also gradually improved. By the end of 2016, China Development Bank had a total asset of 14.3 trillion RMB, and its non-performing loan ratio was kept below 1% over 47 consecutive seasons. Therefore, the bank achieved financial balance, maintained sustainable development, and is able to serve national strategies in the long term. In the BRI construction, China Development Bank only maintains a small profit and does not pursue profit maximization. It first set up a complete market system environment and credit structure, and by solving market absence with developmental finance, it created a sound market order and system rules for the entrance of commercial finance and social capital, and optimized the environment for RMB internationalization. Some major projects in BRI construction are in the blue-sea fields which profit-driven capitals cannot or are unable to enter. China Development Bank entered these fields according to international conventions and market rules; it played a pioneering role and conducted counter-cyclic adjustments. After the success of the projects, the bank will direct commercial capital and various social capitals to flow in, and effectively implement RMB's various international currency functions.

13.3.10 *Learning and Innovation*

China Development Bank has always been learning and making innovations during its growth and development. In a period of 20 years, China Development Bank developed from a registered capital of 50 billion yuan to a total asset of 14.3 trillion yuan, from a policy bank supporting "infrastructure, basic industry and pillar industry" to the largest developmental financial group in the world, and from the first breakthrough in international business to becoming China's largest overseas investment and financing bank. The outstanding success of China Development Bank is attributed to its people's effort to serve national strategies, adjust to domestic and overseas situations and keep on learning and making innovation. It can be said that the capabilities of learning and making innovation is the largest advantage of China Development Bank. Pushing forward RMB internationalization in BRI construction is a grand project which is long-term, systematic, theoretical and involves multiple fields and high level of complexity. It requires China Development Bank to make full use of its advantages in learning and innovation, and become a pioneer which builds its own way. At the new historical starting point, China Development Bank should strive to become a world-leading developmental financial institution, serve national strategies with marketized methods, and play a unique role in economic and social development and the financial system. It should make progress and breakthroughs with a strong willpower and fulfill its national missions with dedication.

13.4 Suggestions for Banks to Push Forward RMB Internationalization

13.4.1 *Closely Cooperate with People's Bank of China to Create a Coordinated Driving Mechanism of RMB Internationalization*

People's Bank of China is our country's central bank and is the main institution in charge of RMB internationalization. China Development Bank should actively cooperate with People's Bank of China, create a coordinated driving mechanism, strengthen RMB credit granting cooperation with central banks and financial institutions of countries along the BRI route, and systematically push forward RMB internationalization. According to the internationalization experience of GBP, USD, JPY and EUR, the joint force created by the central bank, relevant institutions and cooperative countries is the key to achieving internationalization of the domestic currency. The Federal Reserve is the USA's central bank. In the 10-year period following its foundation in 1914, the Federal Reserve enabled USD to become the official foreign exchange reserve currency of various countries, led the construction of international currency system, and established the USD's hegemonic position in the world in aspects of international exchange rate arrangement, currency reserve and balance of payments mechanism. The British central bank effectively solved multiple credit crises of GBP including devaluation and payment crises by currency swaps and overseas loans, boosted the enthusiasm of overseas non-residents to use GBP, and increased overseas GBP stock. Countries along the BRI route have a solid foundation for political and economic cooperation with China. They have high expectations for China's investment as well as trade and financial cooperation with China, and are also highly dependent on the above. Therefore, they greatly appreciate RMB internationalization. People's Bank of China should seize the good opportunity, strengthen effective communication and cooperation with central banks of relevant countries, try to set up a cooperative organization of central banks for BRI, help create a regional currency cooperation system centering on RMB, and accelerate implementation of RMB's international currency functions.

13.4.2 *Achieve a Virtuous Cycle of RMB in Infrastructure and Capacity Cooperation*

Countries along the BRI route are mostly emerging economies and developing countries. These countries have singular industrial structures, and their exported products are mostly primary products. They have large deficits in foreign trade and unbalanced international payments. After the global economic crisis, these countries only have a weak capacity of attracting investment and financing. In addition, many of these countries are in the recovery or rising stages of economic development. They have rich natural resources, a strong demand for development and a large space for cooperation. While conducting infrastructure and capacity cooperation with countries along the BRI route, we should focus on building a global value chain originating in China, always plan before taking actions, and optimize the investment and trade environment for RMB internationalization. To overcome externality in infrastructure construction and prevent investment and financing risks, China Development Bank should pay high attention to credit structure construction and actively take part in integrating the host country's upstream and downstream industrial chains, while supporting Chinese companies and countries along the BRI route to conduct infrastructure construction cooperation. In terms of capacity cooperation, China Development Bank should make appropriate arrangements while supporting China's high-end, medium-end and low-end industrial output, help relevant countries improve industrial structure with RMB capital, and facilitate RMB valuation and settlement with investment and trade. To direct relevant countries to cast off over-dependency on USD in foreign exchange receipts and payments, China Development Bank should actively connect to the development strategies of these countries, help them increase capabilities of production, processing and earning foreign exchanges (RMB) through exports, and also help them make improvements on trade deficits and balance of payments in order to create a currency substitution effect of RMB, increase possibility of using RMB as a foreign investment and reserve asset, and help create a virtuous cycle of RMB in the BRI region.

13.4.3 *Facilitate Regional and Global Economic Integration in Serving Economic Diplomacy*

According to the historical experience of major international currencies, a currency's internationalization process is always accompanied by the issuing country's regional economic integration and economic globalization. The internationalization of GBP is attributed to the foreign trade, investment and financial cooperation conducted by the UK through colonial expansion. The USD's hegemonic position was inseparable from the international rules such as "Bretton Woods System" and GATT led by the USA, as well as the great contribution of "Marshall Plan". The birth of euro took place because the statesmen of European countries transformed the "optimum currency area" theory into reality. The failure of JPY internationalization was because Japan was overly dependent on the USA and Europe and neglected cooperation with Asian countries at the early stage. Later, when Japan put forward the "Asian currency" concept, it had already missed the good opportunity due to economic recession. China Development Bank could make full use of its functions to serve economic diplomacy, cooperate with our country's government departments, focus on emerging economies along "Belt and Road", strengthen cooperation with developed countries, and encourage Chinese companies to expand the overseas market. It should construct inter-governmental cooperation mechanisms in regions along BRI and in Africa and Latin America, remove obstacles which block flows of industry, capital, material, talent and technology, avoid investment and trade frictions, facilitate regional and global economic integration, push forward opening and development of regional financial markets, set up regional currency stability systems and credit systems, create a joint force pushing forward RMB internationalization, establish a two-way optimum flow channel for RMB in China and overseas, and construct a new international system and order, in order to lay a solid foundation of international cooperation for RMB internationalization and facilitate RMB's wide use in surrounding countries, important regions and the entire world.

13.4.4 *Participate in Offshore Financial Market Construction to Increase Liquidity of Overseas RMB Assets*

In the background of managed opening of China's capital account, building domestic and overseas RMB offshore financial markets, expanding the overseas RMB capital pool, making innovation in RMB financial products and pushing forward interconnection of onshore market and offshore market are the essential pathway to achieving RMB internationalization. In addition, RMB offshore financial markets could effectively prevent overseas hot money speculation, isolate international financial risk transmission and protect healthy growth of domestic industries. With the deepening of BRI construction, demands for RMB offshore financial markets and financial products related to trade and investment will increase rapidly. To meet the customers' requirements for RMB capital and financial services, China Development Bank should make full use of the advantages of its Hong Kong branch, Shenzhen branch and Shanghai branch, actively participate in the construction of domestic and overseas RMB offshore financial centers, and build a diversified RMB offshore financial market in qualified countries along the BRI route. China Development Bank could develop bond products, currency fund products, derivative products and foreign exchange products valuated and settled in RMB in the offshore financial markets to meet the investment requirements of global customers and attract domestic and overseas banking and non-banking institutional investors and individual investors. It should make innovation in credit financial products and services, and provide convenience for companies to conduct RMB cross-border financing with fixed-income financial assets such as bank deposits and bonds. On the basis of traditional cross-border businesses such as international credit, bond issuance and foreign exchange trade, China Development Bank should accelerate innovation in RMB investment and financing products and achieve multi-level development of RMB internationalization driven by trade, investment and financial product innovation.

13.4.5 *Provide Convenience for RMB Investment and Trade with High-quality Comprehensive Marketing*

Currently, China Development Bank has prominent advantages in supporting Chinese companies' overseas investment and trade with medium-term and long-term loans. To push forward RMB internationalization in BRI construction, China Development Bank could take advantage of its comprehensive finance license, make innovations to launch various targeted financial products, provide high-quality comprehensive financial services for Chinese and foreign parties, provide convenience for RMB investment and trade activities, and play its role as the main bank in BRI construction. Firstly, it should make a comprehensive marketing plan. China Development Bank should make use of the advantages of the bank-government-company cooperation platform, satisfy the demands of Chinese companies and cooperative countries in BRI construction, and formulate different policies for different countries and companies. Secondly, it should accelerate deployments of overseas branches and institutions. By means of overseas branches, representative offices and work groups, it should construct bank cooperation systems such as agent banks together with domestic and overseas commercial banks and financial institutions engaged in BRI construction. By using the most advanced financial technology, it should integrate the cross-border RMB cooperation and service system. Thirdly, it should strengthen prospective and refined RMB financial product innovation. On the basis of medium-term and long-term credit, it should provide comprehensive financial services in the form of investment, bonds, securities and rentals, such as equity investment, bond issuance and underwriting, investment banks, securities brokerage, asset management and asset securitization, and also provide comprehensive rental services for high-quality customers in the fields of aviation, infrastructure, ship, commercial vehicle and engineering machinery. Fourthly, it should direct social capital to widely participate in BRI construction. While providing comprehensive marketing services, China Development Bank should pay attention to system and credit construction, cultivate a mature and complete financial market, and create a joint force pushing forward RMB internationalization.

13.4.6 *Increase Risk Management and Control Capability to Ensure Smooth Progress of RMB Internationalization*

Foreign financial cooperation is the core content of RMB internationalization, and maintaining financial security and stability is the precondition for the success of foreign financial cooperation. The Central Economic Working Conference at the end of 2016 clearly requested to "attach more importance to prevention and control of financial risks". In the background of economic globalization, overflow effect of financial crisis is prominent, and international financial risks are transferred at a high speed. The risk overflow effect caused by adjustment of currency policies and financial policies of countries along the BRI route could produce major external impact on our country's financial security. To push forward RMB internationalization in BRI construction, China Development Bank needs to realize the nation's specific policy objectives on the basis of marketized operation. Therefore, it is under great pressure of risk management and control. The financial risks it is facing mainly arise from factors including the long investment period, large amount, concentrated industries and customers, international environment and frequent variation of macro-economy. China Development Bank should strengthen comprehensive risk management, continuously push forward risk culture construction, strengthen risk management and control for key countries, industries and customers, steadily improve the risk management responsibility system, and keep enhancing the risk management and control capabilities. In BRI construction, China Development Bank should strengthen country risk analysis and credit system construction, provide financial services by focusing on companies, adhere to the marketization principle in project operation, make use of the advantages of bank-government-company cooperation platform, ensure information symmetry between different cooperative parties, help companies to make prudent decisions and conduct rational project investment, avoid blind decision-making, investment and expansion, prevent failures of major project investments, and ensure smooth progress of RMB internationalization.

13.4.7 *Provide Decision-making Bases for RMB Internationalization Through High-End Think Tank Research*

The grand project of RMB internationalization is a long-term, systematic, theoretical and practical project which closely connects different fields. Without the guidance of proper theories, it is difficult to achieve real effect, and the improper efforts may even cause systematic financial risks. The Belt and Road Summit for International Cooperation advocated the construction of a BRI think tank research, communication and cooperation network in order to provide intellectual support for countries along the BRI route, gather different opinions and reach a consensus. China Development Bank has combined intellect with financing, and established close cooperative relationships with international organizations, Chinese and foreign government departments, companies and financial institutions. The bank has been contributing to BRI construction with macro-policies and financial research by its internal research and planning institutions. Therefore, it is already playing the role of a national think tank. To push forward RMB internationalization, China Development Bank should strengthen capabilities of high-end think tank research, pay attention basic theoretical research of RMB internationalization, take into consideration national policies and strategies, analyze big data of investment, trade and financial cooperation, and put forward practicable operation suggestions. While conducting high-end think tank research for RMB internationalization, China Development Bank should understand relevant positioning and direction, wisely make long-term plans, closely cooperate with decision-making departments responsible for pushing forward RMB internationalization, such as People's Bank of China, conduct prospective, targeted and reserved policy research, make full use of the advantages of developmental finance, identify issues and find answers in practice, make breakthroughs in innovation, and provide scientific bases for the central government to make decisions.

13.4.8   *Connect with and Improve the Currency Payment System of Countries Along the Belt and Road Initiative Route*

Currently, the development of financial infrastructure of countries along the BRI route is unbalanced, and many countries' RMB payment systems are incomplete. It has become a bottleneck in the effort to push forward RMB internationalization. In countries along the BRI route, such as Egypt, where I worked, opening an inter-bank RMB account is a difficult matter for both residents and non-residents, not to mention RMB circulation. These countries need to connect with a payment system which can serve RMB's internationalized functions of valuation, settlement, investment and reserves. An important foundation of currency integration of EU counties is the fact that 16 countries in Europe co-founded the European Payments Union as early as 1950, and effectively solved problems of currency settlement and free convertibility between the countries. Our country should learn from the USA's Clearing House Inter-bank Payment System (CHIPS), and by commercialized operation, improve RMB's Cross-border Inter-bank Payment System (CIPS), and conduct final clearing via the China National Advanced Payment System (CNAPS). Our country should increase clearing efficiency, reduce clearing cost, comprehensively monitor RMB cross-border transaction, provide necessary financial infrastructure assurance for pushing forward RMB internationalization, and provide convenience for RMB capital to support BRI investment, trade and financial cooperation. While implementing the RMB special loans, China Development Bank could help connect to and improve the currency payment system of countries along the BRI route, and build an RMB circulation channel required by financing, trade connection and facility connection.

13.4.9   *Push Forward RMB Valuation and Settlement for Bulk Commodities of Countries Along Belt and Road Initiative Route*

Bulk commodities are the leading commodities in international trade, and mainly include oil, steel, non-ferrous metal, ore and bulk farm products. Among them, oil transaction is the most important and frequent benchmark transaction. One cause of the failure of JPY internationalization was that JPY's valuation and settlement functions in international trade were not fully developed. The USA is a large country of oil consumption. Although it is not an OPEC member, it has great influence on global oil price. In the 1970s, the USA and Saudi Arabia reached an "unshakable" agreement which established the USD as oil's unique pricing currency. And the USA stabilized USD's position in international oil trade by means of oil finance. Bulk commodity trade has a strong currency inertia and is the key to achieving currency substitution in international trade. Iraq and Iran once tried to valuate and settle oil trade with currencies other than USD, but failed due to extra-territorial interference and domestic political turmoil. In 2015, China and Russia successfully tried to settle oil trade with RMB. In 2016, China surpassed the USA as the largest oil import country. Taking this as a starting point, China Development Bank could make use of the advantages of large-amount credit support, vigorously push forward RMB valuation and settlement for bulk commodities such as oil and natural gas in countries along the BRI route, such as Saudi Arabia and Egypt, gradually increase RMB's use in international trade and make breakthroughs in different aspects of RMB internationalization.

13.4.10 *Build a Global Value Chain Originating in China in Countries along "Belt and Road"*

The BRI covers more than 60 countries and districts across Asia, Africa and Europe, including 43 countries in Asia, 16 countries in Middle East, 4 countries in CIS and 1 country in Africa. These countries and districts have a total population exceeding 4.4 billion, accounting for 63% of world population. Their economic aggregate accounts for 30% of the global value, therefore they have a huge market potential. BRI construction will help create a new production network and consumption market across Europe, Asia and Africa, a new space of growth for European, Asian and African economy and even the global economy, and a global production chain and value chain centering on China.

With the healthy adjustment of domestic economic structure, China's industries are advancing toward the high end of global value chain, and China has the capabilities to transfer advantageous capacity overseas and expand foreign trade cooperation. While supporting major projects in BRI construction, China Development Bank could make plans at first, direct Chinese and foreign companies to integrate the host country's resources, reasonably arrange upstream and downstream industries, promote RMB valuation and settlement, optimize the investment and trade environment of RMB internationalization, direct commercial bank capital and social capital into projects, encourage Chinese and foreign companies to participate in BRI construction with different cooperative models such as PPP (Public Private Partnership), EPC+F (Engineering Procurement Construction + Financing), PFI (Private Finance Initiative) and BOT (Build-Operate-Transfer), and create a joint force of investment and financing cooperation. China Development Bank could cooperate with relevant departments of our country, comprehensively connect with developed countries actively engaged in BRI construction and countries along the BRI route, and motivate relevant countries to reduce customs clearance cost and logistics cost, save time and cost of company investment and trade, and increase transparency and predictability of government policies. It should help create a fast and efficient trade environment, enable relevant countries to obtain more benefits from the global value chain, and more stably operate the supply chain of China output in the regions along BRI, in order to create a global value chain originating in China and facilitate RMB internationalization.

14

Breakthrough of RMB Internationalization in Egypt

In January 2016, President Xi Jinping conducted a state visit in Egypt and published a five-year implementation plan on strengthening both countries' comprehensive strategic partnership together with Egyptian president Abdel Fattah al Sisi. According to the plan, both countries would connect their development strategies and visions, focus on infrastructure construction and capacity cooperation, and work together to transform Egypt into a supporting point of the Belt and Road Initiative (BRI). The plan created conditions for the first breakthrough of RMB internationalization in Egypt.

14.1 Basic Information of the Project

On September 17, 2017, China Development Bank and SAI-Bank signed a special loan of 260 million RMB and a special loan of 40 million USD for medium-small companies in Africa in Cairo, Egypt. It was the first landing of the BRI RMB special loan projects in Egypt. On the same day, China Development Bank and Banque Misr signed the *Memorandum of Understanding for "Belt and Road" RMB Special Loan Cooperation Between China and Egypt*, and both parties planned to actively push forward RMB loan cooperation. The special loan of 260 million RMB would be used to support project construction in Egypt in fields of infrastructure, electricity, energy, communication, transportation, agriculture, medium-small enterprises, and "step out" of Chinese companies. The special loan of 40 million USD would be used to support project construction of small and medium companies in Egypt. Song Aiguo, the Chinese ambassador to Egypt, Wang Yongsheng, the vice president of China Development Bank, Ackoff, the vice president of Banque Misr and Magrudi, the vice president of SAI-Bank attended the signing ceremony and made their speeches.

Ambassador Song Aiguo indicated in his speech that China and Egypt have been good friends in history. In the new historical condition, both countries are supporting each other and going hand-in-hand on the way of national development and rejuvenation. With the progress of China's BRI and the steady implementation of Egypt's "new Suez Canal corridor" development plan, China and Egypt have demonstrated more common characteristics, and both countries are welcoming a new historical opportunity for deepening comprehensive strategic cooperation. The RMB loan agreement signed between China Development Bank and SAI-Bank signified the first landing of China's overseas RMB loans in Egypt. It is a concrete cooperative project which implemented the decision of the heads of both countries in the BRICS summit in Xiamen, and an important step in the development of China-Egypt bilateral relationship. China-Egypt relationship has a bright future. China Development Bank, Banque Misr and SAI-Bank contributed a lot to the development of China-Egypt bilateral relationship, and hopefully both countries will cooperate to make more achievements in future.

Mr. Wang Yongsheng indicated in his speech that the special loan equivalent to 250 billion RMB set up by China Development Bank to support BRI construction is an important result of the Belt and Road Summit for International Cooperation held in May 2017. The RMB loan contract and memorandum of understanding signed this time signified the first breakthrough of RMB loans in Egypt. It is also an important measure to implement the decisions of the heads of China and Egypt in Xiamen summit in September 2017. The signing of the contracts has profound significance and a demonstrative effect for accelerating RMB internationalization, promoting China-Egypt capacity cooperation by means of financial cooperation, and facilitating China-Egypt investment and trade. It will provide a strong support for both countries' economic and trade development, capacity cooperation and upgrade, as well as "stepping out" effort of Chinese companies.

Mr. Ackoff, the vice president of Banque Misr indicated that Banque Misr is the second largest bank in Egypt and has a full commercial bank license. It almost participated in the construction of all state-level key projects in Egypt. In January 2016, Banque Misr and China Development Bank signed a special loan agreement of 100 million USD for medium-small companies in Africa. During the Belt and Road Summit for International Cooperation in May 2017, both countries signed a loan agreement of 500 million USD, which signified China's friendly support for Egypt. Mr. Ackoff hoped China Development Bank would continue to support Egypt's comprehensive finance, and that both banks would strengthen cooperation in the fields of RMB, infrastructure, capacity and consortium loans.

Mr. Magrudi, the vice president of SAI-Bank indicated that China and Egypt have a long friendship in history, and share the same values of peaceful coexistence and win-win cooperation. Mr. Magrudi was greatly honored to cooperate with such a great nation of China. The signing of the loan agreement is the first time of cooperation between SAI-Bank and China Development Bank. Mr. Magrudi hoped both banks could establish a mechanism and system for long-term cooperation, and conduct more projects beneficial for the people of both countries in future.

14.2 The Belt and Road Initiative Created Conditions for RMB Internationalization in Egypt

14.2.1 *Basic Information of Egypt*

Egypt is one of the four great ancient civilizations, and its full name is The Arab Republic of Egypt. Egypt's national territorial area is 1.00145 million square kilometers. The population in June 2017 was about 94.6 million. Islam is Egypt's state religion, and most believers are in the Sunnite, accounting for 84% of total population. Coptic Christians and believers of other religions account for 16%, and additionally, there are 8 million expatriates. The official language of Egypt is Arabic. The capital is Cairo, and major cities include Alexandria, Luxor, Aswan and Suez. Egypt and China have been in good friendship in history, and Egypt is the first Arabic and African country which established a diplomatic relation with new China. Egypt is located at the intersection of Asia, Africa and Europe, and the Suez Canal is located in Egypt, therefore Egypt has important geo-advantages and an important strategic position. In terms of politics, Egypt has been the leader of 22 Arab league countries over the long term, and plays a demonstrative role for 57 countries in Africa. It is also an influential country among 17 countries in Middle East. In terms of economy, Egypt's total GDP in 2016 was about 300 billion USD, ranked the 38th in the world, and was only second to Saudi Arabia and the UAE in Middle East, and second to Nigeria and South Africa in Africa. Therefore, Egypt is an important regional economy power.

14.2.2 *Major Obstacles for RMB's Exchange and Use in Egypt*

In history, as with many countries, Egypt's foreign investment and trade cooperation were mostly conducted in USD and EUR. The domestic currency of Egypt is Egyptian pound. In the foreign exchange rate system of major banks in Egypt, the currencies directly convertible with Egyptian pound only include USD, EUR, GBP and the currencies of several major neighboring countries such as SAR. RMB cannot be exchanged and used in Egypt because of three realistic obstacles. Firstly, Egypt is dependent on USD and EUR. Egypt had been the colony of France and England successively, and obtained the USA assistance after World War II, therefore it has close cooperative relationships with the USA and European countries. Most of Egypt's foreign exchange assets are USD, therefore Egypt has strong currency dependency. Secondly, USD has a strong currency inertia in China-Egypt economic and trade cooperation. China and Egypt have a close economic and trade relationship in recent years. The volume of trade between China and Egypt in 2016 has exceeded 10 billion USD, but the major currency for valuation and settlement between Chinese and Egyptian companies is USD. A strong currency inertia is existing between both countries. Thirdly, RMB's convertibility and use in Egypt have not been approved by the Egyptian government. RMB internationalization started in 2009 and has been making rapid progress so far, but it has not reached Egypt. In the global credit currency system, currencies have sovereign properties, and the government's approval is the precondition for any currency to be exchanged and circulated in a country. Our country could enable RMB to be approved by the Egyptian government through the "event driving" process.

14.2.3 *The Belt and Road Initiative Created Conditions for RMB's Landing in Egypt*

Deepened cooperation between China and Egypt on BRI created important conditions for RMB's landing in Egypt. Firstly, the central banks of China and Egypt signed a currency swap agreement, which provided policy assurance for RMB's landing in Egypt. On December 6, 2016, People's Bank of China and Central Bank of Egypt (hereinafter referred to as Egyptian central bank) signed a bilateral domestic currency swap agreement with a scale of 18 billion RMB/47 billion EGP, in order to maintain financial stability of both countries and facilitate bilateral trade and investment. The agreement has a term of 3 years and is extensible upon both parties' consent. Secondly, Egyptian central bank became the borrower of USD loans of China Development Bank. The loan cooperation paved the way for RMB loans. On January 21, 2016, China Development Bank and the Egyptian central bank signed a loan agreement of 1 billion USD in order to strengthen Egypt's foreign exchange reserve and help the Egyptian central bank increase liquidity. It was the first time for China Development Bank to grant credit of a large-amount loan to an overseas central bank. Thirdly, China and Egypt are deepening cooperation in investment and financing, which produced a huge demand for RMB capital. China and Egypt established a coordination mechanism for capacity cooperation and set out multiple priority cooperation projects in the fields of electricity, transportation, port and urban construction, such as the State Grid and Teda Suez Canal Park. Thus, a strong capital demand emerged for RMB internationalization in Egypt. Fourthly, Chinese and Egyptian financial institutions are deepening their cooperation, which provided platforms and channels for RMB's landing in Egypt. As the main bank in BRI, China Development Bank provided loans exceeding 1.5 billion USD to National Bank of Egypt and Banque Misr. Other Chinese banks also provided credit support for Egypt with the marketized operation model. The deepened financial cooperation provided platforms and channels for RMB's landing in Egypt.

14.3 Egypt is an Important Supporting Point Along the Belt and Road Initiative

14.3.1 *Political and Economic Situations of Egypt*

(1) *Political Situations*

A. The military is playing an important role in Egyptian politics

The former presidents of Egypt, including Nasser, Sadat and Mubarak all came from the military. After the "1.25" revolution in 2011, president Mubarak resigned, and the Armed Forces Supreme Council took the power. In June 2012, Morsi, the president of the Freedom and Justice Party founded by Muslim Brotherhood won the presidential election and took office. In June 2013, the supporters and opponents of Morsi held a large-scale demonstration and caused a bloody conflict. On July 3, 2013, the Egyptian military unseated Morsi, suspended the constitution and announced the "three-step" transition road map including constitutional amendment, presidential election and parliamentary election. On August 13, 2013, the Egyptian government appointed 25 provincial governors, among whom 16 have a military background and 1 has a police background.

B. The strong president Sisi steadily pushes forward political reforms

At the end of May 2014, Egypt held a presidential election. The former military leader Sisi was elected with 97% votes and took office in June. Overall, after constitutional amendment in 2014 and the presidential election, Egypt's political situation was getting steady, and the administrative authority's capability of handling the situation was obviously stronger than the period of Morsi and transitional governments. In the middle of March 2015, Egypt held the Egyptian Economic Meeting in Sharm El Sheikh. The meeting was an important measure of the Egyptian government to attract domestic and overseas investment and facilitate Egyptian economic recovery. It was called a "milestone" in Egypt's medium-term economic development plan. More than 2,500 government officials, company representatives, investors and media representatives from 100 countries, 25 districts and international organizations attended the meeting on invitation. In August 2015, the Suez Canal expansion project was completed. The project took a period of 1 year and was completed 2 years before the planned date. The completion of the project boosted the confidence of domestic and foreign investors in the new government and Egypt's future economic development. On January 10, 2016, the new Egyptian parliament held its first meeting, and put an end to the three years' absence of a parliament. Egypt's political transition completed successfully. The new parliament consisted of 596 members, including 448 independent members, 120 party members and 28 members directly appointed by the president. Different from the previous parliament, which was led by the Muslim Brotherhood, the new parliament did not have a leading political party or faction, and the power in the parliament was scattered. The composition of the new parliament reflected the "military strongman" Sisi's absolute control of the Egyptian regime. In addition, the new government obviously relies upon the military's power. Among 27 provincial governors, 17 came from the military. And the military undertook a series of major projects including the construction of affordable housing in cooperation with the UAE government (4.7 billion USD) and the dredging and expansion of the Suez Canal (8 billion USD).

C. Egypt is an influential political power in the Middle East and North African districts

In history, Egypt led the Middle East war against Israel multiple times as a leader of the Arab world. After signing the *Camp David Accords* with Israel, Egypt changed its diplomatic direction, and was dedicated to maintaining stability of the Middle East region. The headquarter of Arab league is located in Egypt, and the president of Arab league is generally an Egyptian according to conventions. Gradually, a new model was developed: Egypt supports other Arab countries politically, and other Arab countries provide economic assistance for Egypt. Egypt has been maintaining a close diplomatic and economic relationship with the USA, Europe and even Israel. Egypt is the first Arab and African country which built a diplomatic relation with China. In June 2006, China and Egypt established a strategic partnership. During president Sisi's visit to China in December 2014, China and Egypt published a joint declaration that both countries will establish a comprehensive strategic partnership. In September 2015, president Sisi attended the commemoration for the 70th anniversary of the success of Chinese people's anti-Japanese war and the world's anti-Fascist war. He actively pushed forward both countries' cooperation in different fields and deepened both countries' strategic partnership. In January 2016, Chinese president Xi Jinping conducted a state visit in Egypt, and it was the first time for China's highest leader to visit Egypt over the past 12 years. During the visit, China and Egypt published the five-year implementation plan for strengthening both countries' comprehensive strategic partnership, and proposed to connect each other's development strategies and visions, and by focusing on infrastructure construction and capacity cooperation, transform Egypt into a supporting point along the BRI route.

(2) *Economic Situation*

A. Egypt's GDP in the fiscal years of 2014/2015 and 2015/2016 achieved faster growth than the previous years

Egypt's GDP has maintained steady growth in recent years; especially in 2014/2015 and 2015/2016, when the growth rate reached 4.4% and 4.3%, respectively. These were relatively fast speeds. According to the

World Bank's global economic prediction report in June 2017, Egypt's expected GDP growth rate in 2016/2017 was 3.9%, which was consistent with the Egyptian government's predictions. As predicted by the World Bank, with the economic reforms of Egypt and the improvement of investment environment, Egypt's economic growth rate will stay above 4% in the next two fiscal years, and is expected to reach 5.3% in 2018/2019. Egyptian economy has typical consumer-driven characteristics. (In 2015/2016 fiscal year, the proportion of consumption in GDP was up to 94.2%.) The consumer-driven characteristics of Egyptian economy and a relatively stable labor force structure (although unemployment rate is high) has guaranteed stability of Egyptian economy and reduced the influence of the political turmoil on economy in recent years.

B. Investment is an important means to boost Egyptian economy

The new government started a series of large investment projects. It proposed to implement an investment package of 500 billion Egyptian pounds, and launched major projects including the Suez Canal expansion, new capital construction, multiple gas power stations and Suez Canal corridor economic belt. Among them, the Suez Canal expansion project, which costed 8 billion USD and took a period of 12 months has been completed. Egypt and the Siemens company of Germany signed an efficient gas power station project (with an installed capacity of 14.4GW) with a value of 6 billion euros. Once the project is completed, the three power plants will have the largest generating capacity in the world. Currently the project has started construction. Additionally, Egypt proposed to construct a new capital project at 45 kilometers east of Cairo. The project will cover an area of 700 square kilometers and a population of 5 million, and the total investment of construction will reach 30 billion USD.

C. Egypt's fiscal revenue is increasing steadily, but there is still a large fiscal deficit

In recent years, Egypt's fiscal revenue has been increasing steadily, but Egypt is still under great pressure of fiscal deficit. In the 2015/2016 fiscal year, Egypt's fiscal revenue reached 491.488 billion Egyptian pounds, in which tax revenue accounted for 71.68% and was 352.315 billion Egyptian pounds. Egypt's fiscal expenditure reached 817.844 billion Egyptian pounds. The fiscal deficit in the same year was 326.356 billion Egyptian pounds, accounting for 12.5% of GDP and has exceeded the 3% international warning line. On May 23, 2017, according to data published by the Egyptian government, the fiscal deficit rate in the first 9 months of the 2016/2017 fiscal year decreased from 9.4% of the same period of the last year to 8%, and is expected to decrease to 10.9% at the end of 2016/2017. In July 2016, IMF declared to loan 12 billion USD to Egypt to support Egypt's economic reforms. And the Egyptian government started implementing a series of reform measures, including reducing subsidies and adding tax, and it announced to devalue Egyptian pound and adopt the free floating exchange rate in November 2016. With the gradual implementation of reforms, Egypt's fiscal deficit is expected to decrease to 9.1% in 2017/2018.

D. The government debt is fluctuating on a high level, while foreign debt is maintained at a reasonable level

In recent years, the Egyptian government's debt ratio (amount of internal debt/GDP) has been staying high. In September 2016, the internal debt reached 2.7 trillion Egyptian pounds, with a debt ratio of 77.7%, and was higher than the international warning line 60%. The main reason was that the Egyptian government's debt issuance has been increasing and maintained on a high level. By September 2016, Egypt's total foreign debt reached 60.153 billion USD, with a debt ratio of 16.3% (international warning line is 20%), a short-term debt ratio of 13.2% and a short-term debt repayment ratio of 40.7%.

E. Egypt's foreign exchange reserve is maintaining a steady growth

Since July 2016, Egypt's foreign exchange reserve has been growing continuously. By May 2017, it reached 31.13 billion USD, and covered

6 months of import. Egypt's foreign exchange earnings mainly come from oil export, the Suez Canal, tourism and overseas remittance. Overseas remittance is one of Egypt's major source of income. Additionally, due to the fall of international oil price and the rampancy of Somali pirates, ships passing through the Suez Canal are not increasing in number, and the income of Suez Canal has been staying low.

In a long-term perspective, since young people take up a large proportion in the population structure, the number of migrant workers will increase, and therefore the overseas remittance will also increase. Secondly, as the government resolutely fights terrorism, social security will improve, and the tourist market will slowly recover. Thirdly, Egypt discovered a natural gas field with a reserve of 850 billion cubic meters (equivalent to 5.5 billion barrels of crude oil) in August 2016. According to the Egyptian government, the gas field could be used for at least 10 years under the current demand of Egypt. Hopefully Egypt could suspend natural gas import for 3-5 years to reduce foreign exchange outflow.

F. Foreign direct investment is growing steadily

Foreign direct investment in Egypt in 2015/2016 fiscal year reached 6.838 billion USD, but it was still behind the 8.113 billion USD in 2008/09 fiscal year. In recent years, the UK, USA and UAE have been the top three countries in direct investment in Egypt, and they invested 5.944 billion USD, 807 million USD and 1.329 billion USD in Egypt in 2015/2016, respectively. In May 2017, the Egyptian parliament passed a new *Investment Law* to replace the *Law for Protecting and Encouraging Investment* in August 1997. The new *Investment Law* updated and improved the content of investment scope, investment mechanism, foreign capital review, capital composition, foreign exchange use, nationalization and requisition, investment dispute resolution and criminal social responsibility. The terms related to policy transparency and investment promotion reflected the Egyptian government's decision to attract foreign capital and encourage private department development. The new *Investment Law* made revisions on improving efficiency of administrative management, including simplifying approval procedures, reducing approval period, and broaden complaint channels. Relevant departments can issue company license and project permission before land is approved. The implementation of the new law will greatly help Egypt attract foreign investment.

G. Egypt's inflation rate has been staying high under the influence of Egyptian pound devaluation

Due to the floating exchange rate reform, Egyptian pound devalued significantly, and Egypt's inflation rate kept rising. Since April 2017, Egypt's inflation rate has reached 31.46%, which was the highest over the past 30 years. According to the Egyptian government's economic reform plan, the Egyptian government will continue to increase the price of oil and electricity and reduce relevant subsidies. In the short term, Egypt will still be under the great pressure of inflation. The finance minister of Egypt indicated that the inflation rate will gradually decrease in the next few years.

14.3.2 *Egypt's Financial, Taxation and Foreign Exchange Policies*

(1) *Financial Policies*

The Central Bank of Egypt (CBE) founded in 1961 is Egypt's baking regulatory agency. The No.88 act issued by the Egyptian government in 2003 and the No.64 presidential decree issued by the Egyptian president in June 2004 set out the main responsibilities of the Egyptian central bank, which include maintaining price stability and stable operation of the banking industry, formulating and executing currency policies and bank credit policies, issuing currency, supervising the banking industry, managing foreign exchange reserves, managing foreign exchange transaction market, supervising national payment system, and recording and tracking Egypt's external debt (including the public and private departments).

Egyptian Financial Supervisory Authority (EFSA) is a new government supervision agency founded as per No.10 decree in 2009 to replace the previous Egyptian insurance supervision bureau, capital market management bureau and mortgage finance management bureau. EFSA is responsible for supervising Egypt's non-banking financial market, including insurance, capital market, mortgage finance, finance lease, asset securitization and factoring business.

On June 15, 2003, the Egyptian government issued No.88 law on the central bank, bank system and currency. On March 22, 2004, the Egyptian government issued the executive regulations on No.88 law, i.e. the No.101 decree. In 2005, the No.93 decree revised the *Banking Law of Egypt*. The above decrees specify details on the banking industry's systems, functions and supervision. The Egyptian banking industry operates on a mixed pattern. It could both provide loans and make investments. And Egypt has set up stock exchanges in Cairo and Alexandria.

In terms of the bank's ownership, Egyptian banks can be classified into state-owned banks, private and joint venture banks and foreign banks (which operate business by setting up branches in Egypt). The three main commercial banks (National Bank of Egypt, Banque Misr and Cairo Bank), which are most influential in Egypt are all state-owned. Private and joint venture banks and foreign banks should be founded according to Egypt's investment law. Although they are private companies, state-owned banks can also participate and hold certain amount of shares in joint venture banks.

Egyptian law does not prohibit banks not registered in Egypt from providing loans for customers registered in Egypt. According to Article 66 of the Egyptian banking law, except when the Egyptian central bank requires data disclosure for purpose of foreign debt supervision, the loan agreements do not need to be notarized or registered at any public institution in terms of its validity, effect and executability. Unless specifically provided in relevant laws, the borrower does not need the approval, authorization, consent, or judgment of any public institution or government departments in signing, submitting and fulfilling loan agreements.

(2) *Tax Policies*

The direct and indirect incomes of all Egyptian natural persons and legal persons are all taxable. Egypt's taxes are classified into direct tax and indirect tax, and mainly include payroll tax, income withholding tax, personal income uniform tax, company profit tax, real estate tax, customs duties, sales tax, stamp tax and development tax. The standard tax rate for company profits is 20%, and the profit tax rate of industrial companies and export companies is 32%. The profit tax rate of non-state-owned oil exploitation and production companies is 40.55%. If the company's annual profit exceeds 18,000 Egyptian pounds, the company should pay the national resource development tax at a rate of 2%. Sales tax applies to finished product manufacturing, operation or processing for the customer, some intermediate services and some tourism services. The sales tax is similar to added-value tax and is mainly levied on imported or locally produced finished products. Manufacturers with an annual sales exceeding 5,4000 Egyptian pounds and all importers and distributors should register for tax payment at the tax bureau. The standard rate of sales tax is 10%. While paying sales tax for goods, the sales tax that was already paid for raw materials and during goods circulation can be deducted from the payable amount. For exported goods, tax reimbursement is applicable.

(3) *Egypt is Implementing Foreign Exchange Control*

Since August 1991, Egypt has loosened foreign exchange control, allowed free convertibility of foreign currencies under the current account, established a national uniform foreign exchange market, and adopted the floating exchange rate policy. The floating exchange rates are listed by the banks every day, and foreign currencies can be freely converted in banks and money shops. State-owned and private foreign trade companies could apply to use foreign exchanges at the banks, and generally they need to prepay 10–35% of the import contract amount to the bank. According to No.117 *Foreign Exchange Transaction Act* in 1991, apart from government authorities and public departments (which have foreign exchange budgets), all natural persons and legal persons can hold foreign currencies, and conduct foreign currency deposit, exchange and international payments, but they must conduct such transactions at banks approved by the government. Egypt's foreign exchange earnings mainly come from tourism, overseas remittance, oil and natural gas, and the Suez Canal.

Egypt has never achieved free convertibility under the capital account. Since 1999, Egypt's balance of payments has been in an adverse condition, and Egypt was short of foreign exchanges. Most banks have specified the maximum amount for one-time foreign currency exchange. Since the end of 2012, banks and currency exchange institutions have been seriously lacking foreign exchanges, therefore it was difficult for individuals to purchase foreign exchanges at commercial banks (the purchase must serve specific purposes specified by the central bank, and the foreign exchanges should be used preferentially to import drugs and essential raw materials). People could exchange Egyptian pounds into foreign currencies in the "black market", but the exchange rate would be 5–10% higher than the official rates published on the website of the Egyptian central bank. Since 2011, the Egyptian central bank has been selling limited USD by auction in the commercial inter-bank market 2–3 times a week, and specified that the companies should preferentially use the exchanges to purchase drugs and necessary equipment.

On March 14, 2016, Egypt declared to adopt a more flexible exchange rate system. Egyptian pound devalued 13% to USD in single time, and the EGP/USD rate became 8.85:1. On November 3, 2016, the central bank declared to devalue Egyptian pound to USD once again from the rate of 8.85:1 to 13:1. The range of devaluation reached 48%, and the central bank declared Egyptian pound as freely floating to USD. In June 2017, as reported by IMF, the Egyptian central bank will remove restrictions on USD deposit and remittance in the next few months.

14.4 Basic Information of the Cooperative Party — Egyptian SAI-Bank

14.4.1 *Overview of Egyptian SAI-Bank*

Egyptian SAI-Bank was founded on March 21, 1976. It was the first joint venture bank set up by Arab Bank in Egypt according to No. 43 investment decree (later revised according to No.230 decree in 1989 and No.8 decree in 1997) of the *Investment Law* in 1974. The issued and paid-up capital of SAI-Bank increased from 4 million USD in 1978 to 150 million USD at present. SAI-Bank has allocated 15 million shares, and each share has a face value of 10 dollars. SAI-Bank has a full license in Egypt and could conduct various banking businesses including investment, loans and rentals. The bank's fields of operation include industry, agriculture, real estate, business and trade. SAI-Bank also provides Islamic financial products and services through its Islamic branches. Meanwhile, SAI-Bank also conducts retail business, company business and investment bank business. By the end of April 2017, SAI-Bank had 33 branches in Egypt and 1,139 employees in total.

14.4.2 *Shareholder Structure of Egyptian SAI-Bank*

The largest shareholder of SAI-Bank is Arab International Bank, which holds 46% of shares. Arab International Bank is an investment bank founded as per international treaties on the contributions of the governments of Egypt (38.76%), Libya (38.76%), the UAE (12.5%), Qatar (4.98%) and the Sultanate of Oman (2.49%). It has certain privileges and is headquartered in Cairo. According to the treaties, Arab International Bank has the following privileges in the member countries: 1. Arab International Bank and its branches are not regulated by supervision institutions, public institutions, public department companies and joint stock companies. 2. Arab International Bank is exempt from all forms of nationalization. 3. The documents, records and files of Arab International Bank cannot be infringed, and the bank is exempt from controls and inspections by judicial, administrative and accounting departments. 4. Arab International Bank is entitled to tax exemptions on funds, profits, dividends and various activities and transactions. 5. Arab International Bank is exempt from taxes and obligations to withhold tax from customers. Arab International Bank mainly conducts banking, financial and business activities related to economic development and foreign trade, especially in its member countries and other Arab countries and districts. Arab International Bank is not allowed to conduct Egyptian pound business and can only invest in local banks.

The second largest shareholder of SAI-Bank is Arab Contractor Investment Co., Ltd., which holds 17% of shares. Arab Contractor Investment Co., Ltd. is a leading construction company in Middle East and Africa. The company has 77,000 employees and cooperates with customers, partners and suppliers from 29 countries. The company has rich experience in the construction industry and supporting services, including public buildings, bridges, roads, tunnels, airports, housing, sewage treatment plants, power plants, dams, hospitals, sports buildings, historical site restoration, irrigation, concrete production, shipbuilding, electromechanical engineering, engineering consultation and steel structure manufacturing and assembly.

The third largest shareholder of SAI-Bank is Egyptian Insurance Co., Ltd., which holds 16% of shares. Egyptian Insurance Co., Ltd. was founded on January 14, 1934, and Muhammad Taha, the minister of economic affairs is serving as the company's chairman of the board. The insurance company provides support for many projects related to national independence of Egypt by gathering social capital.

The fourth largest shareholder of SAI-Bank is Egyptian Insurance Co., Ltd., which holds 11% of shares. Egyptian Insurance Co., Ltd. is the largest professional company in the field of life insurance in Egypt, the Arab world, and even the entire Africa. And it is the largest and oldest insurance company in Egypt. Pursuant to relevant decrees in 1964, Egyptian's 14 insurance companies were merged into four, including 3 direct insurance companies and 1 reinsurance company, most of which are 100% state-owned.

14.4.3 *Corporate Governance Structure of Egyptian SAI-Bank*

SAI-Bank regards corporate governance as an important part of bank operation and development. The board of directors of SAI-Bank advocates integrity and morality by setting up examples. They are playing an important role in formulating bank strategies and policies, appointing, supervising and issuing high payment to senior management staff, and ensuring the bank's accountability for the investors and the authority. SAI-Bank respects the shareholders' rights, and enables the shareholders to exercise their rights and effectively take part in the shareholders' meeting by regularly delivering effective information. The accountability system is the key to SAI-Bank's governance. Power is strictly controlled and the staff members are responsible for their behavior. To ensure accountability, SAI-Bank is maintaining a diversified composition of the board of directors. The responsibilities of the president and CEO are separated for power dispersion. The bank's corporate governance structure is dependent on the board of directors and the senior management. The bank has designed an internal auditing matrix (compliance, risk and internal auditing) as the solid support of the governance structure. And it strives to cultivate a culture of sufficient disclosure to increase transparency and build mutual trust.

The SAI-Bank board of directors has four subordinate committees:

(1) *Internal Auditing Committee*

The committee consists of 3 members who are not members of the executive council and have experience, knowledge and speciality in the finance and accounting fields according to Article 82 of No.88 law in 2003. The committee is mainly responsible for the bank's internal supervision and auditing.

(2) *Risk Committee*

The risk committee is mainly responsible for managing and tracking the bank's risks, and make sure various operations comply with risk management strategies and policies. The committee consists of 3 non-executive directors and 1 executive director.

(3) *Corporate Governance Committee*

The committee is mainly responsible for formulating and providing suggestions for the board of directors on corporate governance policies and guidance, and screen and nominate candidates for the director and committee member positions so that the board of directors could elect and appoint committee members. The committee consists of 3 non-executive directors.

(4) *Compensation Committee*

The compensation committee is mainly responsible for researching salaries and bonuses, checking policies and regulations on salary, allowance, profit, incentive, promotion and sanction, approving benefits for directors and employees according to preset objectives, and submitting suggestions to the board of directors. The compensation committee consists of 3 non-executive directors.

According to information on the SAI-Bank website, currently SAI-Bank has 1 chairman of the board, 1 vice chairman, and 9 directors, as listed in Table 14.1.

According to Table 14.1, all board members of SAI-Bank have an excellent educational background and rich practical experience in finance, project management and supervision. The chairman of the board of SAI-Bank is the former vice president of Banque Misr, the second largest commercial bank in Egypt, and two directors are the former president and vice president of the Egyptian central bank, respectively. It can be concluded that the senior management staff of SAI-Bank are playing a crucial role in Egyptian financial field.

14.5 The Project's Progress and Significance

14.5.1 *The Project's Progress*

In May 2017, Chinese president Xi Jinping declared in the BRI Summit for International Cooperation that China Development Bank would implement an RMB special loan of 250 billion yuan to support infrastructure, capacity and financial cooperation projects of "Belt and Road". As the only Chinese financial institution registered in Egypt, China Development Bank's representative office in Cairo timely reported to the Egyptian banking industry the details and results of BRI Summit for International Cooperation, and introduced the significance of BRI RMB special loan for Egypt in the professional prospective of finance serving real economy. In July 2017, SAI-Bank

Table 14.1   Information of Egyptian SAI-Bank Directors

Name and Position	Resume
Muhammad Taha (Chairman of the board and executive director)	Mr. Muhammad Taha has over 35 years' experience in operation and management in the banking and financial industry and worked in senior management multiple times. Mr. Taha once worked as the vice chairman of the board of Banque Misr, a board member and the risk management director of National Bank of Egypt, a director and the general manager of Incolease and the general manager for credit and risk management of MIBank. Currently Mr. Taha is a board member of an important financial institution in Egypt. Additionally, Mr. Taha is honored to give lectures on bank management and credit analysis in American University in Cairo. He also made contributions for modifying the *Egyptian Financial Lease Act*, and further explained the terms in the economic committee of Egyptian parliament.
Abodai Miguit (Vice chairman of the board and executive director)	Mr. Abodai Miguit is the vice chairman of the board and executive director responsible for implementing the bank's strategies by formulating executive plans in order to ensure effective resource management. He has over 35 years' experience in the banking industry and once worked in many administrative positions in multiple banks. In 1975, he cooperated with Arab International Bank and joined the international investment and finance department. In 1978, he joined the Credit International Egyptian Bank. Afterwards, Mr. Abodai Miguit joined MIBank (1981–1999). Before joining SAI-Bank and working as the executive general manager in 2004, he used to work as the general manager for credit and marketing of United Bank of Egypt (UBE). Mr. Abodai Miguit was elected as a board member and the finance supervisor of Egyptian Banking Association in 2005, and worked as a board member of Incolease. In 2009, Mr. Abodai Miguit was appointed as a board member of the banking department of Egyptian competition management bureau.

Abu Ye Oyou (Non-executive director)	Abu Ye Oyou has a doctoral degree and a bachelor's degree in economic philosophy. He is the economic consultant of Arab economic and social development fund, and became the founder and CEO of Defense and Security System Co., Ltd. in 2012. Dr. Abu Ye Oyou once worked as the CEO of Kuwait International Bank (2010–2011) and the financial consultant of Kuwait minister (2006–2010). After working in different leadership positions in Egyptian central bank, Dr. Abu Ye Oyou was appointed as the president of the central bank (2001–2003). He successfully established the Egyptian Anti-Money Laundering Organization. Dr. Abu Ye Oyou was also the Egyptian general representative of Arab Monetary Fund (2001–2003) and African Development Bank. He used to work as the economic and financial consultant for multiple minister-level economic and financial institutions in Egypt. He is also the board member of multiple entity enterprises. Dr. Abu Ye Oyou published multiple works and academic theses, and is working as the economic professor of Zagazig University.
Muhammad Muharram (Non-executive director)	Mr. Muhammad Muharram is the president and financial consultant of MGM Bank, and the president of Egyptian Mutual Fund Management Co., Ltd. and Cairo Factor Co., Ltd. He is the Egyptian Mutual Fund Management CEO and executive director of Piraeus Bank in Egypt, and worked as the chairman of Commercial Bank of Egypt (2002–2008) and Egyptian American Chamber of Commerce (2006–2008). Since his graduation from the business department of Cairo University in 1974, Mr. Muhammad Muharram has spent most of his career time working in the banking industry. He once worked as the credit and marketing officer of Citibank and the assistant vice president and New York chief representative of Fleet National Bank. Mr. Muhammad Muharram is a board member of multiple famous social responsibility research institutes, chambers of commerce and associations.
Ye Wacker (Non-executive director)	Mr. Ye Wacker has many years' experience in the financial field, including capital, capital market, Islamic banking business and investment banking business. He was appointed as a board member and the managing director of Arab International Bank (AIB) in 2014. Mr. Ye Wacker worked in management and executive positions in Commercial International Bank (CIB) in Egypt (2008–2013), until he was appointed as a board member. He also worked in administrative positions in Islamic banks of multiple countries. Mr. Ye Wacker is also a board member of Egyptian Banking Association.

(Continued)

Table 14.1   (*Continued*)

Name and Position	Resume
Iburahem (Non-executive director)	Mr. Iburahem is the managing director, a board member, an executive committee member, and director of the asset and liability accountability committee of Cairo Bank. He is the first vice president of Central Bank of Egypt and is responsible for the execution of inter-bank foreign exchange and currency policies, reserve management and foreign debts. Mr. Iburahem has acquired rich experience in banking industry in the local and international markets. He worked as the general manager and senior investment director of Arab International Bank in Cairo, vice president and investment consultant of Merrill Lynch in London and Bahrain, and investment consultant of Lehman Brothers in Bahrain. He also worked as the financial director of Gulf Riyad Bank in Bahrain and Arab African International Bank in Cairo. Mr. Iburahem has an MBA degree of American Business and Finance School in Cairo, and has acquired investment certification of New York Stock Exchange, National Association of Securities Dealers and Chicago Board of Trade.
Muhammad Mawson (Non-executive director)	Mr. Muhammad Mawson worked in multiple management positions in Osman Ahmed Osman & Co. and was later appointed as the company's chairman of the board and CEO. Prior to that, he was the director of Egypt's national drinking water and health administration. He is also the chairman of employee insurance foundation of Arab contractors, the chairman of the board of Tourism Development Elite Co., Ltd. and a board member of Tourism Construction Subway Co., Ltd. Meanwhile, he is also the member of several business councils and chambers of commerce.
Mosak (Non-executive director)	Mr. Mosak is the president of Egyptian Insurance Co., Ltd. Through a series of effective reforms, he led Egyptian Insurance Co., Ltd. to achieve outstanding performance in multiple fields. Mr. Mosak has a doctoral degree in economics and foreign trade of Helwan University, and participated in international conferences, workshops and training in multiple business fields.

Name	Description
Sairal (Non-executive director)	Sairal has a doctoral degree and works in public administration in the school of economics and politics of Cairo University. He is also the director of the investment department of Egyptian Life Insurance Co., Ltd. He has over 32 years' experience in the fields of investment, finance and management, and did excellent work in financial analysis, feasibility research, planning of the finance of non-performing companies and management restructuring. He also participated in formulation of merger and acquisition plans, real estate and financing lease, stock valuation, credit research and review and project financing plans. Dr. Sairal is a member of the investment committee of Egyptian Life Insurance Co., Ltd., and a board member of Gulf Bank and Housing Development Bank in Egypt. He published multiple research works in finance, economy, restructuring, governance and management.
Ye Barudi (Non-executive director)	Mr. Ye Barudi is the vice president of Osman Ahmed Osman & Co. He has a bachelor's degree in civil engineering of Einstein University. He has over 36 years' experience and worked as important leaders. Mr. Ye Barudi led and supervised several strategic departments and major projects, including housing and mining department, electromechanical department, feature buildings and industrial buildings, Central Bank of Egypt's construction project and Cairo stadium construction project. He is also the vice president of the joint venture of Bibiotheca Alexandria project of Balfour Beatty and RodioTrevi, and is responsible for leading and supervising the Dar Al-Hadith auditorium construction project of Madinah-Saudi Arabia.
Ebrahim (Non-executive director)	Ms. Ebrahim has over 25 years' experience in the diversified business and investment field. She has an MBA degree of Arab Academy for Science, Technology and Maritime Transport. She attended a variety of business courses and was appointed as the director of the investment department of Misr Insurance, one of the largest insurance companies in Egypt.

Source: Official website of SAI-Bank.

expressed its appreciation for RMB's landing in Egypt, and formally submitted a loan application to China Development Bank. After two months' review and contract negotiation, China Development Bank successfully granted credits to SAI-Bank. On September 17, 2017, China Development Bank and SAI-Bank signed an RMB special loan contract of 260 million yuan in Cairo. The special loan contract signified BRI RMB special loan's first landing in Egypt. On the same day, China Development Bank and Banque Misr signed the *Memorandum of Understanding for China-Egypt BRI RMB Special Loan*, and both parties promised to actively push forward RMB loan cooperation.

14.5.2 *The Project's Significance*

Egypt is an important supporting point along Belt and Road. Egypt's inclusion of RMB as its foreign exchange reserve currency will have a great impact on the Middle East and African districts, and will serve as an example for the smooth progress of RMB internationalization and BRI construction. BRI construction requires a large amount of capital, and dependency on USD or other extraterritorial currencies is both risky and unsustainable. Therefore, our country must push forward financial cooperation with domestic currencies centering on RMB. The special loan of 260 million RMB granted to SAI-Bank will be used to support project construction in the fields of infrastructure, electricity, energy, communication, transportation, agriculture, medium-small companies and "stepping out" of Chinese companies. It signified Egyptian currency authority's official approval for RMB's convertibility and use in Egypt, and was a precondition for pushing forward direct convertibility between Egyptian pound and RMB and achieving wide use of RMB capital in China-Egypt investment and trade cooperation. The use of RMB will bring tangible benefits to Egypt. It will provide more capital channels for China-Egypt infrastructure and capacity cooperation projects and motivate more Chinese companies to invest in Egypt. The 260 million RMB credit granting project of SAI-Bank was a beneficial attempt of both countries to push forward RMB internationalization in BRI construction, and created a win-win situation for both countries.

Chapter

15

Conclusion: Policy Suggestions

15.1 Lay a Solid Foundation of Domestic Economy and Steadily Push Forward RMB Internationalization

15.1.1 *Always Ensure Steady Development of Domestic Economy*

According to the experience of major international currencies, a currency's internationalization follows certain rules and is the result of the issuing country's political and economic position. The steady growth of domestic economy is the precondition for the lasting success of RMB internationalization. We should seize good opportunities in pushing forward RMB internationalization, but should not be overly hasty. Nor can we compromise the steady development of domestic economy in this process. Therefore, in a public opinion environment with loud voices calling for RMB internationalization in China and overseas, China should keep sober, make progress steadily, adhere to currency policy independence, give priority to steady growth of domestic economy, prevent domestic industry hollowing during overseas investment, and achieve tangible results in supply-side structural reforms.

15.1.2 *Maintain RMB Value Stability*

If a currency's value is unstable, countries in the world will have a negative expectation for the currency, and have scruples about accepting the currency in settlement, investment and reserves; and in a worse case, the international society will dump the currency. The quick flow-in and flow-out of speculation capital will seriously harm the healthy development of domestic economy. According to historical experience, the substantial devaluation of GBP and the substantial appreciation of JPY caused great harm to the economy of both countries, and seriously frustrated the internationalization process of GBP and JPY. To tackle the pressure on RMB exchange rate imposed by the USA and other western countries, we should learn from the regionalization experience of German Mark and euro, and by conducting regional cooperation in investment and financing with countries along the Belt and Road Initiative (BRI) route, we should create a currency cooperation system to share RMB's devaluation or appreciation pressure, adhere to the managed floating exchange rate system, and maintain relative stability of RMB value.

15.1.3 *Steadily Push Forward Capital Account Opening*

The liberalization and marketization of financial market will effectively facilitate currency internationalization, but failed regulations may also cause a destructive shock to the country's economic and financial system. According to the internationalization experience of major currencies, capital account opening is crucial and will influence the width, depth and liquidity of a country's financial market, but it is not a precondition for currency internationalization. Chinese economy has made great achievements in the decades following the reform and opening-up of the country, but there are still many problems in the financial field. For example, domestic financial institutions are not sufficiently internationalized, onshore and offshore financial markets are underdeveloped, the government lacks experience in cross-border financial supervision, and financial infrastructure for RMB cross-border flow is still backward. Currently, while pushing forward RMB internationalization in BRI construction, our country should strengthen RMB's valuation and settlement functions in cross-border trade, make innovation in developing RMB financial assets, construct RMB onshore and offshore financial centers, solve our country's above-mentioned weaknesses in the financial field, and steadily push forward managed opening of capital account.

15.2 Strengthen Economic and Financial Cooperation on the Principle of "Discussion, Co-development and Sharing"

15.2.1 *Construct an Economic Cooperation Framework in Countries Along the Belt and Road Initiative Route*

An important cause of the failure of JPY internationalization was that Japan heavily depended on the USA and neglected cooperation with Asian countries. When Japan put forward the "Asian currency" concept, it already missed the good opportunity for JPY internationalization. As the largest suzerain, England closely cooperated with other countries in economy and laid a foundation for GBP internationalization. The key to the success of euro internationalization was the close cooperation between Eurozone countries. Due to economic integration of Europe, resources flowed frequently between the European countries, and currency internationalization was naturally achieved. As a large trading country, China has built close economic and trade relationships with various countries. With the healthy development of domestic economic structure, China's industries are advancing toward the high end of global value chain; therefore China is capable of transferring advantageous capacity to countries along the BRI route and expanding trade cooperation. China should learn from the experience of international currencies, actively construct economic cooperation framework with countries along the BRI route, and establish multi-lateral institutions facilitating economic integration when necessary, in order to divert pressures of the USA and other western countries and create a favorable regional cooperation basis for RMB internationalization.

15.2.2 *Set Up a Central Bank Cooperation Organization in Countries Along "Belt and Road"*

The internationalization of GBP, USD, JPY and EUR was inseparable from the joint force of central banks of various countries, with the domestic central bank as the center. Therefore, the key to pushing forward RMB internationalization in BRI construction is to create a regional currency cooperation system centering on RMB with wide participation of central banks of relevant countries. The countries along the BRI route have a solid foundation for political and economic cooperation with China, and have high expectations for, and high dependency on China's investment, trade and capital. China should seize the favorable opportunity, set up a central bank cooperation organization in countries along the BRI route, create a regional currency cooperation system focusing on the central banks of relevant countries, facilitate investment, financing and trade cooperation of relevant countries, and accelerate implementation of RMB's functions for internationalization.

15.2.3 *Connect to and Improve the Currency Payment System of Countries Along "Belt and Road"*

Currently, countries along the BRI route have unbalanced development of financial infrastructure, and the RMB payment systems of many countries are not complete. The situation has become a "bottleneck" restriction in pushing forward RMB internationalization. In some countries where I worked, opening an RMB account in a bank is a difficult matter for both residents and non-residents, not to mention RMB circulation, payment, valuation, settlement, transaction and reserves. An important basis for currency integration of EU countries is that 16 countries in Europe founded the European Payments Union as early as 1950, and effectively solved problems of currency settlement and free convertibility between different countries. Therefore, we should connect to and improve the currency payment systems of relevant countries on the principle of "discussion, co-development and sharing" in order to open up channels of RMB capital flow for financing, trade connection and facility connection. In addition, we should learn from the USA's Clearing House Inter-bank Payment System (CHIPS), and improve the RMB's Cross-border Inter-bank Payment System (CIPS) with the commercialized operation model. And we should perform final settlement with China National Advanced Payment System (CNAPS), increase clearing efficiency, reduce clearing cost, and comprehensively monitor RMB cross-border trade, in order to provide necessary financial infrastructure for pushing forward RMB internationalization in BRI construction, and support BRI construction with RMB capital.

15.3 Optimize the Belt and Road Initiative Investment and Trade Cooperation Environment

15.3.1 *Build a Global Value Chain Originating in China in Countries Along the Belt and Road Initiative Route*

The BRI covers districts in Asia, Africa and Europe. The 65 countries along BRI have a total population exceeding 4.4 billion, accounting for 63% of world population. Their economic aggregate accounts for about 30% of global economic aggregate. Most of these countries are emerging economies and developing countries and are generally on the rising stage of economic development. They have rich natural resources and a huge market potential. In investment and trade cooperation with countries along "Belt and Road", China should make plans before taking actions, learn from the currency internationalization experience of the UK, USA, Germany and Japan, integrate upstream and downstream resources, create appropriate distribution of high-end, middle-end and low-end industries, promote RMB valuation and settlement, infuse RMB capital and optimize the investment and trade environment of RMB internationalization. China should sufficiently communicate with developed countries actively engaged in BRI construction and the countries along the BRI route, and work together to reduce customs clearance and logistics costs, save time of investment and trade, and increase transparency and predictability in districts along the BRI route, in order to create a fast and efficient trading environment, enable relevant countries to obtain more benefits by taking part in the global value chain, more stably operate the supply chain originating in China on the basis of the countries along the BRI route, and build a global value chain originating in China.

15.3.2 *Solidify Policy Communication Results with Free Trade and Investment Cooperation Agreements*

Playing a leading role in foreign investment and trade is the precondition, important means and necessary choice of currency internationalization. China should strengthen policy communication with countries along the BRI route, facilitate trade and investment, solidify communication results in the form of legal documents and enter into agreements facilitating free trade and investment cooperation, in order to lay a solid foundation of policy and legal assurance for RMB internationalization and more effectively implement RMB's functions of valuation, settlement, trade and reserves. In recent years, Chinese government has signed economic and trade cooperation agreements with 30 countries. China's Ministry of Commerce, relevant departments of more than 60 countries and international organizations co-published a cooperation initiative for pushing forward BRI trade connections during the BRI summit. On this basis, China should continue to push forward economic and trade cooperation with countries along the BRI route, enter into bilateral or multi-lateral free trade and investment cooperation agreements, and encourage and direct RMB's use in investment and trading activities.

15.3.3 *Direct Capital to Major Projects by Providing RMB Special Loans (Funds)*

Conducting foreign investment and providing foreign assistance with the domestic currency had been an effective means of internationalization of GBP, USD, JPY and EUR. In May 2017, China declared to provide capital support for "Belt and Road", add 100 billion RMB to the Silk Road Fund, and encourage financial institutions to conduct RMB overseas fund business with an expected scale of 300 billion RMB. China Development set up a BRI special loan of 250 billion RMB (for infrastructure, capacity cooperation and financial cooperation). Exim Bank of China set up a BRI special loan of 130 billion RMB. China is strengthening support for countries along the BRI route by providing RMB special loans (funds). These measures will not only motivate relevant countries to improve their RMB payment systems, but also solve the financing gaps of major projects in the beginning stage of construction, create a good expectation of positive energy, direct private capitals to invest RMB funds in BRI construction, expand the capital pool and liquidity of overseas RMB and create a greater "siphonic effect" of capitals.

15.3.4 *Encourage Preferential Use of RMB in Foreign Investment and Trade Cooperation*

According to the internationalization experience of major currencies, the main cause of successful internationalization is the large proportion of use of the domestic currency in foreign investment and trading activities; while the main cause of failure is the currency's weak valuation and settlement functions in foreign investment and trading activities. Currently, RMB's use does not match China's position as a global power in trade and investment. China still relies upon USD and EUR for valuation and settlement in foreign investment and trade, and RMB cannot be directly converted with the currencies of many countries along the BRI route. It can be said that a major obstacle in our country's investment and trade cooperation in countries along the BRI route is the low degree of RMB internationalization. Therefore, our country should make full use of the advantages of the BRI leadership group in planning and coordination, unify various functions of People's Bank of China, Ministry of Finance, Ministry of Commerce, National Development and Reform Commission and State Administration of Taxation related to the BRI, strengthen policy communication with countries along the BRI route, remove obstacles in laws and financial infrastructure to RMB's use, issue policies and systems encouraging preferential use of RMB in foreign investment and trading activities, and by adopting various methods such as preferential financing, tax preference and fiscal subsidies, encourage Chinese companies to preferentially use RMB in investment and trading activities in countries along the BRI route.

15.4 Strengthen RMB's Valuation and Settlement Functions in International Trade

15.4.1 *Push Forward RMB Valuation and Settlement for Bulk Commodities of Relevant Countries*

Bulk commodities are the leading commodities in international trade, and mainly include oil, natural gas, steel, non-ferrous metal, ores and bulk farm products. Among them, oil trade is the most important and frequent benchmark trade. A cause of the failure of JPY internationalization was that the JPY's valuation and settlement functions in international trade were not sufficiently implemented. The USA is a large country of oil consumption. In the 1970s, the USA and Saudi Arabia reached an "unshakable" agreement, which set up USD as oil's only pricing currency. Since then, the USA has been tightly controlling the valuation and settlement of international oil trade with USD, and has controlled oil finance and many oil producing countries. Although the USA is not an OPEC member, it has great influence on global oil price. Bulk commodity trade is the key to currency substitution in the international trading field, and has strong currency inertia. Iraq and Iran once tried to valuate and settle oil trade with currencies other than USD, but eventually failed due to political turmoil and other reasons. In 2015, China and Russia successfully tried to settle oil trade with RMB. In 2016, China surpassed the USA as the largest oil import country. Taking this as a starting point, China should make use of its comprehensive advantages in investment and financing, vigorously push forward RMB valuation and settlement for bulk commodities such as oil and natural gas in countries along the BRI route, such as Saudi Arabia and Egypt, gradually increase RMB's use in international trade and implement RMB's important functions for internationalization.

15.4.2 *Direct Cross-border E-commerce to Conduct RMB Valuation and Settlement in Relevant Countries*

One important reason for the success of GBP and USD internationalization is that the issuing countries established their currencies as top currencies for valuation and settlement in international trade by a variety of means, such as innovation. Cross-border e-commerce combined the advantages of e-commerce and international trade, and could effectively facilitate global free trade. Our country made great achievements in cross-border e-commerce. It cultivated a complete industrial chain and ecological chain, and formulated a set of management systems and rules favorable for the development of cross-border e-commerce. In 2015, China's cross-border e-commerce had a trade scale of 5.4 trillion yuan, with a year-on-year growth of 28.6%. In the trade scale, cross-border export was 4.49 trillion yuan, and cross-border import was 907.2 billion yuan. Hangzhou became the first comprehensive pilot zone of cross-border e-commerce. In the beginning of 2016, 12 cities including Guangzhou, Shenzhen, Tianjin, Shanghai, Chongqing and Dalian set up comprehensive pilot zones of cross-border e-commerce, and reproduced Hangzhou's experience of "six systems and two platforms". Our country's cross-border e-commerce industry has strong comparative advantages in countries along the BRI route. It could change the consumers' habits and help build the model of valuation and settlement with RMB and the domestic currency of the partner country. The consumers will gradually develop currency dependency in the new shopping mode. Therefore, cross-border e-commerce has great potential in pushing forward RMB internationalization.

15.5 Strengthen RMB's Financial Transaction and Reserve Functions

15.5.1 *Increase Diversity of RMB Offshore Centers and Financial Products*

To implement RMB's internationalized functions, China needs to learn from the issuing countries of other international currencies and build a highly developed financial market as the support. While maintaining managed convertibility of domestic capital account, building RMB offshore centers, making innovation in RMB financial products, and pushing forward interconnection between onshore and offshore markets are the essential pathway to RMB internationalization. With the deepening of BRI construction, demands for RMB offshore markets and RMB financial products related to trade and investment are becoming prominent. For example, companies could conduct RMB cross-border trade financing with RMB fixed deposits in the offshore market or fixed-income financial assets such as bonds, and banks could develop RMB currency funds, RMB-valuated derivatives and RMB foreign exchange transaction products in the offshore market to meet the investment demands of global customers and attract overseas banking and non-banking institutional investors and individual investors. Therefore, China should build diversified RMB offshore centers in qualified countries along "Belt and Road", accelerate development of RMB investment and financing products on the basis of traditional cross-border businesses such as international settlements, foreign exchange trade, bond issuance, international clearance and international credit, and achieve multi-level development of RMB internationalization driven by trade, investment valuation and financial product innovation.

15.5.2 *Strengthen RMB's Investment and Foreign Exchange Reserve Functions with Currency Swaps*

In history, the British central bank effective solved the GBP credit crisis by currency swaps. Japan constructed a regional currency cooperation framework in East Asia district by currency swaps. So far, People's Bank of China has signed bilateral domestic currency swap agreements with central banks of more than 21 countries and districts along the BRI route, with a total scale exceeding 1 trillion yuan. The currency swap agreements signed between China and countries along the BRI route can not only help the countries provide liquidity support for each other, but also promote RMB as the bilateral trade settlement currency, facilitate direct investment and financial asset investment with RMB as the valuation currency, and on the above basis, motivate countries along the BRI route to increase RMB foreign exchange reserves. Reserve currency refers to assets or deposits valuated in a foreign currency, and it is mainly held by the government or official institutions as foreign exchange reserves. In September 2010, the Malaysian central bank purchased RMB-valuated bonds of 10 billion USD in Hong Kong as its foreign exchange reserve, and it was the first time for RMB to become a reserve currency of the central bank of another country. By December 2016, RMB assets accounted for 1.07% in IMF's database of official foreign exchange reserve currencies, and at least 40 countries and districts included RMB as their reserve currency with different methods. In recent years, many countries along the BRI route has been seriously lacking in USD liquidity, therefore they have a strong demand for our country's liquidity support. Motivating countries along the BRI route to increase RMB foreign exchange reserve by currency swaps is an effective means of marketized operation.

15.6 Improve the Quality of Financial Services

15.6.1 *Increase the Number of RMB Clearing Banks and Agent Banks Along "Belt and Road"*

According to the internationalization experience of USD, EUR and JPY, forming a certain scale of overseas stock is the foundation for a currency's circulation in the international market. Therefore, our country could separately handle the RMB cross-border clearance of relevant countries and the domestic clearing businesses, improve the overseas RMB business clearing network and set up a highly efficient RMB capital clearance channel. By May 2017, China has set up 23 overseas RMB business clearing banks around the world. Among them, only 7 are located in countries along "Belt and Road", and could not meet the realistic requirements of financing for BRI construction. Many companies gave up RMB settlement due to the high cost of clearance and settlement. To make full use of RMB capital in BRI construction and further increase efficiency of using RMB capital, our country should set up RMB clearing banks in more qualified countries along "Belt and Road". In unqualified countries along "Belt and Road", we should actively promote the "agent bank" model, i.e. allowing and encouraging local financial institutions to open RMB inter-bank transaction accounts in Chinese banks' domestic or overseas institutions in order to conduct cross-border settlement and clearance with RMB capital, and provide more convenience for using RMB capital to support BRI investment, trade and financial cooperation.

15.6.2 *Accelerate Chinese Financial Institutions' Distribution Along "Belt and Road"*

The international currencies have a common characteristic: Their issuing countries have a highly developed and globalized banking industry, and the overseas distribution of bank branches of these countries could basically meet the overseas financial service requirements of domestic companies. The banking industries of these countries flourished around the world by providing financial support for domestic companies. For example, in 1959, the HSBC Bank, subsidiary of HSBC Group of England purchased the Middle East Bank of England and set foot in the Middle East market. And it set up Saudi British Bank in Saudi Arabia in 1978 and Egyptian British Bank in Egypt in 1982. In 1976–1979, the Deutsche Bank of Germany set up branches in a dozen countries successively. By 1988, it expanded to another 12 countries, including the countries in Asia Pacific region. So far, most employees of Deutsche Bank have worked in foreign countries before. China's banking industry has been developing rapidly in recent years, and 4 banks are ranked among the top 10 in the world. The distribution of Chinese bank branches is similar to that of the Japanese banking industry. The branches are mostly concentrated in countries and districts with the most developed finance and a large economic aggregate, but their distribution in countries along BRI still lags behind. There aren't sufficient branches of Chinese banks in those countries. Currently,

Chinese companies' investment and trade cooperation in countries along BRI is developing rapidly; therefore Chinese financial institutions should actively set up bank-government-company cooperation platforms and branches, design financial products, provide financial services and control financial risks in those countries according to government policies, customers' requirements and local conditions.

References

Abdi. *Study on the Political Order of Arab District in 21st Century*, doctoral dissertation, Jilin University, 2017.

Ba Shusong, Yang Xianling. Currency Anchor's Selection and Exit: Re-Investigation of Optimum Currency Rules. *International Economic Review*, 1st issue, 2011.

Bai Ruomeng. Economic Growth, Chance Equity and Social Unrest: Experience of Inclusive Economic Development Concept in Arab Countries. *Academic Journal of North University of China*, 2nd issue, 2017.

Barry Eichgreen. *Exorbitant Privilege — The Rise and Fall of the Dollar.* Beijing, China: China Citic Press, 2011.

Bian Weihong. Offshore RMB Market Entered a Staged Adjustment Period. *International Finance*, 1st issue, 2017.

Bond Principles, *2017. 6 Green Bond Principles 2017: Guidance on Voluntary Procedures of Green Bond Issuance.*

Cai Yuchen. *Influence of the Europe and USA's Sanctions Against Russia on China-Russia Trade.* 2015.

Cao Yuanzheng. RMB Internationalization, Capital Account Opening and Financial Market Construction. *Finance Forum*, 6th issue, 2016.

Chen Jie. A Brief Analysis of Unemployment in Arab Countries. *Arab World Studies*, 6th issue, 2009.

Chen Miaoxin. Optimal Currency Area Theory and Thoughts on Single Currency Zone in East Asia. *Journal of Finance and Economics*, 2nd issue, 2002.

Chen Yuan. *In Between the Government and Market — China's Exploration of Developmental Finance*. Beijing, China: China Citic Press, 2012.

Chen Yulu. Acceleration of RMB Internationalization Through "Belt and Road" Initiative. *Economic Information Daily*, 8th issue, 2015.

Chen Zhi, He Jingjing. Anniversary of Exchange Rate Reform: RMB Won Three Counterattacks. *21st Century Financial Report*, 10th issue, 2016.

Cheng Siwei. *The Pathway of RMB Internationalization*. Beijing, China: China Citic Press, 2014.

China Development Bank. *Annual Report of China Development Bank 2016*. 7th issue, 2017.

Cohen B J. *Future of Sterling as an International Currency*. New York: St. Martin's Press, 1971.

Cohen B J. *The Geography of Money*. New York, NY: Cornell University Press, 1998.

Cowan E. *Topical Issues in Environmental Finance*. Retreived from Economy and Environment Program for Southeast Asia (EEPSEA) website: www.eepsea.net/pub/sp/10536141350ACF346.pdf.

Ding Jianping *et al*. *RMB Internationalization During "Stepping Out"*. Beijing, China: China Finance Publishing House, 2014.

Fan Xiaoyun *et al*. RMB Internationalization and Stability of International Currency System. *World Economy*, 9th issue, 2014.

Ge Qi. Application of Macro-Prudential Management Policies and Capital Control Measures in Cross-Border Capital In-Flow and Out-Flow Management of Emerging Market Countries and the Effects of Such Application — Analysis of China's Choices in Capital Flow Management Policies During Capital Account Liberalization. *International Finance Research*, 3rd issue, 2017.

Geoffrey G. Jones."International Financial Centers in Asia, the Middle East and Australia: A Historical Perspective", in *Finance and Financiers in European History, 1880–1960*, edited by Y. Cassis, Cambridge University Press, 1992.

Guo Tianyong, Ding Xiao. International Comparative Study of Inclusive Finance — From the Perspective of Bank Services. *Studies of International Finance*, 2nd issue, 2015.

Han Long. Proposed Solutions for Major Legal Problems in RMB Internationalization. *The Law Journal*, 10th issue, 2016.

Hong Yousheng *et al.* The "Belt and Road" Initiative and Changes of Current International System. *Academic Journal of Nanjing University*, 6th issue, 2016.

Hu Huaibang. Facilitate "Belt and Road" Construction with Developmental Finance. *Contemporary Financial Expert*, 5th issue, 2017.

Hu Huaibang. Make Use of Developmental Finance to Serve "Belt and Road" Strategies. *Globalization*, 5th issue, 2015.

Hu Huaibang. Seize the Opportunity of RMB Internationalization and Accelerate Construction of Shanghai International Financial Center. *New Finance*, 6th issue, 2011.

Hu Huaibang. The National Mission of Developmental Finance. *China Finance*, 8th issue, 2014.

Huang Runzhong. The Road of British Economic Development. *Academic Journal of University of International Relations*, 2nd issue, 2000.

Huang Xiaoyong. Pathways of Implementing Natural Gas RMB Strategies. *Academic Journal of Graduate School of Chinese Academy of Social Sciences*, 1st issue, 2017.

Jiang Boke, Zhang Qinglong. Currency Internationalization: A Research of Conditions and Influence. *New Finance*, 8th issue, 2005.

Jiang Chuanying. The Middle East Upheaval's Influence on the Economy of Arab Countries in Change. *Arab World Studies*, 6th issue, 2012.

Jiang Fachen. *SWOT Analysis of CRRC China's Exploitation of Russian Market*, 2016.

Jiang Zhenjun. The "Changeable" and "Unchangeable" in China-Russia Economic and Trade Cooperation. *European and Asian Economy*, 2nd issue, 2017.

Jin Ling. The "Belt and Road": China's Marshall Plan?. *International Studies*, 1st issue, 2015.

Jin Ruiting. How to Output Energy-Saving Products, Technologies and Services. *China Economic & Trade Herald*, 3rd issue, 2016.

Jin Xin. *Study on China-Russia Sovereign Wealth Fund Cooperation*, 2016.

Johnston. *Sequencing Capital Account Liberalization and Financial Sector Reform*, IMF Paper on Policy Analysis and Assessment, PPAA/98/8, July 1998.

Labatt S., White R. R. *Environmental Finance: A Guide to Environmental Risk Assessment and Financial Products*. Hoboken, NJ: John Wiley & Sons, 2003.

Li Guohua. Inclusive Finance Practice in "Belt and Road" Construction. *China Finance*, 9th issue, 2017.

Li Jianjun *et al.* Search Cost, Network Effect and the Channel Value of Inclusive Finance. *International Finance Research*, 12th issue, 2015.

Li Jihong *et al.* Study of RMB Internationalization Process by Analyzing RMB Settlement Trials in Overseas Direct Investment. *Journal of Regional Financial Research*, 5th issue, 2011.

Li Junfeng *et al.* Guidelines on Core Principles of Inclusive Finance Application. *Financial Supervision Research*, 2nd issue, 2017.

Li Lili. Saudi Arabia's Economic Development Condition and Sustainability of China-Saudi Arabia Economic and Trade Cooperation. *Economic Forum*, 10th issue, 2015.

Li Mei, Ding Hui. Construction of China's Green Finance System in "Belt and Road" Framework. *Environmental Protection*, 19th issue, 2016.

Li Wei. The International System Basis for the Rise of RMB. *Contemporary Asia Pacific Studies*, 6th issue, 2014.

Li Xin. *Research on China Nuclear Power's "Stepping Out" Strategies in the Framework of 21st Century Maritime Silk Road*, master dissertation, Party School of the CPC Central Committee, 2016.

Li Xinyin. Necessity and Methods of Green Finance Tool Innovation. *Academic Journal of Liaoning Socialist School*, 4th issue, 2006.

Li Zhonghai. Rouble Internationalization Strategies — Domestic Currency Settlement in China-Russia Trade. *Russian Studies*, 4th issue, 2011.

Lin Hongshan. Design of the Macro-Prudential Management Framework of Capital Account. *Fujian Finance*, 7th issue, 2017.

Lin Lefen *et al.* The "Belt and Road" Construction and RMB Internationalization. *World Economy and Politics*, 1st issue, 2015.

Lin Na. *Analysis and Evaluation of Development Capabilities of China's Renewable Energy Industry*, master dissertation, South China University of Technology, 2016.

Lin Nan. Actively Expand RMB Settlement for Oil Trade. *Foreign Economy and Trade*, 1st issue, 2017.

Liu Di. Cross-Cultural Human Resource Management of French Companies in China. *French Studies*, 1st issue, 2012.

Liu Min *et al.* A Brief Analysis of the Impossible Trinity and RMB Exchange Rate System Reform. *China Economy and Finance Observation*, 1st issue, 2008.

Liu Yuefei. *Currency Internationalization Experience and RMB Internationalization*, doctoral dissertation, Dongbei University of Finance and Economics, 2015.

Ma Chengfang. *Gradual Progress of RMB Capital Account Convertibility*, doctoral dissertation, Jilin University, 2013.

Ma Jun. Construction of China's Green Finance System. *Finance Forum*, 5th issue, 2015.

Ma Yunfei. Petroleum Rouble and Petroleum RMB — Challengers of Petro-Dollar. *China Economic Herald*, B02 column, May 31, 2014.

Mai Junhong *et al.* Research on Factors Influencing Our Country's Green Finance Based on Joint Analysis. *Macroeconomic Study*, 5th issue, 2015.

Mckinnon. *The Order of Economic Liberalization: Financial Control in the Transition to a Market Economy*. Baltimore, MD: Johns Hopkins University Press, 1991.

Meng Gang. *China's "Belt and Road" Investment and Financing Cooperation in Australia*. Beijing, China. People's Publishing House, 2017.

Meng Gang. Enlightenment of Currency Internationalization Experience on Pushing Forward RMB Internationalization in "Belt and Road" Construction. *Globalization*, 10th issue, 2017.

Meng Gang. Experience and Enlightenment of Public-Private Partnership (PPP) Model of Australian Infrastructure. *Overseas Investment and Export Credit*, 4th issue, 2016.

Meng Gang. Lead "Belt and Road" Financial Innovation with Green, Inclusive and Domestic Currency Finance. *New Finance*, 11th issue, 2017.

Meng Gang. Push Forward RMB Internationalization During "Belt and Road" Construction. *People's Daily*, theoretical column, January 17, 2018.

Meng Gang. Pushing Forward RMB Internationalization Through "Belt and Road" Construction. *Developmental Finance Research*, 3rd issue, 2017.

Meng Gang. Strategic Thinking on Pushing Forward RMB Internationalization in "Belt and Road" Construction. *Shanghai Finance*, 10th issue, 2017.

Meng Gang. The Missions, Advantages and Strategies of China Development Bank to Push Forward RMB Internationalization. *Developmental Finance Research*, 4th issue, 2017.

Meng Gang. The Values, Pathways and Obstacles of Developmental Finance System Construction. *Developmental Finance Research*, 2nd issue, 2006.

Milton Friedman, Anna Jacobson Schwartz. *A Monetary History of the United States*. Beijing, China: Peking University Press, 2009.

People's Bank of China. The Continuous Progress of RMB Internationalization. *China Financial Stability Report*, 2016.

Qi Shaozhou, Fu Zexi. Analysis of China-Russia Trade from the Global Value Chain Prospective. *Business Studies*, 6th issue, 2017.

Qiao Yide *et al*. RMB Internationalization: Interaction Between Offshore and Onshore Markets. *International Economic Review*, 2nd issue, 2014.

Research Group of Investigation and Statistics Department of People's Bank of China. Push Forward Reforms of Interest Rate and Exchange Rate and Capital Account Opening in a Coordinated Manner. *Financial Market Studies*, 2nd issue, 2012.

Sachs. *Understanding Shock Therapy*, Social Market Foundation Occasional Paper, No. 7, 1994.

Salazar J. *"Environmental Finance: Linking Two World"*, A Workshop on Financial Innovations for Biodiversity Bratislava, 1998.

Shen Jianya. *Currency Competition and RMB Internationalization*, master dissertation, Southwestern University of Finance and Economics, 2013.

Sun Haixia. Euro Internationalization: Process and Enlightenment. *Zhejiang Finance*, 11th issue, 2011.

Sun Haixia. USD Internationalization: Process and Enlightenment. *Academic Journal of Lanzhou Commercial College*, 1st issue, 2012.

Sun Jie. Cross-border RMB Settlement and RMB Internationalization. *Global Finance*, 4th issue, 2014.

Sun Miao. Current Situation and Characteristics of Germany's Direct Foreign Investment and Use of Foreign Capitals. *International Economic Cooperation*, 6th issue, 2001.

Sun Shaoyan, Shi Hongshuang. China-Russia Cross-Border RMB Settlement — An Analysis Based on RMB Internationalization and the USA and Europe's Sanctions Against Russia. *Northeast Asia Forum*, 1st issue, 2015.

Tang Bin, Zhao Jie, Xue Chengrong. Problems in Domestic Financial Institutions' Acceptance of the Equator Principles as Well as Implementation Suggestions. *New Finance*, 2nd issue, 2009.

V.K. Chetty. Measurement of Near Money. *American Economic Review*, 9th issue, 1969.

Wang Erde. Three Causes of Developing Renewable Energy in Middle East. *21st Century Economic Report*, 22nd issue, 2013.

Wang Honggang. China's Participation in Global Governance: Opportunities and Direction in the New Age. *Foreign Affairs Review*, 6th issue, 2017.

Wang Jipei. BRICS Bank Development Orientation. *Financial View*, 9th issue, 2014.

Wang Junhua. "Green Revolution" of the Financial Industry. *Ecological Economy*, 10th issue, 2000.

Wang Junhui. RMB's Inclusion into SDR Basket and Its Influence. *Globalization*, 1st issue, 2017.

Wang Weihan. RMB Settlement for China's Oil Imports in View of RMB Internationalization. *Finance & Trade Economics*, 1st issue, 2011.

Wang Yu *et al.* Opportunities and Challenges of the Petroleum RMB Valuation System. *Futures and Financial Derivatives*, 5th issue, 2016.

Wen Xueguo. Building Urban Agglomerations with Global Influence. *Wen Wei Po*, 5th column, September 1, 2016.

Wu Lei. Challenges in Economic Development of Arab Countries During Social Transformation. *Arab World Studies*, 5th issue, 2014.

Wu Nianlu. *Euro-Dollar and European Currency Market*. Beijing, China: China Financial and Economic Publishing House, 1981.

Xu Poling. The Nature, Content and Policy Logic of Import Substitution of Russia. *Russian, Central Asian & East European Studies*, 3rd issue, 2016.

Ye Bin. Outlook on Negotiation of China-Europe Bilateral Investment Treaty. *World Outlook*, 6th issue, 2015.

Ye Hua. *Study on Strategic Framework of RMB Internationalization*, doctoral dissertation, Party School of the Central Committee of CPC, 2013.

Ye Zhendong. Push Forward RMB Internationalization with the New Round of Capital Account Opening. *Globalization*, 1st issue, 2016.

Yin Hong, Cui Zheng. Russia's Economic Situation and Policies Under Western Sanctions. *International Economic Review*, 3rd issue, 2017.

Yin Jianfeng. RMB Internationalization: "Trade Settlement + Offshore Market" or "Capital Output + Transnational Companies"? — The Lesson of JPY Internationalization. *International Economic Review*, 4th issue, 2011.

Yu Qi. How to Construct a Green Finance System under "Belt and Road" Strategy. *Times Finance*, 3rd issue, 2016.

Yu Yongding. *The Last Barrier: "Capital Account Liberalization and RMB Internationalization"*. Beijing, China: China Eastern Press, 2016.

Zhang Guangyuan, Liu Xiangbo. Why Stressing Inclusive Finance in "Belt and Road" Construction. *Securities Daily*, A03 column, May 20, 2017.

Zhang Hongxia. Sanctions and Anti-Sanctions: The Difficult Situation of Russian Economy and the Way Out. *Russian, Central Asian & East European Studies*, 6th issue, 2016.

Zhang Hongxia. The Causes of China-Russia Trade Decline and Relevant Strategies. *Reformation & Strategy*, 2017.

Zhang Qi. The Imminent Energy Reform of Arab Countries. *China Energy News*, 8th issue, 2013.

Zhang Shuangshuang. *Empirical Study of China's Potential of Exporting to Arab Countries in the Strategic Background of "Belt and Road"*, master dissertation, Shandong University of Finance and Economics, 2015.

Zhang Wenzhong. Multi-Level Financial Cooperation on "Silk Road Economic Belt": Creating a Financial Chain of Central Cities. *Xinjiang Finance and Economics*, 5th issue, 2017.

Zhang Xiaofeng, Wu Shan. RMB Internationalization in Africa: Challenges and Outlets. *International Studies*, 3rd issue, 2016.

Zhang Yun. Top 10 Keywords on Energy and Power in the Two Sessions. *State Grid*, 4th issue, 2016.

Zheng Zhijie. Seize the Historical Opportunity and Serve "Belt and Road" Construction with Developmental Financial Services. *People's Daily*, 8th issue, 2016.

Zheng Zhijie. Strategic Thinking on RMB Internationalization. *China Finance*, 6th issue, 2014.

Zhihuan E. New Driving Force of Hong Kong Offshore RMB Market. *China Finance*, 22nd issue, 2016.

Zhou Xiaochuan. Four Constructive Ideas on "Belt and Road" Financing. *Shanghai Securities News*, 6th issue, 2017.

Zhou Xiaochuan. Prevent Systematic Financial Risks in All Cases. *People's Daily*, 6th column, November 12, 2017.

Zhou Xiaochuan. The Prospect and Pathway of RMB Capital Account Convertibility. *Journal of Financial Research*, 1st issue, 2012.

Zhou Yueqiu. Pushing Forward Green Finance Development and RMB Internationalization in a Coordinated Manner. *Financial Times*, 9th issue, 2017.

Zhu Yina. *Influence of RMB Settlement in Cross-Border Trade on Foreign-Related Business, Modern Communication*, 2016.

Zhu Zijing. *The Complementary Nature and Influential Factors of China-Russia Trade*, 2016.

Zong Liang. The Cooperative Effect of "Belt and Road" and RMB Internationalization. *International Finance*, 3rd issue, 2017.

Epilogue

In recent years, with the rapid development of Chinese economy and the further opening of China, RMB has become increasingly used in the world as a medium of exchange and a means of reserve and payment, and RMB internationalization has gradually become a hot topic. On September 30, 2016, RMB was formally included into International Monetary Fund's (IMF) Special Drawing Right (SDR) basket, making an important step in its internationalization process.

While bringing about huge political and economic benefits, currency internationalization will also create uncertainties in the domestic economy and influence the regulation based on the issuing country's macro-economic policies, especially financial policies. Therefore, we need to keep sober and actively create conditions to obtain benefits and avoid harms. In the present day of economic and financial globalization, China must push forward RMB internationalization in order to establish its position in the competition of world financial resources.

RMB internationalization is a gradual process which will not be going smoothly. Many problems will emerge in this process, including political interference, limitation of economic strength, and financial risks. We should study carefully, push forward this process steadily and solve problems safely. We need both theoretical research and practical explorations.

Because of working in the Bank field, we have a deep understanding of financial issues, extensive theoretical knowledge and a rich practical experience accumulated in his long-term overseas work. This book is the latest research result. It explained the great significance, historical opportunities and theoretical foundation of RMB internationalization, summarized the currency internationalization processes of developed countries, and put forward practicable policy suggestions based on the author's empirical research and work experience. Therefore, this book has great value of reference.

As pointed out in the 19th National Congress, China has stepped into a new age with Chinese characteristics. We hope for more domestic or overseas thinkers and researchers to combine theory with practice and to make contributions to theoretical and practical innovation in the new age with Chinese characteristics.

MENG Gang
July 2018

Index

CPSIA information can be obtained
at www.ICGtesting.com
Printed in the USA
JSHW020214051119
2157JS00004B/2